ONE WEEK LOAN

Right Hand Left Hand

RIGHT HAND LEFT HAND

DOROTHY LIVESAY

Published in October 1977 by Press Porcepic Ltd., 70 Main Street, Erin, with the assistance of the Canada Council and the Ontario Arts Council.

All efforts have been made to locate copyright holders. Any information on uncredited sources would be appreciated.

ISBN 0-88878-104-0 (cloth)   ISBN 0-88878-105-9 (paper)

Cover design by Catherine Wilson
Printed and bound in Canada by the Hunter Rose Company

1 2 3 4 5   81 80 79 78

Distribution:

CANADA	U.S.A.	U.K. & EUROPE
Musson Book Company	Press Porcepic Ltd.	Books Canada Ltd.
30 Lesmill Road	70 Main Street	1 Bedford Road
Don Mills, Ontario	Erin, Ontario	London N2 .
M3B 2T6	N0B 1T0	England

Canadian Cataloguing in Publication Data

Livesay, Dorothy, 1909-
   Right hand, left hand

Bibliography: p.
ISBN 0-88878-104-0 bd.   ISBN 0-88878-105-9 pa.

1. Livesay, Dorothy, 1909-   —Biography.
2. Women poets — Canada — Biography.   3. Canada—
History — 1918-1939.* I. Title.

PS8523.I8Z5   C811'.5'4   C77-001487-9
PR9199.3.L56Z5

I000452024

For My Son
Peter Macnair

Acknowledgements

My grateful thanks to my editors, David Arnason and Kim Todd for their patience and devoted work. Also, to the many others who have provided material and support; Jean and Stafford Johnston, Allan Ricketts, W.T. Lawson, Oscar and Toby Ryan, Louis Muhlstock, Irene Kon, Peter Hunter, Mac Reynolds, Barker Fairley, Charles Comfort, Wilfred Eggleston, Robin Endres, Sophie Livesay Stewart, Ingham Sutcliffe, Robert Kenny.

Contents

Right Hand Left Hand
(a fragment)

We who are working have no visitors.
Nobody comes to enquire: and how
much gas do you use per month?
We are not seen by relief investigators, nurses, social workers, coal men,
gas collectors, dietitions, apologetic postmen. The butcher and the baker
cannot say 'hello'. Only the milkman, seeing the note hid in the bottle,
knows we are alive.

And the boss, the boss knows.

> *Mrs. Sutton, your hair is untidy today. If marriage is going to let you slip
> up on your appearance, why we will have something to say—*

(Johnny cut his hand this morning. I shouldn't have bandaged it.)

> *Miss Nightingale! Those togs must not be allowed to litter the floor!
> Pick them up with your left hand while your right hand pulls the lever!*

(I know not what my brother doeth)
We who are working have no laughter.

Introduction

The thirties in Canada were a time of massive contradictions. The depression provided some of the worst poverty we have ever seen, and certainly the most widespread misery we as a people have ever felt. Millions were out of work, hungry, desperate — first for survival, then for dignity. The insecurity, anger and fear generated have left a legacy from which we have by no means recovered yet. At the same time, there was, at least for many, an optimism we had hardly felt before, and certainly have not felt since. For if the old system was in a state of collapse, surely that meant that a new order was being born. Over it all, the wealthy and the secure skated as though the depression were a mere flaw in the otherwise unblemished stretch of history that would carry them inevitably to their destinies in their own good time.

When it was over, and the war had saved us, history closed over the depression like thin skin over a suppurating wound. Nobody now, much wanted to remember the bad times. Winners and losers together conspired to treat the depression as a bad dream. A legend has grown around those times, made in equal parts from romantic visions of the dust bowl, bread lines, Bennet Buggys, rod-riders and gallows humour. For the most part, the literature of the period is escapist, recollections by raconteurs, and first hand accounts, filled with pathos and bad grammar.

It was against this view of life in the thirties that writers like Raymond Knister, A.M. Klein, F.R. Scott and Dorothy Livesay were setting forth a realist and satirical antidote.

Dorothy Livesay, born in Winnipeg in October 1909, moved with her family, in 1920, to Toronto where she went to school and then the University of Toronto. Aside from regular escapades that exasperated and secretly delighted her newspaperman father, J.F.B. Livesay, she did well in school, won awards for her poetry and was generally a "blue-stocking." Then, the growing misery of the depression, a year in Paris where social fermant was concentrated, and some personal awakenings turned the upper-middle class girl into a tough-minded social radical. What followed is part of the history of The Canadian social and literary scene.

The history of Canadian writing from the perspective of the political left dates back before Confederation but the tradition is so obscured that many are not aware of it. In the nineteenth century Alexander Maclachlan and Isabella Valancy Crawford wrote poems which expressed their sympathy for the poor and the oppressed. Agnes Maule Machar and M.A. Foran wrote novels which expressed a working-class sensibility. Archibald Lampman and Duncan Campbell Scott found Victorian capitalism repellent, though they turned towards ideals of beauty rather than to social remedies. In this century the "bohemian" poets, including Tom McInnes, Wilson Macdonald, Robert J.C. Stead and Douglas Durkin foresaw the coming day of the common man and wrote poetry filled with broadly sympathetic pictures of the working man, investing him with all virtue, and contrasting him with the evils of the rich. They wrote a poetry intended to be read by the working man as well and their rhythms were strong, their rhymes pronounced and unsubtle, their approach sentimental. They are accused now of having written doggerel, though none of these writers was personally unsophisticated. Unfortunately for their reputations, the day of the "common man" has been a long time coming.

The rise of the socialist party of Canada in the period before the first war and the appearance of its organ, *The Western Clarion,* allowed for a more specifically ideological statement of working class sympathy than anything literary had permitted before this time. Brilliantly clear essays explaining Marxism and arguing its inevitability appeared in the *Clarion's* pages. One of its founders, Wilfred Gribble, wrote scattered poems and short stories that are more coherently Marxist than anything before the thirties. Gribble, however, was tried for sedition in 1915 (he spoke in favour of pacificism in Saint John, N.B. at the height of a white feather campaign). He disappeared into Saint John prison and there is no trace of him after that, nor any continuous expression of a left wing literary sensibility that we know of at present. The summing-up address by the judge, Mr. Crocket, is worth quoting:

I am disposed, however, to make some allowance for the condition of mind under which you laboured and which, I have no doubt, was due to those pernicious, false expositions of doctrine or belief, with which you most unfortunately have been feeding your intellect. These expositions, as you have understood them, have apparently engendered in you, as they are bound in time to engender in all men who accept them in a like sense, a spirit of unreasoning discontent and distrust, which sees nothing but slaves in themselves and tyrants in all the rest of mankind. These fruits of this teaching—this discomfort, this suspicion, this hate—are the tyrants which in reality enslave you. It is not your fellow men, who by energy, by enterprise, by their own genius and labour and their own resources find employment and wages for you, which you may or may not accept at your will and pleasure. It is not the state, which educates and enfranchises you and gives you every conceivable badge of freedom, but it is those ideas themselves, which, recognizing no benevolence, no public spirit, no patriotism, no unselfishness, no excellence of any kind in others in truth imprison you within yourselves and shut out from your vision, the light of all inspiring and enobling thought and feeling.

For your present difficulties, therefore, I blame to a large extent the dangerous teaching of which you have become unfortunately a misguided devotee, and I believe that you and others have already, by means of this prosecution, been taught a salutary lesson as to the trouble which such teaching breeds.

This suggests the sort of attitude against which any left wing thought was forced to contend.

The events of the thirties appeared to demonstrate that, beyond the simple inequities of the capitalist system, there were internal contradictions which made its final and complete collapse inevitable. Only then, did there arise in Canada a literary movement that combined sympathy for the working class and the oppressed with a clear ideological framework and a set of revolutionary social remedies.

The first years of the depression, 1929 to 1931, were years of confusion for the literary intellectuals of the country. In the pages of the *Canadian Forum,* writers such as Leo Kennedy and A.J.M. Smith were busy dismantling the colonial literary legacy left by Bliss Carman, Charles G.D. Roberts and Archibald Lampman. During the twenties, magazines had proliferated, mainly to carry advertisements for the new technological age, but they had also offered space for poetry and short stories. Now, in a period of economic crisis, they were disappearing as fast as they had appeared. The most significant (because nationalist) publisher of the period, Graphic Press, went under, a victim of the depression.

1932 saw the first grouping together of writers with an interest in the left. In March of that year, thirty-five people gathered together in Toronto to form the first Progressive Arts Club. Among the founding members were Maurice Granite, Ed Cecil-Smith, Dorothy Livesay, Stanley Ryerson, Oscar Ryan, Helen Nelson, Sam Kagan, Avrom Yanovsky and Richard Taylor (RIC). They decided to publish a monthly club journal to be called *Masses.* The club, in reality an offshoot of a discussion group that had been in existence since 1928, provided an opportunity for members to discuss and articulate the proper concerns for literature, both in the present and in the new age that was to follow. *Masses* provided a vehicle for that literature. The Progressive Arts Club had a section for writers, another for artists, and a third for theatre workers. Similar Progressive Arts Clubs sprang up over the next year in Winnipeg, Montreal, Vancouver, Halifax and London as well as in several small Ontario centres.

An offshoot from the Progressive Arts Club was the Workers' Experimental Theatre. On May 6, 1932, they produced their first play, *Deported,* at the Ukrainian Labour Temple in Toronto. Interest in agit-prop theatre quickly spread, and workers action theatre groups evolved not only in the major cities in Canada, but in a surprising number of rural areas as well. Most of the plays produced followed closely the patterns of international workers theatre, but many were written by Canadians. Among them was *Eviction,* a play about the police murder of a Polish immigrant in Montreal named Nick Zynchuk. He was killed when he tried to reclaim his furniture from the house out of which he had been evicted. The event captured the imagination of writers on the left, and became the theme of plays, stories, and poems. A number of the founding members of the Progressive Arts Club wrote agit-prop plays. Among them were Stanley Ryerson, who wrote *War In The East,* and Oscar Ryan, who wrote *Unity.* Dorothy Livesay wrote *Joe Derry,* an agit-prop pantomime for children.

The most significant play produced by the Workers Experimental Theatre was *Eight Men Speak,* written collectively by Oscar Ryan, Ed Cecil-Smith, Frank Love and Mildred Goldberg. It concerned the imprisonment of eight members of the Communist Party, including its leader Tim Buck. After a series of initial successes both in Toronto and elsewhere in 1932 and 1933, the Workers Experimental Theatre went into decline in 1934. In 1935, under the leadership of Jean "Jim" Watts, the Toronto Theatre of Action came into existence. Its first production was *Waiting for Lefty* by the American writer Clifford Odets. The play was a great success, well attended, and, surprisingly, critically well received.

Writers of the left during the thirties tied literature strongly to action. *Masses,* during its run from April, 1932, to April, 1934, continually reiterated its demand that the writer be a political organizer as well. Its position was essentially revolutionary. Its successor, *New Frontier* magazine took a much more reformist stance. The editorial in the first issue suggested that the purpose of *New Frontier* was "to acquaint the Canadian public with the work of those writers and artists who are expressing a positive reaction to the social scene; and to serve as an open forum for all shades of progressive opinion."*Masses* had regarded even the C.C.F. as a part of the enemy. *New Frontier* was prepared to deal with a much broader range of left wing opinion and idea.

The editors of *New Frontier* included William Lawson, Dorothy Livesay, Barker Fairley, Margaret Gould, J.F. White, and, for a while, Leo Kennedy. Among its associate editors were Jean Burton, Felix Walter, Fritz Brandtner and Sam Hayakawa. The less revolutionary stance of the magazine is not surprising. Certain of its editors and writers were involved in organizations like the League Against War and Fascism, which joined various groups under a single umbrella. Dorothy Livesay, for instance, had been a member of both that group and the Youth Movement for Peace. As well, 1935 was the year of the Comintern and the establishment of the united front. The various groups on the left were beginning to work together, as the threat from the extreme right loomed as a larger and larger menace. For all of the left wing groups, certain events became central symbols: the miners' strike at Estevan, Dominion Day "riot" at Regina, the Long Trek to Ottawa, the sit-in at the Vancouver Post office and art gallery. Increasingly, world affairs, such as the Italian invasion of Ethiopia, became matters of central concern.

More than any other event, however, the Spanish civil war deflected interest from the struggle at home to the world at large. That war appeared from the perspective of the thirties as a kind of Armageddon, a final confrontation between the forces of the right and the forces of the left. Canadian intellectuals either took direct part in the war, or spent much of their time and effort in creating support for the forces fighting Franco.

Then, in 1939, Stalin signed the Soviet-German pact and the Cold War began. Dismayed by Russia's manoeuvrings and by the increasingly convincing evidence about the nature of the Soviet trials, Canadian intellectuals began to turn away from the moral leadership of the Communist Party. Then, the hot war was upon us, and all efforts were thrown into that struggle against Nazism and Fascism.

When the war was over, the Canadian left had lost its focus. Several of its leaders were dead. The rest had seen their lives so wrenched out of the directions they had taken that to go back seemed impossible. The spirit of solidarity was gone, and Canadian writers and artists turned to other, and usually more personal, concerns. Their work had been published in quite deliberately ephemeral outlets, and few were interested in republishing it. Once more, the new age had failed to arrive. The evidence of their work is now available only in scattered archives. This book is an attempt to make known an important part of our literary heritage, through the eyes of an active participant and sensitive poet.

David Arnason

Conventions

The author's commentary is typeset in Garamond Italic.

News articles, pamphlets and letters are set in Times Roman and have bylines accompanying them.

Stories, plays, and poems are set in Andover Roman with titles italicized. All material is written by Dorothy Livesay unless otherwise indicated.

Toronto—Paris—Toronto
1928-1932

*"And I'm not lost, Jinny. FOUND. One straying
poetess in Paris!"*

I was born in Winnipeg, on October 12, 1909, in a
snowstorm. Thus, for the larger part of each year I
am ten years younger than the twentieth century.
The other Canadian artists of my era were those
men born soon after the turn of the century: Raymond Knister, Earle
Birney, Robert Finch, A.J.M. Smith, A.M. Klein (1909), Leo Kennedy and
Irving Layton (1913). No companion women poets were born until the
end of the First World War: P.K. Page, Miriam Waddington, Ann Wil-
kinson, Anne Marriott, Margaret Avison and Phyllis Webb. So until they
began to make their mark in the forties, I always had the feeling I was
struggling alone to make a woman's voice heard. I admired the men —
particularly those who encouraged me — Knister, Klein and (for a time)
Smith, but I felt curiously detached from them in a literary and life-style
sense.

My roots were in the prairie soil and in Ontario's tight Victorian city,
Toronto, where we came to live in 1920. My parents were both journalists and had met on the Winnipeg Telegram. They married and lived
in Winnipeg until my father returned from the First World War as a war
correspondent; and then went to Toronto to be manager of the Canadian
Press. He immediately bought land at Clarkson where he built a cottage
and, later, a house.

Flung from rural innocence into urban sophistication, I was challenged by the mysteries of the city — particularly the rigidity of the class structure; the poverty of the immigrant Jewish "Bathurst and College" community versus life in the tall sequestered duplexes of "The Annex" in which our professional family dwelt, on Walmer Road. Early poems illuminate that dichotomy — particularly "Hermit", "City Wife" and "From the Multitude." They were written in Clarkson where we spent summers and weekends.

My education also tended to isolate me from the pounding pulse of the city. My parents were both the products of private boarding schools and it seemed they never even considered sending me to the local public school, Harbord Collegiate. Instead I walked past the elitist boys' high school, U.T.S., down Spadina Avenue to Glen Mawr school (now a residence of the University of Toronto). By the time I entered the Fifth Form (Upper and Lower) I was aware of "not belonging" to the socialite Sixth Form circle of girls who came from Toronto's "best" families. They were well-to-do, good at basketball and skating, rigorous in their lady-like behavior patterns — vying with each other for a dance with the Prince of Wales. Whereas I was an unathletic "frump" — a "square" in today's terms — a freckled girl with glasses who always "came first" when the monthly reports were read aloud at Prayers by the Principal, Miss Stuart.

Undoubtedly in self-protection, I sought out other isolates who at heart were rebels also, against authority and "proper" behaviour. Of these, one was bent on an academic career, Erica Mundy with whom I later went to Trinity College. The other was "Jim" Watts, who later became Jean Watts Lawson of the MacKenzie-Papineau battalion in Spain — an extraordinarily stimulating but wilful and wayward woman's liberationist. And there were two teachers who played quite a part in encouraging my individuality, perhaps because they were not Torontonians but came from the older, more mature culture of the Maritimes. Mary Irick Jennison, my English teacher, was plain, plump, red-faced like a Toby jug, with stringy black bobbed hair; but her eyes were a wonderful Irish blue and wide like her mouth. After school, on the side, she was taking courses in economics and political science with a view to becoming a social worker. Her approach to literature was intensely stimulating, for she related the novels and poetry to the world they sprang from. She challenged us with questions about atheism and socialism. In my last year in the Sixth Form (preparing for Senior Matriculation, grade XIII) Jim and I had an ill-concealed "crush" on our mathematics teacher, Margaret Ford. Young, dark, elegant, her mind was keen as mustard so we longed to know her better. The chance arrived when — of all things — Emma Goldman came to Toronto on a lecture tour.

How could it be that Jim and I were attending those literary (and political and feminist lectures) at the Masonic Hall above Bloor, on Yonge Street? My father, J.F.B. Livesay, was at that time one of a kind — "a radical and agnostic" he called himself. As a young reporter in Winnipeg in 1908, newly out from England, he had been sent to cover Emma Goldman's lecture on Gorki. Her knowledge of Russian literature and her admiration for his heroes — Ibsen and Shaw — must have impressed him so much that when twenty years later he heard she was to give a lecture series in Toronto he decided my education needed expanding. He arranged to take Jim and me to Goldman's lecture on Tolstoi; and thereafter, for several weeks we went alone, evenings, not only to the literary lectures but to lectures on feminism and on birth control.

A young anarchist girl whom I should have met then, but didn't alas, has described Emma Goldman in these terms:

The first time I saw Emma I saw the very warm human person — like a Viking to me — though she was a teensy *woman, five feet, five inches, like Queen Victoria! Long blond hair turning grey, deep blue eyes [hidden under] very thick lenses . . . a sunshiny person with wonderful humour and a wonderful smile . . . and yet tremendous strength [behind it]. The most dynamic kind of person [one could meet]. Her stance had that kind of solidity of a piece of sculpture. . . . There was no fear in this woman. She took a stand. Everything about her was taking a stand.*

Undoubtedly Emma Goldman's dynamic interest in anarchism and the rebels of literature led us, by the time we were at university, to George Bernard Shaw's The Intelligent Woman's Guide to Socialism and Communism *and to Ibsen's* The Doll's House.

* * *

Jim had registered for courses in anthropology and psychology and was planning to be a doctor (whereas I was in the "backwater" of French and Italian studies). That was the kind of person Jim Watts was — always alert to new ideas, and I was very much the follower. She kept exploring everything. She delved into books on sex and trial marriage and so on, long before I did, and told me all about them. She got particularly interested in politics, philosophy and psychology. We were both inter-

ested in women as creative people and were mad about poets like H.D., Emily Dickinson, Elinor Wylie and just daft about Katherine Mansfield.

My father perhaps wanted to stimulate me in these ways, but because he was my father I would, in a sense, resist. But he stimulated my friend so much that she leaped ahead and the things she discovered, she brought to me. I remember she brought us something by Engels on the "Origin of the Family", and that just shook us to death. Engels completely mesmerized us. It was years before I recovered from that book.

By this time we were both very "anti-family" — though hers held her to a far more rigid schedule than did mine. But a conscientiousness and sense of duty had kept me longer "toeing the Christian line." Because Jim was so strongly a rebel it was easier for her to challenge and then renounce all her bourgeois parents' beliefs and standards. When my mother saw that I was being influenced towards atheism she sought to enlist the reasoning of our teacher, "Jennie" who was at the time a devout Anglican. However, as she became radicalized by the study of Marxism, the counter-evidence against Christianity which we, her pupils offered was too great. Thus, by the age of eighteen, at Trinity College, I protested vigorously at having to take "R.K." — Religious Knowledge. Actually, there turned out to be a lot of ferment among the theological students concerning "The Historical Jesus." A series of lectures at Trinity on new archaeological finds did much to support the concept developing in my mind of a "real and human Jesus", not a mysterious godhead. And then, on The Varsity *newspaper where I worked as a cub reporter there exploded the dismissal of our editor, Andrew Allan, for daring to state that "eighty per cent of the student body is atheistic." All these challenges to "received opinion" (including those of John S. Mill himself) prepared the way for my acceptance, by my fourth year, of the theories of dialectical materialism.*

* * *

My own writing was also a source of pleasure and frustration. Since I was a child I had particularly wanted to write prose — and I did a great deal of that in my teens and early twenties — while studying in France in 1928-29 I wrote a novella. I think my first poem was published in the Vancouver Province *when I was thirteen and I received a cheque for two dollars. Probably if mother hadn't been in the literary life and writing poems and stories herself, I mightn't have had the temerity to go ahead and publish. She more or less organized that. My first book,* Green Pitcher, *was published before I was nineteen. But I was very unsatisfied with that at the time.*

Apr. 20/28

The proofs of "Green Pitcher"
have comes. As I imagined, all
interest is gone from me. It
seems brazen to bring it out now:
how can I know anything better
will follow?

As it is, people will probably call it "charming." Unfortunately, that will be true. As
yet I have not reached any
greater beauty than charm.
What I long for is power,
fire: these perhaps will be
gifts of experience, if it ever
happens that experience be given
to me.

How little poetry matters
to me! I must confess it.
Terrible achings after the elusive
power-depriving story-telling possess
me.

Dorothy Livesay, aged nineteen.

and resigned oneself to a dull existence. — But the question follows: is the reality more important than the imagined Does it last longer really? Some how, the advantage seems to be with the imagination, for there there is no end and no fly in the ointment: there are no finalities, and no disappointments. And moreover is not the importance of the event itself insignificant as compared with its effect on the mind, the imagination, afterwards?

One immediate reason for this question is the fact that I went to dinner last night with Andy and found that Roberts and Bliss were to be with us. There

Andrew Turkel

25

was little reality in it, at the
time ......I felt perfectly at ease,
and could talk without feeling the discomfort of professional
mockery. Bliss advises me to
get my degree, even if it is
a grind — perhaps because
it is one. Talked to him
about his Sappho, and
Hérédia. Remember his half-
senility, his "softness", above
all, his hat. Oh, these
artistic creatures, who are
afraid of newspaperwomen &
yet do their best to catch
the public eye! Charles J. S.
is more careful, nay, exceedingly
careful of his appearance: he
realizes that in the long run
elegance is more attractive aux
dames.

June 2 '28

This constant frustration is
agonizing, eternal. If only I
could accept it.

I cry to the world: "Take, eat,
this is my body" — and the
world jeers.

I wish I had a barbaric yawp!

*I was awarded the Jardine Memorial for English
Verse by the University of Toronto while in my
second year there, 1927-28, for my poem "City
Wife", which was written as a result of drives, with
my father and friends, through Ontario farm country.*

GIRL WINS COVETED PRIZE

TORONTO POETESS

**Miss Dorothy Livesay, University
Student, Awarded Jardine Memorial
For English Verse**

Miss Dorothy Livesay, a second
year Moderns student of Trinity College, was last night announced as the
winner of the University of Toronto's
most coveted literary prize, the Jardine memorial for English verse, val-
ued at $100. Her winning effort is a
description in verse of a day in the life
of a city woman who married a farmer
and went to live in the country.

Previous to her attempt at the Jardine Memorial, Miss Livesay has had
a number of her poems published in
Canadian periodicals and last year a
collection of her most outstanding
efforts was published in book form
under the title the "Green Pitcher."
The book attracted favorable attention from literary critics of such
publications as "World Wide," the
"Forum," Toronto Saturday Night,
The London Times Supplement, and
from a number of Canadian dailies.

A member of the faculty in English
at the University stated last night that

only a poem of considerable merit can win the Jardine prize, as one of the conditions of the award, which is most strictly adhered to, is that it need not be given in the event of the examining board deciding that the poems submitted are not up to the required standard.

"Miss Livesay's poetry is remarkable, not only for its freshness and spontaneity, but for a mastery of word values rarely found in the work of so young a poet," he said.

WROTE SINCE CHILDHOOD.

Miss Livesay, who has been writing since her childhood, comes from a family of literary folk. Her mother is well known as a poet and has had several books published, and her father, J.F.B. Livesay, who is general manager of the Canadian Press, is the author of "Canada's Hundred Days" and other works. In addition to her writing Miss Livesay has succeeded in gaining honors in her course at the University and finds time for editorial work on her college magazine and is a member of the St. Hilda's College Literary Executive.

Following are two stanzas selected from Miss Livesay's prize winning poem, "City Wife."

Oh, I have followed where the first
    bare maple
Suddenly turned to gold, where
    deeper still
There flamed in red a different maple
    tree
Boldly against the sober evergreens;
And even farther I plunged, until too
    soon
The other end of the wood was
    reached, and broke

Into a line of pale wild cherry trees
Too lovely to be startled by a sound,
Too young to be enchanted by the
    wind.
I soon ran there, thinking I would not
    turn
But follow along the swiftly curving
    road
Until I knew that silence was swinging
    back,
A golden pendulum above the wood —
No! for the sweetness was too much;
    a voice
Seemed to cry loud and louder: Turn!
    Turn once —
As long ago one thought he heard a
    voice
And could not move until he called
    her name;
The name of all names surely loveliest,
Of lost, forever lost, Eurydice.

Miss Dorothy Livesay

At the end of my second year at Trinity College, my father got me a job as "cub" reporter on the Winnipeg Tribune *through his newspaper colleague M.E. Nichols. I was none too happy in this situation but made the best of it — as the following letter shows.*

Winnipeg 2.7.29

Darling Papa

Monday's mail always makes me feel affectionate, there's always such a heap of it. Yes, I saw your name twice in the *Free Press'* Washington despatch. My only criticism of your style would be that it is too intricate (!) Yes, m'love, brevity is a newspaperman's by-law. Never use a colon if you can get away with a stop: never use a dash if you can utilize a comma. . . . But 'fess up now, aren't you a bit Carlylian?

Col. Porter is one cooing dove for lies. In the first place I've never met the man, let alone seen him — and he certainly doesn't know anything about my meagre copy.

Great joke — yesterday being a holiday, they were terribly hard up for news — result three stories of D.K.L.'s played up to beat the band. I filled up the paper — but it was nearly all fiction. Following in Papa's footsteps.

I have been given part of Mrs. L'ami's beat — so am more ensconced here. But dry as dust stuff is still hard to write. I had a talk with W. Patten and he said that I underwrite and do not go in for enough detail. In other words I condense too much. You may talk about my imagination, but it does not spread its wings at all when facts are to be related. As for pounding out a story in five minutes on a typewriter, it's beyond me. The necessity for seeing everything first in pencil and scratching it out, prevents all thought of a journalistic life pour moi. N'est pas vrai? You should have warned me of this instantaneous writing.

Well, my money has been waiting for me in the bank all this time. Mr. Clung alias Flurry alias Sprung informed me of this, when pressed. I go for it demain matin. I pay back Turner then.

You might see what on earth Jim's doing. Couldn't you give her a job? I am afraid as it is she will end up in the gutter (you needn't say I said so). Lunch her or something.

By the way, did you ever look Jinny up?

You evidently took my last letter as a personal affront. You're an awful old ass. Please, when you write, use a typewriter. I cannot read your hand.

Isn't this a newsy letter from a poet who can't write poetry, a shy young virgin caught in the newspaper vortex and determined to stay there because of the fifteen dollars she may save each month? Well, it may be

29

more than that: even if I am a nuisance to Nichols he would be a greater nuisance to you if I decamped — you would suffer from me (O yes!) even as I suffer from you. I hate being my father's daughter. Your anonymosity is the only asset. Yah yah

—Your obedient Pup

I had been in France during the year 1929-30 and this was a very enriching experience. The university, on the basis of first class honours in Modern Languages, permitted me to spend my third year abroad studying French and Italian. On the advice of Constance Charlesworth, wife of Louis McKay, both of them French experts, I chose the University of Marseille, situated in Aix-en-provence. This was Mdme de Sevigne's town and I was transported into her world. I lived in a pension in the route de Tholonet, next door to Cezanne's "Chateau Noir." Mdme de Lombardon, who owned the house, was a charming and fascinating woman. She was very knowledgeable, we had great arguments about Rousseau, for instance. I got very interested in him and she thought he was the devil incarnate and would give me Catholic books to read instead.

Later I came to recognize it was a town known to Mireille, Milhaud, Cezanne and Van Gogh; as well as having known Julius Caesar.

Amongst the farm people also one saw suddenly a Saracen woman, for the moors had been here: and Mont Ste. Victoire, the nearby mountain which Cezanne has painted, was the scene of a bloody battle against the Christians; they were, I was told, obliged to hide in the caves along its precipitous sides. I explored the mountain with some French young people, and it figured largely in my novel written the following year. A chapter from that novel was published as a short story, "The Last Climb." Aside from learning French, attending lectures on French literature and Italian romantics at the university in Aix, I had a fruitful time in writing — letters, a diary, short stories. I felt very much in Katherine Mansfield's and D.H. Lawrence's atmosphere — indeed news of his death came to me by an odd chance when a daft young Frenchman arrived at our pension from the Cote d'Azur. He had been in the pension where Lawrence died, the week previous.

But all my reading and writing I kept separate from the French family life into which I was drawn — an old-world, aristocratic, poverty-stricken but proud way that bore no resemblance to the twentieth century. I coached the young son in English — he was entering Saint-Cyr military academy; and I became devoted to the seventeen year old sister and identified with her desire for emancipation. Much of this atmosphere, though transplanted to Canada, is to be found in the short story written that year, "The Glass House." I sent the story to my father, who was very flattering about it; he sent it to the Atlantic *and* Harpers *but there was no bite. It lay forgotten in a drawer until his papers were sent to me in 1946 or 47. Thus it was not until twenty years later it was published in* Northern Review, *and then re-published in Foley's* Best Stories *of 1951. Had the story met the same success when I was nineteen or twenty, there is every likelihood, I feel, that I would have stuck to writing prose solely and not attempted to have any different career.*

* * *

Before returning home to Canada and the depression I spent the month of June, 1930 attending the Imperial Press conference with my father in London; that is to say, I went in place of his wife! There was only one other Canadian newspaperman who brought a daughter instead of a wife, so I was really deeply bored by the whole affair. However, I had a glimpse into English society and spent a weekend at Lord Somebody's country house. I was invited to an evening with George Bernard Shaw, and was greatly disappointed when my father decided he was spending that day in a trip to his home on the Isle of Wight. Whilst exploring the Isle of Wight and meeting my aunts, we made up our differences; but things were never quite the same between us and the tension increased yearly as I chose first, social work as a career, and then communism as a belief.

* * *

In my fourth university year my academic standing collapsed completely because I got in with a group of young people who were centred around a Professor of Economics who had come over from Holland — Otto Van der Sprenkel, a very brilliant man. He had a way of gathering students into his apartment and talking only about the new literature and new politics. He had been to Russia and we had great arguments about why he wore silk pyjamas because if he was communist he ought to wear cotton!

This was my first encounter with the ideas of communism — he did it to all of us! Jim and Otto had a long prolonged affair that year. They eventually went to Europe that next summer. Then he abandoned her and she telephoned me long distance asking me to please come to Paris — she was going to commit suicide if I didn't arrive!

By this time, my father was very disapproving of me but my mother came up with the money to send me — since I was going anyway, to write a thesis at the Sorbonne.

31

SPECIAL LUNCHEON
35ᶜ

Macaroni with Ham
or
Cottage Cheese Salad
Bread and Butter
Fruit Cup Custard
or
Strawberries and Cream
Tea, Coffee, Milk

Sandwiches

Date Salad	10ᶜ
Egg Salad	10ᶜ
Tomato and Lettuce	10ᶜ

Nut Bread	10ˢ
Raisin Bread	10ᶜ
Ice Cream	10ᶜ

Charlotte's Coffee Shop, St. George Street, Toronto.

*That summer before I went to Paris was the end of innocence — poli-
tically speaking as well as emotionally and physically. But it would take a
long time — months and years — before the bourgeois literary world I
had grown up in would brush off and leave me naked, stripped, a most
vulnerable young woman making gestures of repudiation but finding it
hard to change herself, psychically.*

*The group centred around Charlotte's Coffee Shop was supportive. It
was just a little one-room place in a cellar but we gave lunches and the
students and teachers who were still left around would drop in. Most of
the students I had spent the winter with — playing poker, going on sleigh
rides, drinking Italian wine — had disappeared when school was over.*

*My sister, Sophie, starting her individual route through art school
worked with me as waitress more from the fun of it than for any
monetary reward I was pleased to give her. In fact, she gave up her share
in order to help me pay the boat fare to Paris. My father didn't think
much of the whole venture.*

* * *

Toronto
June 5, 1931

My dear Kitty:

Marjorie will arrive in Montreal Sunday evening and I will meet her
there. She lands when this Family is in one of its periodic gales. A friend
of D's took over a tea shop near the University which has been running
successfully but has been closed during the summer months when of
course everything is very quiet. As I gather this friend is going to Europe
or somewhere and won't be back until Aug. 8 and D. undertook to run
the thing from May 25 until then, though she is faced with an almost
certain loss. I was not consulted and realize I may have to put up a little
money, but I was content to do that because it is an interesting
experience. So far they have just made both ends meet, D. and Sophie
working about twelve hours a day and making just nothing at all out of
it. But they have a slack season ahead. Both of them seem to enjoy it
very much, but they are literally tied by the leg from Monday morning
until Saturday noon. Obviously D. had Marjorie in mind to help her out.

But I have told her Marjorie is
entirely a free agent and I will not
have her roped into anything she
does not want to do. Also I hope to
take her with us down to the
Maritimes towards the end of July.

That was the situation until yesterday morning, the Family being in
town at Rosemount Ave. and I being
in Clarkson where I am building a
log cabin, "a Room of My Own."

D's great friend, "Jim" Watts, doing psychology at the University, who has a little money of her own, decided to go over to Europe this summer, and offered to pay D's expenses as she herself knows neither Europe nor languages. I put it to D. she cannot take this money except as a loan and it would have to be a definite loan which meant I would have to pay it back within, say, a year, which I am not in a particular position to do. You understand D. is going over to the Sorbonne anyway in October. So D. gave up that idea and went into the tea shop, sacrificing a good job on *The Toronto Star*.

For the past two or three days hysterical cables have been arriving from the erratic "Jim" in Dublin, saying she must have D. or she will be sunk. Florrie phoned me yesterday morning D. was leaving last night for Southhampton. However, she could not get a berth and it is put off a week. I am to have a talk with her in my office this afternoon and perhaps the crazy scheme will fall through.

What I wanted to know and don't know yet is whether they intend carrying on the tea shop. Certainly Sophie cannot do it alone and quite certainly I am not going to see Marjorie pitchforked into a proposition of that kind, with all the responsibility attached, even if I put up the inevitable loss. It is along that line I shall talk to D. I am writing to you now because I would like you to know the situation as it stands.

What I have written puts D. in a rather unfavourable light but I cannot help that. The trouble about D. is she is intent on living her own life and in some ways is strangely irresponsible. No doubt she will succeed, but she will leave a good many corpses in her victorious career.

Affectionately yours,

J.F.B. Livesay

A mutual friend in whom Sophie and I confided our secrets (concerning men) was Jean Morton, a U of T student who had become one of Otto's admirers. He sent her off to the London School of Economics "to be politicized" but it was a great mistake (she says now). She should have gone in for journalism where her gifts lay. (She became Jean Johnston, author of Wilderness Women). *Several letters to Jean confirm the swift change in my attitudes to literature when I became, in Paris, committed to communism. Others frequently at Charlotte's were Gilbert Murrell-Wright, a perennial student who dabbled in the arts and did indeed produce a magazine on campus,* The Privateer. *It was his unconventionality which had led me (and other young women) to fall in love with him . . . a first and distant love. I think this was because he was so non-macho, as we would say now. He accepted women as equals and companions. So did Grant Smith, a reporter on the* Toronto Telegram. *I came very close to him and respected him highly; but I could not fall in love with him. And*

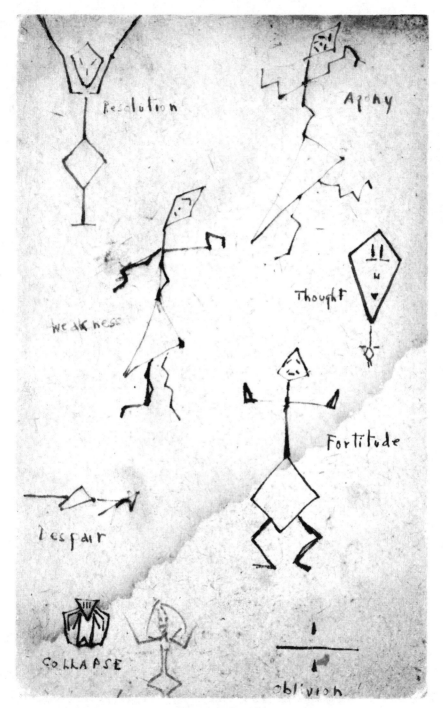

"D.L. in Love"

this separation of the physical from the emotional came as a shock to my intelligence. Why could there not be harmony between men and women at all levels?

I seemed to have found that ideal in Paris. By the time I got there, Jim had fallen in love with someone else and was in no danger of killing herself! Tony, another friend from Toronto, was there, with a lot of other Canadian students — Leon Edel and three Levy sisters from Montreal, Louis Muhlstock, a sculptor and many more, all centred around the Cité Universitaire. Tony was a year behind and decided to stay when Jim and the others went back to Toronto. That year he and I shared bed and board in a sixth floor attic apartment on Boulevard St. Germain.

The depression and the Nazi movement and the feeling of war was all abroad in Paris in 1931 and 32. We spent all our time associating with what was going on politically, that is to say we spent the day in the Bibliotheque Nationale and evenings went to meetings or watched parades. There was a great deal of pressure against the unemployed and the factory workers. I remember coming out of one meeting and the police were there waiting. Everybody coming out of the building was forced to go right down into the Metro. We weren't allowed to wander around the streets. They just took their sticks and whacked us until we went the right way. Oh, but we saw the brutality of the French police — there were workers killed and wounded who had been demonstrating and parading in March, celebrating the Paris Commune, at the cemetery of Père-la-chaise.

It was a revealing time — but dependent entirely, as I scarcely seemed to realize, on the generosity of my parent. The poetry written in this period reflects the complete dichotomy between the old way of thinking and the new. At the same time I was writing intimate love lyrics, I was struggling to express the world's woe and the world's hope as we saw it then.

* * *

Jinnie Morton

Charlotte's, July 1931

Dear Jinnie:

It will be great seeing you, as I missed you when you were leaving. Awful things have happened (here) but I'm not telling people for fear of injuring the business, which is attempting to keep open all summer.

We are meeting expenses. That's all, so far. Gilbert has been swell, keeping accounts, eating, *and* en-

36

couraging. He's a good person to confide in. Thanks for your congrats (re exams) and the same to you.

Dee

July, 1931

Have you seen the second year results? Really, Tony ought to be kept in a museum — except for his sense of humour, which would disturb the caretaker. He and Jim and Otto are doing glorious things together (in Europe) and they want me and I can't go and anyway I shouldn't be telling this to you because I'm telling nobody. But I remember how you were faithful with one person's secret and so I'm thinking you'll be faithful with mine.

Clarkson, July, 1931

Last night it took nearly three quarters of an hour to start Harry's car. Wilfred directed operations very scientifically, explaining just what was the matter. Gilbert and Grant worked. They cranked and they pushed, they sweated and they growled. After the most violent exertion Grant muttered: "God's teeth!" — "What's the matter, old man?" says Gilbert. "It's all right, Gilbert, I was just swearing behind my teeth." And they both laughed and were suddenly friends. So I was very happy.

Harry and Gilbert sat in the back seat with me in the middle. And so I didn't talk to Grant at all and he sat there very silent and then from my house Harry drove him to his Oshawa bus, with Gilbert staying behind with me. We talked for hours on the sofa and I told him everything (except the one thing I told you). And he told me everything too (about his fiancée). We sort of realized how alike we were and what deep friends we had always been. And then he's so wise, he understands me, he told me things that have helped tremendously and I think I know what to do now. I think everything will be all right, Jinny.

So good-bye, my dear, and bless you, and thank you.

August, 1931

A lot of important but painful things happened to me this week-end I can't write about them, probably I won't be able to talk about them. So don't expect the impossible from yours in a muddle, Dee.

August 15, 1931
Aboard the Duchess of York, CPR Steamships, for Paris.

Ah Jinnie, your very swell letter arrived all right, with a long long telegram from Gilbert, a short short one from Grant; and a letter from Ross and from Harry.

They all came down to see me off. I'm terribly well fixed — for friends. It makes me ashamed sometimes because I feel how ugly I can be. Not what they think of me. Write me a letter telling me my bad faults, Jinnie. Please I know them, but I need to know them from friends. Just now I'm too conceited.

Jinnie, I'm hoping it will be Grant. Just now it is, very much. The next three months will prove things.

No, I should never have told you what I did: the excitement of the moment made me lose my good sense. Not that I fear your knowing: but you weren't ready for it. Do you mind if I whisper how much older you have to grow, Jinnie.

You see, I did it, not because either of us lost our heads — *he* was very reluctant, because of the future. But I said I must have something to remember him by. And for that reason it's the best thing that could have happened, Jinnie. Really. There are other things in life more important but that at the moment was the only important thing. It will always have significance, whatever happens.

Socially and morally it means nothing to me: personally it was everything. It made all the difference.

I shouldn't have told you; but since I did, I must tell you all.

Dee

August 30, 1931
Hotel L'Oasis, Arromanches-les-Bains, Calvados, Normandie.

Suppose you think me dreadful. But besides my having been ill for a bit and Jim also, only much worse, in Paris, I've been through the most fearful times of my life. Everything now is quiet and settled, just about. But I can't tell you of it because it concerns other people besides myself. I'm telling nobody, Jinnie: so don't think I'm cryptic — merely wise and old and a different person from the Dee you know. Like Kashak Mechak and Abednego. After the Burning Fiery Furnace. Forgive me Jinnie, please, because I love you. You know I would talk to you if I could. Have sympathy for me, because it's the most necessary thing in the world for people to have.

This sounds as if I'm unhappy, which is a big lie. Nay, the reverse. And I'm not lost, Jinny. FOUND, one straying poetess, in Paris!

Dee

Doves

Doves dive up and down
Across our window
Silver and shot amber.

Clouds drift
As snow drifts from hemlock
At a breath of wind.

If we lean out
From the window—
Paris
Irony of Eiffel
Tour Saint-Jacques
Sturdy Notre-Dame—
Under the smoke.

Preferable to imagine:
And to watch only, from within
Clouds, silver-spotted,
Doves, slow-circling,
Peace.

c/o Royal Bank of Canada
3 Rue Scribe, Paris
September, 1931

Ah Jinnie,

Many thanks for all your letters. They all arrived finally, and I answered two together — then I found it was entirely too wrought-up an answer: so it was thrown to the basket. That explains why you've had no letter from me. Even though I think about you often. Even though this morning I was exceedingly homesick and thought (among other things) what joy it would be to pop into the Varsity office and talk to Jinnie. Do tell me all the news, every scrap; and if the old paper exists at all.

Not that it isn't very lovely here — with perfect weather and the Seine making Paris seem like a dream city because of its bridges and the constant flutter of yellow leaves upon it. And everyone stopping to smell the air, walking among the high trees of the Tuileries to forget the nervous whistle and screech of Paris traffic. And I too walking along, peering at bookstalls along the quais; or art exhibitions in the Rue de Seine. In three weeks, the University begins! But I haven't been able to see any professors yet, armed as I am with letters of introduction from Felix: they (the profs) are still *en congé.*

Gradually I'm getting some of my symbolists read, and that is interesting. And so is making omelettes; and eating one meal out at a twenty-five cent restaurant. A tight pull even that will be, with me losing ten dollars a month on account of the exchange. And I only had ten dollars extra, to count on after food and room! So the theatres I went to last month are probably the last I'll see. One was Ben Jonson's Volpone translated and re-arranged by Jules Romains. Very swell indeed. And another was a Provence play — a tragedy — called Marius. And a third interesting, but not so good as a play, was "Macchiavel" by Mortier — excellent acting.

All these I saw with Tony. So you realize I am not lonely. I suppose everyone knows he is taking his third year here. Tonight we go to an open communist meeting protesting against the Polish imprisonments. Ought to be good stuff. Certainly Europe's in one hell of a mess. I don't see any way out but the death and burial of Capitalism.

My love to all you think would be cheered by it. Meanwhile keep the secret well — of how terribly happy I am. Thine, Dee.

Paris, Nov. 5

Jinnie, hello, you didn't even tell me what job you are holding down on the *Varsity*, who the editor is, who else is about, what Ann Adler is doing, whether Willie Ann is getting paid, if Charlotte's is a success, why the duece Nat is at O.C.E. who the hell let the octogenarian back on the staff, excuse me I like the lad but he's a professional and damn it all what's the *Varsity* anyway, a garbage can, resurrection palace or an honest to god 'fore the devil STUDENT NEWSPAPER?

Now I are mad. Because the rag could be so much that it isn't. Sure it's a rag we all know that I'm not slamming it I'm saying shouting and bellowing from the other end of the world, "Rag, Be Thyself." Where's Andy anyway. GERMANY? VIENNA? Or Peterboro? Saw him the day I left on Young street and he was red-eyed and vague. See I've forgotten how to spell that dazzlin' avenoo.

And Victorious Lange? Où donc est-il, fils d'une biche.

Society is corrupt, I've decided. Diderot says that Woman has spent the centuries learning how to wear her fig-leaf becomingly. That is doubtless why the French pronounce
                    High Life
to rime with   Fig Leaf
Only they don't know that, the Innocents abroad.

Which reminds me I once wrote an article for the *Privateer* about a ship and entitled it cleverly "INNOCENTS ABOARD". It appeared in print "ABROAD" and I wept bitterly.

After all, the smallest of my troubles.

I'M WORKING. That is to say, I'm taking a rest. This week only.

Can't concentrate. In love again? Any way, I've seen my profs and I have two lectures precisely per week. One on the theory of comparative literature and one on How To Work. No professors on the Art of Loving; no professors on the art of enduring a stifling classroom; of eating bleeding beef or mumified veal; of being nonchalant when your pants break down on the BOULEVARD SAINT GERMAIN. Well, it's like that.

To continue my queries. Is the Guild really existing without me and Paul and its unacting president? (Which reminds me that Betty Sims fell down a flight of marble steps at the Sorbonne and landed at our hero's feet. Thus they met. (I have not yet encountered her.)

This was to say further good luck to the *Varsity* and more particularly to the Frat. Who-all is new? Jocelyn? Tell me what schemes you concoct to make them work. And what you have for supper.

There may be a brief article of mine in the *Star* on student life, which you can copy into the *Varsity* if you would like it. Had to send it Starwards, not to you, on account of needing moneys, always and forever. . . .

As I am,

Dee

And hoping this letter convinces you how Paris is depraving me.

Old Trees At Pere La Chaise

Old trees drift silently all down the hill,
And stop beside the green grass at the gate.
Encaged with tombs, they feel the wind, and wait.

Beyond, the dust lies with a difference.
The crumpled dead lie huddled in these streets
Belleville and Memilmontant, Gambetta
The dead in cold damp tombs slip up and down
The stairs of bleak and shattered houses, grope
Into the bedroom, kitchen, lavabos in one—
Move there, and hate, and bring forth child
And then go creeping from the window's dust
Into the shrouded bed, the heavy sleep.
The sulking dead lie huddled in these sheets
Only to wake and stumble through the maze
The choking air of unenlightened streets.
What more can women do, so pitiful
With bundles of their own small flesh and bone
The wrinkled babies of the labourer
Than struggle from beneath the roots, the dust

Of Paris corner-stones and roofs, and crawl
With the old men, beside the jobless young
Up to the sunlight of the Cimitiere?
There, green grass growing in lush patches lies,
Shadows the stones; a little wind will play
Softly amid the canopy of trees.

The skulking dead lie huddled in these roots—
Old trees with spring wound round their head
And the sky's blue parasol above—
The crumpled dead, laden with urns and tombs
Slink downward from the sturdy, living roots
That clutch the earth for sweetness, to find there
The faded taste of dust, the choking air.
Old trees at Pere la Chaise that strive to rise
Above this stony city, carefully planned
A junk heap to immortalize
The body, since the soul is shrunk—
Old trees, live longer! till a wilderness
Has covered stone and bone
And among the sunwarmed grasses
Eager children run!

Chez Mlle. Andrée Lévy
51 Rue de Bagneux,
Montrouge, Paris.
January 4, 1932

My Dear Jinnie:

Glad you had such a good time in London, in spite of the getting there. I regret that I was both ill and mentally occupied while you were here. Hope Paris made up for it. I've learned, I've been learning that the proverb "the world loves a lover" is utterly false. Family, friends and concierges loathe lovers. Doubtless the species is objectionable; in that case it should be regarded as a disease and left to run its course!

Tell Sonie I'm going to write her a long letter on the joys of married life. Tell Gilbert also that I send him thanks for his card, and wish I was at home to give him some advice.

No! That last might kindle his wrath. Leave him alone, send him my constant, very friendly love.

And so, for the moment, good-bye; and good luck to you. Study hard, take not the world too seriously. The people you cannot understand, leave alone.

I *am* in a position to sermonize — how many miles away? Love ever,

Dee.

Chez M Le. Levy
51 Rue de Bagneux
Montrouge, Seine
France
2 Fevrier, 1932

My dear Jinnie:

You'll think I'm a turner-about-face, doubtless: but I've decided that all newspaper people (i.e. my father, Grant, you) should write typewritten letters. And now you will repeat your last announcement: "I am not going in for journalism." Why on earth not? Expliques-toi. Have your desires lapsed like mine into an urgent desire to do nothing in the world but run a bookshop? A Sylvia Beach bookshop, bein entendu. I have been sitting in hers all day reading up old reviews and listening discreetly to the talk of people, such varied people, who come in to buy, sell, borrow or chat.

The best was an American who had a little boy at the Montessori school and is trying to get her collected verse published. It has been printed in all the right magazines — but no real publisher advances with smiling hands. *I* should feel damned lucky to have Eayrs (Macmillan) take mine. D.V., nothing happens to it.

This is James Joyce's birthday; and the 10th anniversary of Ulysses. Sylvia had white lilacs sent to her by him. But where is he, that reclusive man? Oh, for a glimpse.

Ask Jim, should you see her, whether she has Wallace Stevens' "Harmonium." Very worth while having.

Glad you enjoyed London so; but Otto would make one enjoy Siberia — n'est-ce pas?

Had a lively visit from Marjorie Price, on her way to Russia. I showed her the hidden Paris; and then we talked and talked — international politics!

This Chinese war is terrifying. Who knows whether we'll ever see Canada again, we two here? Anything may happen.

Best wishes to the Frat and its doings. And love again to yourself, "Nasturtium"; and many many thanks for your unconscious propaganda about my sad plight — which led to a raised allowance. Angel!

Your *old* Dee.

La Chope Latine, Boul Mich.
3 June, 1932

Dear Jinny,

Expect you are cross with me because of no news. If you knew how I had been working these last two months you would understand. It's not over yet, for though my essay is in I won't know whether it will be accepted until next week — then, if so, three exams which have me already in a state of dread, since I never took any Anglo-Saxon and cannot translate John Donne. Voilà!

Lately I've been to the races, to a couple of theatres; but only once (yesterday) to the country — that is, the forest of Versailles. It was lush green, since every day brings showers — hail — then sudden bursts of sunshine. Like April weather at home.

Spring fashions are shiny black straw hats, horrid; and the men, instead of ties, are wearing pom-poms! Red, white and blue. The most awful effect you can imagine, with yellow and red checked shirts. God, what a country.

Still, that's not saying I am running it down really, because I adore it — especially since Christmas. And Toronto of course is the last thing I want.

We have no clothes at all! So Jim and Anne had better bring Canadian sackcloth to ship me home in. That date is still uncertain — and meant to be.

. . . No news of what Otto plans to do. But I expect Felix will tell us. Hoping to see him on the eleventh. *Dear* Robert Finch is here, along with Douglas Duncan — who's a nice soul though with too much money. The Sims left for Germany and Victor last Sunday, expecting to be shot (reasons unknown) in the Hartz mountains.

You will perhaps guess that I am feeling ironic at present, not wanting to come home. But I hope a week at sea will soften and sweeten me, so I will be able to keep my mouth shut and my disappointment hid when I get back! I shall see you, I hope, at Clarkson.

Good for Gilbert's paternal instinct! Hope it's a boy. Is it too early to be so rash as to bring home a baby's plate?

No use asking questions! I'll be home to have them answered.

Love, as ever, Dee.

Clarkson, Ont. July, 1932

Dear Jinnie,

This is hardly a time to write to you, as I am very depressed. Grant has just cancelled a luncheon party (to meet his wife). Ainsi soit-il. But I thought I had better tell you that you had better not count on me for any doings, as I expect to be going to Muskoka within a week, chez Tony. But don't let that interfere with your coming here or taking S. to the

Glen. We will be on a better footing, I hope, with each other, by September. As for communism, it's a working-class movement and I realize now that it's no use trying to spread it anywhere except within the proletariat. It is alien to the other classes, they do not *feel* that way and so they cannot think that way. I want to think and belong to, work for, the proletariat; and so we will not talk about it any more. On that subject you and I are strangers. For Otto was right.

Now, let it rest. And be my old Jinnie. And remember that I am more or less in a Tunnel now, as a person, without any illusions or much interest in anybody. You'll have to accept that. — Dee.

Interview with Mrs. "Jim" Lawson Tuesday, May 9, 1967.

J.L. You see, the father and mother were so completely different. There was a constant pull for the two girls between them. And the father was, well he was quite a neurotic character, with a rather marked speech impediment. But a very brilliant man, and as I guess you know he was the founder of the Canadian Press. And the mother, while she wrote, it is true, I would think that she was a very minor writer. The main thing about her was that she was extremely traditionally religious; she was a very staunch Anglican. Of course, Livesay's aim at home was to horrify her at every step. So every meal was a kind of bravado anti-religious thing on the part of Livesay with Mrs. L. kind of sighing and tearing her hair. Oh, he used to do things like pasting up rather insulting, and quite funny poetry on the walls about one or other of the family. Of course, she couldn't reply, this wasn't her means of defense. In fact, she had no means of defense. As well as that, she was the most appalling housekeeper—the house was mad. They used to have New-Canadian maids, a series of them, none of them ever stayed very long. As soon as they learned English—and a lot of them seemed to be writers, poets and things in their own language—they weren't really cut out to be maids. And they would do things like move the bathtub to wash under it, plus pulling out all the plumbing. So the house had some lovely old things, stuff Dee still has—old chests—still it was a mad place, but full of books.

Well, I grew up there because it was so much pleasanter than my house. Livesay was terribly interested in the girls. His whole life centred on those two girls and their friends. And he used to treat us all like grown ups and invite us to lunch at the Royal York and have green turtle soup and fresh strawberries in December, and that sort of thing. When you're fourteen and you've been taken out to lunch by a real grown up man, it is a tremendous thing. And they never really treated them as children really; they were part of the adult world.

Anyhow, of course, they both married men older than themselves, which was obvious. Girls brought up such a way. . . .

C.B. *Binky Marks thinks that Dee revolted against her parents, do you agree?*

J.L. She may have been rebelling against her mother but not against her father. I think her father really belonged to . . . he completely approved of her activities. Wouldn't you say? He wasn't ready to join the Communist Party or anything like this, but he was a born iconoclast, so as far as rebelling against the family as a unit is concerned, no, I don't think so at all. And actually Dee's earlier life was really quite traditional. I remember summers that I would stay out there and sleep in the wood shed and we would talk all night. She was getting confirmed. And I was then an atheist and we would have long, long conversations lasting literally all night about religion. When do you get confirmed, fifteen or sixteen? Anyway she was still quite traditional then. Her main interest wasn't in social things at all. She wasn't a social critic then. It was purely literary. She spent her whole youth reading and books were the thing she was interested in. It was only much later she became interested in social problems and one could hardly help it because we graduated in the 30's.

Actually, both of us, we went to a rather small girl's school and so there wasn't a very big group in each class. But both of us were completely outside that world of running around with boys which at that time wasn't quite as advanced as it is now, goodness knows. But still at fourteen and fifteen you were terribly interested in boys and neither of us were. We were awful blue stockings. It's true she wasn't terribly attractive physically at this time, which I suppose is not very pleasant to not be. But I don't think it bothered her very much except perhaps at the university and then I know there were occasions when it was quite obvious that she wished she were glamorous.

Like everybody at this age, she had a tremendous thing going for someone at the university. He really couldn't see her for trees. Being a poet, well maybe it wasn't worse for her than anybody else, certainly she could verbalize it, the whole agony of the situation. And so she did.

Then later her sex life took a fine upswing and she had a wonderful year in Paris. This was really very satisfying and she blossomed, she just blossomed.

But I don't know anything about her life after she married. I never had the feeling that their marriage was any great shakes. But I never knew Duncan at all; I only really saw them once when I came out here to visit them very briefly just before the war. In fact I was here when the war broke out. So I never got to know him. But it seemed to me that her sex life was rather truncated at this point, but I don't know.

C.B. *Do you think she represents the woman's point of view.*

J.L. For me that's a rather meaningless generalization. I don't know what *the* woman's point of view is.

C.B. *Well, then a woman's point of view.*

J.L. Well, obviously she represents *a* woman's point of view.

C.B. *Take the love poetry at the end of her last book, do you identify with it, understand it?*

J.L. Yes, certainly. Yes, but can't men identify with it too? I mean is love poetry so divided between the sexes? Such things are only significant to women? I don't think so, then of course, I am not a man.

I was quite swept away by Paris and my first real love affair that year. But the tragedy was that I was awakened to a desire for home and man and children rather than for a career; and Tony had thought of me as a thoroughly independent, modern young woman who would not load him with responsibilities. Undoubtedly I gave that impression! It was I who made the discovery about myself and he did not take to the emerging person. I think all this had a rather damaging effect on my psyche. To be so ripe and not to be plucked!

What followed was my most painful year; back in Toronto taking social work at the university and having to endure a mutually-agreed-upon separation from my lover, whilst all the while encountering him, as we both became more involved in the communist movement.

July, 1932

My Dear Jinnie

Forgive the silence. After such a happy time with you I should have written at once to thank you for it. We were thrilled to hear that you had the energy and will power to knock down a thug after leaving me. Perk was very excited and woke me up the next morning with the story. Bravo!

I've been in town lately, delivered my book to Eayrs, bought some exciting material. But impossible to find a dressmaker who charges less than thirty dollars or more than four. Don't know what to do. Tony is due the beginning of August and may spend a few days out here.

Tomorrow I see Olya and I hope get in touch with things. Had lunch with Ross recently and found he is on the labour beat — damned interesting. I've started writing a series of articles on French life (sic) which I hope to syndicate.

Sophie and I wonder whether you could manage the Glen during the week, say after Wednesday. As I may go to Montreal next week-end and she to Wasaga. Don't do this unless convenient. There's all of August ahead of us.

Love and expecting news, Dee

 *That summer of 1932, back in Toronto after a year in Paris, was a crucial one for friendship and love, as the letters to Jinnie reveal. My political convictions became the dominating obsession of my life. This lost me friends, split me away from parents, disrupted my relationship with my lover. It was at this point that Raymond Knister came back into view. In my teens I had had a strong emotional pull towards him because of his critical brilliance and because his poems and stories about farm life in Ontario were so direct and meaningful. He was ignored by the current literati because he was so modern. I saw in his imagist poems a new source for Canadian poetry. I felt his penetrating criticism was just what was needed. By 1927, when he was twenty-seven, he seemed to be heading for a brilliant career, meeting people like the Leo Kennedys and the Wilfred Egglestons, all young marrieds whose aim was to rejuvenate and modernize Canadian literature. But Knister was desperately poor. Wilfred Eggleston has told me that he happened to be living in an apartment below the Knisters in Toronto's Parkdale and knew that they were visited by the bailiff for non-payment of rent. They had to move. By the time I met Raymond again he had moved many times and was living in a cottage at Port Dover. My long conversations with him, crowded into two days, were polemical. He wanted me to keep on writing lyrical poetry and I wanted him to write political novels! We could not come to terms.*

Two weeks later I was visiting Leon Edel at his flat in Montreal when the phone call came from Leo Kennedy saying Knister had been drowned and this was a frightful shock to me. I thought immediately that I was the cause of his death.

It was only in 1943, at the urging of Lorne Pierce, that I revived my memories of Raymond Knister, began collecting his poems and wrote the preface which is herewith published again. It has been somewhat abridged through the good offices of Robert Quickenden.

Raymond Knister: A Memoir

by Dorothy Livesay

It must have been true that I knew Raymond Knister years before I actually met him. Perhaps it dated from the time I was ten years old, when we left the wide silence of prairie skyway, our senses stunned by the close-up to come: apple-blossomed orchards, upstanding elms by the snake fences, unknown wild flowers in the cool woods. This was Ontario — self-contained, enclosed — but where man had somehow struck a compromise with nature.

That farm country which, when understood, becomes an intense experience — that was Knister's milieu, the central column of his thought. He made excursions away, but always he returned to the fields he had tilled in boyhood — hating, yet loving them.

Turn under, plow,
My trouble;
Turn under griefs
And stubble.

Turn mouse's nest,
Gnawing years;
Old roots up
For new love's tears.

Turn plow, the clods
For new thunder.
Turn under, plow,
Turn under.

("Plowman's Song.")

Throughout my own early adolescence the land, and a blue-shirted farmer behind the plow, were a part of existence as well as of dream. Reading romantic poetry, and writing it with the distorted, unreal idealism of the very young, I seemed nevertheless to sense an essential rhythm, a relationship between the man, the beast and the land, which had symbolic significance.

How different was the real-life encounter with the farmer who was poet, too! I must have been thirteen or fourteen, self-consciously sitting in the sun in my father's woodland garden at Clarkson. My dog, a noisy but dowdy old Airdale, suddenly began to bark violently. Someone was coming up the drive, a wiry, small-built man. As the dog bounded toward the man, I called him back, I knew, quite fruitlessly. The stranger approached. Wearing an unbecoming dark suit, his red, sunburned face was flushed from the June heat. He came up warily and when he began to talk I thought the dog had terrified him.

"Rab's all right," I said. "He's quite harmless and dull."

49

The man smiled, his serious face transformed. "I — I was looking —"

"For my mother, Mrs. Livesay?" Mother often had strange callers, depending upon what literary project engaged her attention at the time.

"No. I must have seen a m-m—" He paused, struggling. Then: "I have come to see Mazo de la Roche."

"Oh, I see! Well, you've come too far. Look, her cottage is just back there, through the trees."

Mazo, with several books to her credit, was working steadily away at *Jalna,* and Raymond Knister was bringing his own novel to her for criticism. I remember afterward, as she was coming through our woods with her pail for the milk, she said that Knister talked in a torrent of words, and, once started, his stuttering was eased. His manuscript interested her. He wrote about three thousand words a day, at which she marvelled.

The following winters Knister sometimes appeared at our Toronto house as well, for my mother was preparing an anthology of Canadian verse (never published) to which Knister contributed. Robert Finch, she told me, thought highly of these bare, unmusical imagist verses. And in reading them I, too, was suddenly stirred, as if I had found my own voice speaking.

The quiet snow
Will splotch
Each in the row of cedars
With a fine
And patient hand;
Numb the harshness,
Tangle of that swamp.
It does not say, The sun
Does these things another way.

Even on hats of walkers
The air of noise
And street-car ledges
It does not know
There should be hurry.

("Quiet Snow.")

Raymond Knister was born (at Ruthven) near Comber, Essex County, Ontario, on May 27, 1899. Elizabeth Banks, his mother, was an Ontario-born schoolteacher, of Scottish parentage. Robert Walter Knister was the youngest of thirteen born to German Canadians who had settled in Ontario one hundred years ago. He was a man of perseverance and foresight who imported pedigreed Clydesdales from Scotland and became the first man to grow soy beans in Kent County.

The centre of the community was the Methodist church, in which both parents were active. The 'non-conformist conscience,' which grew out of this religious atmosphere, must have had its struggles beside the lively historic sense which drove the young Knister to his books. His father also inculcated in the young man a conscientious aim toward perfection which, when combined with an extreme sensitivity, made every criticism a spur and a defeat. It may have been some such half-humiliating incident, too painful to be consciously remembered, which sent the small seven year old boy home from school one noon, unable to speak coherently. He tried to tell his mother what had happened, but could not. From that day on he stuttered badly. As a result, Knister's mother wanted to keep him out of school for a year, but the father insisted that his education must begin. And therefore, it would seem, the transitory shock which led to stuttering became so strong a habit that later efforts to correct it failed.

His life at this period was divided between farm work and books. At eighteen Knister decided that words would be his field and he turned to the writing of poems and fiction. Characteristically, he wrote from the heart, from direct experience. Better than people, he knew sun and snow, spring and autumn; he knew a boy's job of farm chores; he knew animals. For instance, he hated feeding the pigs, but he found a poem in the trough ("Feed"). He loved the stable and the character of horses. These he described with a tender simplicity and intensity. It was these poems, without apparent music, straightforward as a man talking, which won their way into the best poetry magazines of the United States, and into *This Quarter*, Paris.

These poems were more than a promise of powers to come. They were a complete statement about life on the farm. The emotion in them is not that of conflict, so much as resignation. The harmony in them comes from an inner music, close to the rhythm of speech. The fresh, original descriptive quality comes from direct observation. Some of the poems fail. They try to be something they are not, something stylized. Or they take on a moral tone, ending with a philosophical tag. But these are immaturities common to any young poet.

In 1919, Knister went to Victoria College, Toronto, but a bout of influenza followed by pneumonia sent him back to the farm where he worked fourteen to sixteen hours a day to regain his health. His need to write was now becoming more certain, as he himself has written: "There was something about the life I lived, and all the other farm people around me, something that had to be expressed, though I didn't know just how." He wrote poems which were published in American little magazines, while in London *The New Criterion* praised his poems for their "objectivity." But Canadian editors continually rejected his work. He did not know why at the time. He had to go to the United States and then return, in order to find out. Even after that he never fully understood: and the sense of injustice grew, however courageously he fought to down it.

Canada, in the twenties, was coming to grips more seriously than ever before with the idea of nationhood. In material aspects unhurt by the war, the early depression years were imperceptibly flung off, as a bad dream fades on waking. There was a feeling of boom in the air, a quest for excitement which, however, had none of the carnival cynicism about it which attacked American life and literature. We are not a boisterous people, nor given to extremes. We had been brought much closer, culturally, to the United States, but bouts of cynicism like Hemingway's were not adolescent meat: we repudiated them for a more robust romanticism. All that was positive in the imagist movement in poetry, all that was realistic in prose like Dos Passos' — this had appeal and influence.

In a country steeped in the sapling tradition where the first need has been to lean on England, and the second to snuggle up to the United States for stamina, original creative writing was not to be expected. Morley Callaghan, the most hopeful prose writer of the late twenties, was aiming at American markets or at *This Quarter*, the magazine of the American Paris. Mazo de la Roche, after her first novels, *Possession* and *Delight*, which had a real native flavour, turned her attention towards England and began writing of English characters and customs in a rural Ontario setting which failed to convince Canadians.

Knister was also an exile by virtue of the very honesty with which he described the soil and the people he knew. He now turned his attention to the American Midwest and the small magazine, *The Midland*. In an article on Knister in *The Canadian Forum*, Sept., 1932, Leo Kennedy recalled H.L. Mencken's earlier judgement on *The Midland* as "probably the most important magazine ever founded in America." It was here that Knister published stories marked by that "objectivity" that Kennedy so highly praised: "In the stories . . . we find . . . Canadian farm life depicted with faithfulness and warmth, and a realism quite sufficiently literal."

At this time, Knister's object in writing poetry was to present the object seen, the thing felt, as simply and feelingly as possible. His concern was to "interpret beauty: not becoming bogged down with the moral preoccupations of Wordsworth, nor finding the be-all and end-all in the sense, as Swinburne." It was this idealistic, uncompromising young man who, in Iowa and Chicago, met with many of the coming American writers, particularly the regionalists like Ruth Suckow. This was a happy period for Knister, as his letters show. It was also a period of self criticism in which he wrestled with the problems of his art: "I incline to find more and more that the short story is one of the trickiest of forms. How to impart a hint of the wonder and mystery behind the circumstances, and yet remain true to these latter. This can be done through humour — and is — once in a blue moon, but it takes a mature artist, at least."

Despite his success on *The Midland*, Knister felt a need to return to the place of his roots. In Canada, names like Wilson Macdonald and E.J. Pratt were coming to the fore in poetry, and Mazo de la Roche and Morley Callaghan in prose. Though Knister met them on infrequent trips to

Toronto, he kept on working at his own writing regardless of theirs. A letter of January 2, 1925, from Blenheim, Ontario, reveals his constant concern with the problems of the "mature artist." He describes the difficulty of achieving simplicity, the continual "toil and rewriting" required. He touches on the temptations of writing for money and the frustrations of dealing with editors. He expresses his belief that there is an "appreciative public" which his work cannot reach because of critics and editors. The letter also reveals a tension between an anxious desire to "perfect" himself and the belief that "art is probably taken too seriously." As Knister developed, this balance between humour and seriousness swung more and more towards the latter. His passionate search for perfection led him to think of himself as an artist and nothing else. In his last notes for the unwritten novel, *Via Faust,* he calls this stage in the writer's life the second phase:

> He decides a la Keats that the truth about life is its beauty and struggles to put this into his novel, realistic — a dramatized study of personal relations (people doing him in business and so forth). . . . He decided all this malevolence is really only the life urge. Self-assertion naturally becomes selfishness. It is necessity, and it is something else. It is life, the urge and spring of things; life cannot be stagnant. It has to move, and if the living being is not gifted with brains and imagination, the stirring is bound to be of seeming malevolence.
>
> As life cools in himself, life, of whatever sort, seems to be the thing to be valued.

This point of view is important to stress, because it is one which Raymond Knister's work did not go beyond. He had planned where it would go: the direction would be, like Kierkegaard's, away from the aesthetic to the moral stage: what he called "the Dostoevsky prophet role." And he fully realized, before the end, that such a direction would lead him into an ethical world, a world where creative action mattered more than aesthetic interpretation. The three stanzas called, "Moments when I'm Feeling Poems" give a hint of the goal toward which Knister was working: one of humility and acceptance. But that "third stage in a writer's life" was not to be. Instead there was: "all this malevolence."

In 1927 Knister married Myrtle Gamble, a girl who had grown up in the same countryside as Knister. She was quiet, reserved and hard of hearing; perhaps it was her very simplicity and innocence which attracted him as being part of his childhood knowledge. In his youth and early manhood he had had little to do with women. The one girl to whom he had been officially engaged in 1925-1926 was a Southerner and a Roman Catholic, not approved of by his mother. Her father had intervened to forbid the marriage. Despite his strong ambition, at twenty-seven he was emotionally immature and seems to have held a highly idealistic conception of what a woman should be. "I have already seen you in my dreams," he told Myrtle with dramatic earnestness.

In a letter written to a friend at this time, Knister expresses the hopefulness which still rules his nature. He again makes an appeal for a Canadian literature which will be free of English or American influence. Having read through a collection of poems written for Dominion Day, he writes: "Reading these my wife suggested that I should have written something out of the soil for the occasion like "After Exile," what Canada meant to one Canadian, instead of laudable sentiments anent impersonal institutions, and individually regarded with very mixed feelings during their lifetimes. I said, 'Oh God, when is Canada going to have a poet instead of an advertising man!' But the time is not yet, nor am I the man. Aweel."

Shortly after writing that statement he gave up journalism and turned his attention to *White Narcissus,* a novel about which he later confessed with perfect honesty: "At that time I did not know anything about human relationships." The novel was accepted for publication by Macmillans, for whom he was also at work compiling a volume of Canadian short stories. Apart from these projects Knister was also doing critical writing; an essay on Archibald Lampman in the *Queen's Quarterly* shows strong insight combined with a sense of tradition and language.

Knister was also in contact with a group of poets who congregated in Ottawa and Montreal. Leo Kennedy, Leon Edel, A.M. Klein, A.J.M. Smith and F.R. Scott had rejected the native tradition and, under the influence of Eliot and Spengler, had begun to think of themselves as citizens of the world. They had formed *The Canadian Mercury* and were very active in the newly founded Graphic Press in Ottawa. They offered a yearly prize of one thousand dollars for a Canadian novel which Knister won in the second year, with his novel on the life of Keats, *My Star Predominant.* However, the press went bankrupt and Knister was able to collect only seven hundred dollars, much of which was used to pay the legal fees resulting from the difficult struggle to get the money.

The novel itself is a paean to beauty and death. Perhaps, because he felt the same struggles within himself, Knister has recaptured the feverish sense of urgency which activated Keats in the four years leading to his death. He portrayed the poet as demanding the utmost of himself in his desire to deliver the vision of beauty to the world. He was deeply impressed with Keats' urge to fight against obstacles and ability to hold fast to the vision and express it at all costs. Leo Kennedy described the novel as "the dramatic account of the soul and character development of the poet."

Such a treatment of an historical novel was not popular at the time it was published (Ryerson, 1932). But it may well be, when the rage for scandal and eroticism has subsided, that Knister's substantially honest, penetrating and glowing picture of a great poet will be read appreciatively and with relish.

At this time Knister was continually harassed by material and economic pressure. And he was far from alone in his failure to earn a living. The vast army of the unemployed was beginning to gather voice and writers were taking sides politically. Some were pushed to the wall without fully understanding what was happening to their world. Others, still economically secure, began to participate intellectually in the world conflict of ideologies. Knister's life fell in with these contradictions. He was one who had to suffer personally, yet who remained grimly determined to stay with his ambition.

He continued looking for help and found it in Lorne Pierce of Ryerson Press. Pierce did everything possible to secure the release of the manuscript of *My Star Predominant* from the defunct Graphic Press and also set Knister to work on an anthology of Canadian prose. While on a holiday at Lake St. Clair Knister wrote to Pierce about his difficulties in writing and his need for money. Pierce was alarmed by the desperate tone of the letters and left for Lake St. Clair to offer Knister whatever personal help he could give him. He arrived only to learn that Knister had been drowned.

Weeks after the funeral, which took place near the scene of the drowning, in Port Dover, and which was attended by many writers and critics, Myrtle Knister came to our house for dinner — shy, quiet, but troubled. She told us of that last day spent by the lakeshore, when they were preparing to go to Walkerville for a visit with Knister's sister. She has since written down what occurred that evening: "He followed me about my work all that day, as I swept and packed and cooked, talking incessantly. He had such an uplifted feeling, as though he had just come into some great powers. He said Keats and perhaps Shelley too had felt the same way, and then, just as these new vistas of consciousness opened up to them, everything was snatched away. He ended talking on the note that perhaps man was only permitted a rare glimpse of what all his life he had been seeking, and then it was over."

Half an hour later Raymond Knister went to the shore for his usual afternoon swim. His wife was too busy to accompany him, as had been customary. Knister took the rowboat out some distance from the shore, to get closer to deep water. Before Myrtle and wee Imogen, watching from their cottage could believe it, he had disappeared, his body seemingly sucked down by an undertow. It took three days of dragging to find him.

The shock of Knister's going affected many people outside his own family. It seemed as if in him Canada had created a writer who believed in the land and the people, who might be at the beginning of new powers of expression. To Leo Kennedy, fellow poet who had known him through his hardest year, in Quebec, he had come through with flying colours and was 'on his way up,' with 'all his creative powers quickening' within him. To Lorne Pierce, Knister's death meant the loss of 'a magnificent spirit, the promise of a kindling force in Canadian letters.' Morley Callaghan, on the other hand, believed that Knister had already made his 'rendez-vous with death' some years before. To me, the problem that his life posed never left me. Knister seemed to epitomize the struggle of a generation, and one which will again come to the fore, even more pressingly.

Knister had come again to Woodlot, two weeks before his death. He drove me along the lakeshore that fascinated him, with its cold blue water, dazzling sunshine, colourful crowds. That evening I had a longer talk with him than ever before, five or six hours of uninhibited inter-change. Once he began to talk, he could not stop. In this way he met his speech handicap head on and, from the force of his intensity, sur-mounted it. But listening to him that night was like hearing the voice of one who had gone a long way down a dark road. He had lost, somewhere, his sense of direction. He admitted that he had been searching the philosophical poets — Goethe and Rilke especially. He had talked with religious men, seeking a way to calm himself. But he felt he had been frustrated too long, cheated of living the complete and harmonious life which he believed was the creative artist's right.

Ever and again he returned to the other theme close to his heart: the importance of creating beauty; of losing no time; of wasting no moment in the present, however urgent its turmoil. "If one could get completely away from the world, as our painters do, to some remote northern lake. That would be the way to start searching for truth."

This was too escapist for me. "But how could one live that way? It is in the process of living — that is, of working with and loving people — that we learn the truth about life."

In my belief he did not want that reply, nor any reply. He had already chosen. To save the integrity of his creative life he was willing, nay, he felt it necessary, to blot out the obligations and compromises of everyday life. Before his marriage he had said in a letter: "I can't stop writing, even to get married." Now that decision, as he told me of it, had become much more intense.

Such are my impressions, after fifteen years, of Raymond Knister's mood before his death. Today these impressions are sustained when I turn to the last book in which he was immersed, those final weeks: the *Duino Elegies* of Rilke, together with an appraisal of them by Hester Pickman in *The Hound and Horn* (April-June, 1931). Aside from the evidence of significant passages underlined by Knister, it is clear that the German poet's philosophy found ready ground in the German-Canadian spirit of Knister. Rilke's message is forthright: no compromise. He enshrouded this in his own particular mythology, which Hester Pickman described as follows:

> In the *Elegies* Rilke is no longer searching, because he has found all that is necessary to him in the possible immortality of man's spirit. I say possible, because it is clear that to Rilke immortality was only for a few; for those

whom he calls heroes, and for those who die young — that is, for those who have escaped the slavery of worldly standards which must necessarily kill the soul.

How completely in accord with Knister's views, imbued as he was with the Keatsian spirit and the hero-worship of Keats, who died young! These themes of Rilke — the belief in the perfection of childhood, the supreme importance of sorrow, the death that may lead to immortality — these "have now become the permanent values that lie at the vanishing point of all human perspective" (Hester Pickman). Had they not also become the permanent values of Knister? Over and again Rilke refers in his poems to the theme of the "Fruhentruchten" — "the early snatched away."

> He only makes it clear that the slight imperfection of their lives is something we must remedy, that they may detach themselves from earth. His is a conception akin to that of purgatory. But even more important than the help we give them, is the sorrow they cause us and which we need. Their death is the eternal sorrow that feeds the heart of man, as in Greek legend the mourning over the death of Linos was the origin of music.

One cannot help wondering what extraordinary effect these lines, and the poetry behind them, may have had on the overwrought, oversensitive spirit of Knister. Such a philosophy implies that the temptation to flee the world is not one of cowardice, but of self-sacrifice. Self-immolation to save the world — how often in the history of mankind has that theme been the portent of tragedy!

Whatever the truth of his death may be, it is the life of Raymond Knister which is symbolic for us today. His struggle has been the crux of almost every writer's life in our time. It is a struggle more bitter and desperate in Canada than almost anywhere else. How it is resolved determines a man's creative output. Some creative figures, like Sir Gilbert Parker, will gradually "go commercial" to sell their stuff and live by the trade; others, like Frederick Philip Grove, will die in poverty and resentment, idealists to the end. That the problem is so often resolved into an uncompromising idealism is due more to our synthetic culture, our schools, our philistinism, than to the individual's weakness. If the creative life were everyone's to share, if it were an accepted part of our community life, there would be no dichotomy. Writers and artists who need the fulfilment of marriage and child-rearing should be given that opportunity, free from the great destroyer, economic fear.

For Raymond Knister that opportunity was not guaranteed. What he was able to leave us is the record of that effort, that struggle. The prose he longed to write never reached its full flowering; but there is enough of it, in the short stories, to guide and stimulate serious writers of the future. This prose, poetic and interpretive of our countryside and our people, succeeds because of its utter simplicity and honesty. Stripped of all pretension and wordiness, beneath the bare style there is revealed an undercurrent of passion, of emotion, which gives it lasting significance for us.

But of all the legacies which Raymond Knister has given Canada, the finest is his poetry. The headstone of his grave at Port Dover, Ontario bears the following words which may serve as a tribute to his troubled spirit and to the achievement of his art:

> The sea breathes, or broods, or loudens;
> Is bright or is mist and the end of the world;
> And the sea is constant to change.

> I shall not wonder more, then,
> But I shall know.

---

20 Rosemount Ave.
December 8, 1932

Dear Jinnie, [at L.S.E.]

Thanks for the pamphlet and the nice letter. I suppose this will hardly catch you before you are gone. Unfortunately I lost your address the other day, and mother mailed you my book not noticing the number of the house was missing. Do you suppose you will ever get it? It's just out, with a few to-be-expected romantic reviews from Canadian critics. Happily this satisfies the family, for they are much more interested than I.

I am in the midst of exams (for the School of Social Work) which have to be good because of maintaining a scholarship. I am almost tempted to apply for a new travelling research scholarship that is being offered for next year; on the other hand, it's better to stick to this and get some practical experience. Meanwhile I shall have to be satisfied with the Marxian attitude as an approach, not as action. With Tony it is wholly action, he is so busy I doubt if he will get any scholarships. His whole energy is turned violently in one direction. I don't know what will happen to him.

There's little more to say. Haven't been near Gilbert and feel very guilty about it. He was extremely sympathetic one night and then had a violent reaction the next morning — or so it seemed — and so depressed me that I am literally terrified of seeing him. I assure you, it's no use at all trying to make it up with him; he is finished and you might as well make up your mind to that.

Did you know a girl called Maysie Roger at Vic? She's in my year and course (social work) and interests me quite a bit. She's reserved though, so it won't be a galloping acquaintance. But quiet and non-emotional relationships are my sole aim from now on. Peace is after all essential: and Jim and Tony are the reverse of peaceful. Rationalization! But it's fairly true, by god.

Merry Xmas — and don't be getting twins and *don't* use chemical contraceptives.

Yours cheerfully,

Dee

20 Rosemount Ave.
Toronto.
May First, 1933

Dear Jinnie: (Please don't read this letter until you are feeling disgruntled and fed up with yourself. Letters always sound worse than conversation, and I think this one is pretty bad. I hope you understand why).

I answer at once, because I won't have another breathing space for two months. Last week I finished all my exams, and today I started my field work — very interesting, with unmarried mothers and their offspring. The maddening thing was that I had to observe a mental health clinic in the afternoon, and so missed a demonstration in Queen's Park. However, there'll be a meeting tonight. The P.A.C. Drama Group is putting on a very swell play.

Meanwhile, my P.A.C. Writers' Group comes on apace. Two of the men (unemployed) are writing novels which are extremely interesting — thus utterly disproving the Trotskyites' contention that there can be no working class literature until world socialism is established.

Tell Nina. . .before you depart that

1) I haven't compromised

2) that Lola's example sank deep; and now my new poetry is approved not only by intellectuals of the (Leon) Edel ilk, but more important — by workers and communists. It's only a small step forward, but there's no going back.

What do you want sympathy for? Psychologically speaking, sympathy is an attempt to imagine the other person's situation, but that can only be done in terms of one's own experience. Well, my own experience tells me inexorably that I despised myself when I was in the same state of mind as you. All, therefore, that I can possibly hope for is to see you get out of it — quick. Ross and Olya are just the same: a complete pre-occupation with their own ego, so that they are unaware of any social relationships and in a constant state of self-dramatization. I can say all this, because it is still uncomfortably near to me. Even though you never speak to me again, I am not afraid of being quite ruthless with you. Every paragraph of your letter is a pose, an attempt to say things as you expect people want you to say them. I leave it at that. I feel that education has spoiled you, made you false. You imitate instead of living.

Such harshness would be quite unnecessary if I thought you were a hopeless case. You have enough sense to realize, I hope, that I do this because I am perhaps the only one who really believes something can be done about you.

About other things. Surely you realize that schools are closing all over Canada, teachers are unpaid and literally hundreds are without jobs? To go to Normal School would lead you absolutely nowhere. O.C.E. ditto.

Why not something like Occupational Therapy? Some line like mine which is ever demanding new recruits.

As for "writing", you'll forget it when you are doing something active and useful which makes you socially conscious. If you mean writing for its own sake, you surely realize that that game is utterly played out; the last word in decadence has been said. The art of the present and the future must be functional, must be aware of social movements. Even André Gide, the most art for art's sake of all possible writers, has come to this conclusion. His is a marvellous commentary on capitalism.

Lastly, "career" is a slogan of the nineteenth century feminists. Forget it.

It is a good sign, though, that you do want something. But when you get to the point where you are too busy to analyse yourself, that will be better.

Dee

"Woodlot", the Livesay home at Clarkson.

Decadence in Modern Bourgeois Poetry

Radio Talk given on CBC in 1936 by Dorothy Livesay

Because Marxist criticism of bourgeois art has had to do, mainly, with novelists and prose writers — such as in Plekanov's analysis of the French nineteenth century, or Calverton's recent interpretation of American literature — this does not mean that the poets of today do not offer a good a field for research. On the contrary, modern poetry reflects the decadence of bourgeois society in an amazingly clear way. To illustrate this point, I am going to study mainly the work of two representative poets: T.S. Eliot and Edith Sitwell. But to do so, it is necessary to jump back, first to seventeenth-century England; and then to the late nineteenth century in France. Why do we do this? Because modern poetry derives its chief inspiration from these two periods.

The seventeenth century in England was essentially a transition period. The new commercial middle class was still encumbered by the remnants of mediaevalism. Side by side with Bacon and Hobbes, another group of intellectuals remained firmly attached to the church, to feudalism and scholasticism. And they were so far from being scientific that they were fascinated by the problems of astrology and alchemy. The best example of these two trends was certainly John Donne, poet and preacher: a man who combined a baroque mysticism with passion and a lively intellectual curiosity. In his poetry, the result of this fusion takes the form of symbolism. In order to prove, for instance, that two souls are one, he compares them to the two points of a compass:

If they be two, they are two so
As stiffe twin compasses are two
Thy soule the next foote make no show
to move, but dothe, if the other doe.

And though it in the centre sit
Yet when the other far doth roam,
It leans, and hearkens after it,
And grows erect, as that comes home.

Such wilt thou be to me, who must
Like t'other foot, obliquely runne;
Thy firmness makes my circle just,
And makes me end, where I begunne.

This fantastic play with words is essentially mediaeval; at the same time

61

there lies behind it a great deal of healthy lust. Donne's love poems never saw the light in a Victorian drawing-room. But because he is a mystic occupied with the flesh, and because, too, the decaying mediaevalism of the time smelt of death, John Donne is much concerned with the decay of the flesh. He is always writing words like these:

> When my grave is broke up againe
> Some second ghest to entertaine
> (For graves have learned that woman-head
> To be to more than one a bed)

He is essentially, like his fellow poets, the fantastically religious Crashaw and Vaughan, a poet of his own class, but with roots still in the past.

We must turn now to another situation. The first half of the nineteenth century in France was one of triumph for the bourgeoisie. The chief poet of that time, Victor Hugo, is a romantic optimist, patriotic towards the nation, sentimental about the family. He maintains a mistress to flatter his muse. Physical well-being, industrial expansion, scientific invention all find their place in his poetry. But by 1848 things weren't going so well for the nation; by 1870 Paris was for two months in the hands of the Commune. The bourgeoisie had created its own antagonist. It was not rooted in the past, but it had reached the peak of its expansion and development. It was already decadent. The poetry of this later period marked the change. Baudelaire had led the reaction against optimism. The deepest depression, stamped with a violent hatred of the "rabble" and a violent turning aside from life into a continuous torture of self led him eventually to become a perverted mystic: he worshipped the devil outwardly, but the fear of sin coupled with his own sterility made him, in reality, turn to religion. He has written:

> My soul is a tomb, where, evil cenobite,
> Since eternity I run through and inhabit.

These same features occur and give rise to symbolism not merely as a part of poetry, but as poetry itself. The symbolist school in France represents an attempt to escape from bourgeois materialism into a world where the individual alone mattered, and there he set himself up as the interpreter of the universe. And naturally enough, from a Marxian point of view, all these poets were essentially depraved and decadent in themselves. They were either homosexual, as Verlaine and Rimbaud; or they were ascetic, like Laforgue, due to their own sexual inhibitions or sterility. And all this was inevitably reflected in the tone of their poetry which was cynical, bantering, fantastic or mystical. Always, it was strained. Laforgue's refinement of thought for instance, led him to employ such an inventory of words that no one but himself could grasp their significance.

How then, does this background affect modern poetry? The period of the war is reflected in society, not only in chaos, but in a lack of any positive meaning anywhere. Capitalism is much nearer to death than it was in 1870. The poets of today are in the position of having no positive side, even, to react against. Consequently, negation expresses itself by a complete jump backwards. From seventeenth and nineteenth century poetry, modern poets take their themes: the very basis, then, is sterile.

T.S. Eliot was born in puritan New England, of a professional family. He might easily have grown to be a staunch poet of the American bougeoisie. Instead, from the very beginning he reacted. He fled to Europe. He is now an English citizen and calls himself a "classicist in literature, royalist in politics, and anglo-catholic in religion." What is the poetry that is the result of this self-willed grafting process? It also is a small root with innumerable branches grafted on from John Donne, Webster, Baudelaire and Laforgue. In one of his poems, "The Waste Land," for instance, he has inserted into the text innumerable lines from Shakespeare, Webster, Dante, Middleton, the seventeenth century dramatist, Kyd and Marvel. He gives the references in notes at the back of the book. Moreover, to display his learning, six foreign languages, including Sanskrit, are incorporated. And he rationalizes this by saying, in an essay, that "It is more convenient to use, if necessary, the philosophy of other men, than to burden oneself with the philosophy of a monstrous brother in one's own bosom."

All modern poetry has this same tendency, which arises from the theory of art for art's sake: namely, to appeal to a very small group of people who happen to have had the same prolonged education and the same refinement of the senses. Who is to know, for instance, who is to care, whether in the following lines:

> But at my back from time to time I hear
> The sound of horns and motors, which shall bring
> Sweeney to Mrs Porter in the spring

Eliot is combining phrases and rhythm from two seventeenth-century poets? Whose but a mind extremely like his own enjoys a Baudelairian comparison such as:

> Let us go then, you and I
> When the evening is spread out against the sky
> Like a patient etherized upon the table.

One needs sophistication and cynicism to appreciate the following bachelor:

> And when I am formulated, sprawling on a pin,
> When I am pinned and wriggling on the wall,
> Then how should I begin
> To spit out all the butt-ends of my days and ways?

Obscurity of language is the next limb of our tree. Here is inventiveness for you:

Polyphiloprogenitive
The sapient sutlers of the Lord
Drift across the window-panes
In the beginning was the word.

And I assure you that the context does not help matters. Moreover, the symbolism which we have seen as the inevitable result of this poetry, serves most often, only to obscure the impression. He is trying to express sterility by describing a dry, sandy plain. This is how he does it:

We whisper together
Are quiet and meaningless
As wind in dry grass
Or rat's feet over broken glass
In our dry cellar.

And to express the thoughts of a man who has had a chance, which from fear, he failed to take, the poet says:

I have seen the moment of my greatness flicker,
And I have seen the eternal Footman hold my coat, and snicker
And in short, I was afraid.

Needless to say, this poetry is modern again because its ideas and subject-matter are dissociated. There is an absolute lack of socially valuable meaning in Eliot. He writes of a housemaid, and this is what he says:

They are rattling breakfast plates in basement kitchens,
And along the trampled edges of the street
I am aware of the damp souls of housemaids
Sprouting despondently at area gates.

In general, the themes are three: sterility, death and mysticism. The atmosphere of impurity, of sexual impotence that we found in the consumptive French poet Laforgue, is replaced in Eliot by a definite drawing away from the flesh. He speaks with agony of;

The awful daring of a moment's surrender
Which an age of prudence can never retract.

Sometimes he hides this retreat in cynicism over the stenographer who;

Turns and looks a moment in the glass,
Hardly aware of her departed lover;
Her brain allows one half-formed thought to pass:
"Well, now that's done: and I'm glad its over."

He renounces then; and he renounces in favour of death.

D.S. Mirsky has made an interesting point in this regard. He asks the question, "Why didn't Eliot choose Fascism as his main theme? Why is he not the poet of the last stage of bourgeois imperialism?" The reason is that the active struggle of the bourgeoisie against the revolution is ideologically sterile. And Eliot, whatever his faults, has an extremely strong historical sense. He could not support Fascism because he feels that the death of the middle class is more imminent than Fascism. This is Mirsky's interpretation. He concludes moreover that death is the only historically valuable and sincere theme which is possible for a bourgeois poet of today, and because he has chosen it, Eliot is socially valuable.

I maintain, however that he is socially valuable only to a very small coterie of bourgeois intellectuals. And since his other theme manages to cover a great portion of his work — I mean mysticism, I fancy this detracts rather from his social importance. In "The Waste Land," Eliot's longest poem, it is not wholly the feeling of death that concludes the poem. He begins with

> Prison and palace and reverberation
> Of thunder of spring over distant mountains
> He who was living is now dead
> We who are living are now dying
> With a little patience

But he goes on

> I have heard the key
> Turn in the door once and turn once only
> We think of the key, each in his prison. . . .

But his conclusion affirms a certain philosophical mysticism. "Ash Wednesday", a later poem, shows that he has found his safety-valve — religion. Listen to this new disciple:

> Because these wings are no longer wings to fly
> But merely vans to beat the air
> The air which is now thoroughly small and dry
> Smaller and dryer than the will
> Teach us to care and not to care
> Teach us to sit still

Like the Greek philosophers, Eliot attempts to purify himself by sitting still.

Lest you should think that Eliot is only one, we shall turn now to the three Sitwells, a family of English poets who began writing during the war. No better proof that literature reflects unerringly the environment and class ideology of the writer could be found than in the work of the three Sitwells. It is well to remember that the influence of the seventeenth and nineteenth centuries shows itself very strongly throughout their work.

We find at once in the poetry of Edith Sitwell the same appeal to the intellect, to erudition, to a small group. Aristocratic wit and a constant attempt to render sensations at all costs, by all manner of means, abound in her work.

> The fire is furry as a bear
> And the flames purr

She says.

> The busy chatter of the heat
> Shrilled like a parakeet.

Or

> The crude pink stalactites of rain
> are sounding from the boughs again.

Only her own brothers can really appreciate the following:

> There still remains Eternity
> (Swelling the diocese)
> That elephantiasis
> The flunkeyed and trumpeting sea.

Needless to say, the poet's language will be obscure. Archaic and foreign words are deliberately used:

> Trains that sweep the empty floors
> Pelongs, bulchauls, pallamphores,

I say deliberate, because Edith Sitwell has no wish that her vocabulary should express sense: sensation is all she wishes to convey. There is a great deal of technique in her writing; a great deal of time and care has been spent on it. But the question arises, has it any sort of value at all? It might have a jazz value, if only words had the same appeal as music. But they haven't. This deliberate confusion of the senses is to be found in all modern poetry. To my mind it has the same appeal to the modern intellectual as negro jazz has for the wealthy business man: it dopes him. But I doubt if the intrinsic value in jazz has any place when transplanted to poetry. Humour is all that is left.

Due to her highly specialized manner, Edith Sitwell's thought processes are more difficult to follow than T.S. Eliot's. Once his symbols are grasped, the meaning flashes clear. But Miss Sitwell's symbols are so remote from real life that it is difficult to know exactly where she is leading us. A glimpse at her own philosophy might help: she is watching a Russian ballet and this is what she feels:

So we sit, in the loneliness of identity, watching the movements growing and ripening like fruit, or curling with the fantastic inevitability of waves seen by a Chinese painter; and thought is never absent from these ballets. In Petrouchka we see mirrored for us, in these clear sharp outlines and movement all the philosophy of Laforgue, as the Puppets move somnambulantly through the dark of our hearts. For this ballet, alone among them all, shatters our glass house about our ears and leaves us terrified, haunted by its tragedy.

It is obvious. Tragedy for her is the tragedy of a child's world. She sees life with a capital L as if it were a stage where puppets played. This is her escape from the burden of an ancestral hall. Osbert Sitwell, who is definitely a realist, has written a whole book of poems about old family servants from the point of view of a benign landlord.

Lest you should think that there is only one side to Edith Sitwell, let me point out that her most recent long poem, *Gold Coast Customs* is a different and extremely important piece of work: the theme is identical with that of Eliot's "Waste Land": sterility, death, and finally, mysticism. The more specific theme is ironic: namely, the comparison between the so-called brutal customs of the Gold Coast natives, and the customs of an English society lady holding parties oblivious of London's poor. To my mind this poem is socially valuable, in spite of its mysticism. The knowledge in it that death is coming to destroy the present system is exceedingly marked. This theme has meaning for a dying bourgeoisie: this theme is a confession of defeat. It adds one more important conviction to the certainty that bourgeois art is dead, that a new art, the art of the proletariat is being born.

Montreal 1933-1934

"Painted on many shop windows you will see a blue-bird. The merchant inside will tell you that this sign is a guarantee that none of his goods have been bought from Jews."

Growing Up

So damn little I knew
Wanting, since fifteen, to work in a shirt factory.
Terrible longing to *understand*.
And it was stifled, so many years stifled,
With leisure, literature, learning.
But the womb was clamorous:
Ah, too many abortions
Life's ecstasy reached, fruit formed.
Then the cold instrument's function.
Now I have broken free!
Sent prejudice sprawling
With my quick thrust into living.

Now I am alive, having created
My breath one with yours, fighter and toiler
My hands ready, with yours, young worker
To crush the boss, the stifler
To rise over his body with a surge of beauty—
A wave of us, storming the world.

69

Rain in April

Give us rain in April; for rain is harsh
Reveals the sidewalks where we tread
Cracked, and caked with mud. It blows and beats
Against the worn-out shutters and the walls,
It sweeps away the lethargy of spring.

We must be bolder now; sharp, and more cunning.
The winter was so cold it numbed us rather,
Left us frightened for the tasks ahead.

Give us rain in April; rain will seek
Our very roots. Our understanding trembles.
We must thirst for our own travail, grow
Through our own hunger to the final fight.
Give us thirst and hunger! Rain, defy us,
Sting us into movement, into pain.

We must be made ready, as the fields prepare
For May, and the flowering of our may-day hour—
For the sweep from uncertain April into red growth,
For the bursting of our shackles, into power!

Twenty Years After

Deep in August, wind has a warning sound:
Month of betrayal, when the working world
Proffered itself to destruction, and was hurled
In the name of freedom into the muffled ground.
Now in this August, bombing planes have found
Alaska's borderline; the warning's whirled
To Moscow, where forever alive, unfurled
Red flags of peace signal the world around.

Across the sea, the mighty hiss and groan
Of factories are still: blood on the picket-line.
The sun in deeper mockery has bled
Our fields to dust, beside the farmer's bones—
But common hunger welds the common sign:
A bulwark against war, demanding bread!

70

Members of the "single unemployed" march up Bathurst Street in Toronto.

Canada to the Soviet Union

I believe in the beauty of your faces, brothers and sisters,
I receive the challenge from your eyes, and tremble with joy.
Mine are the restless millions, the women broken,
Stamped on a child's thin body.
Mine are the homeless, degenerate! Desperate young thieves,
    prostitutes;
Mine are the breadlines the hostels crawling with vermin—
(One week's rations in a sack for a family of nine).

"In this country" (Archbishop Gauthier has spoken)
"Let us be thankful that no one has died of starvation."
In this country a certain Harry Spencer
Committed suicide on Prince Arthur Street.
In this country we do not die of starvation, we live it.
In this country we are forced back to the land
At twenty cents a day—
"That's less than army pay," Sir Arthur Currie should whisper
Far from Flanders fields.

Yet I believe in the beauty of your faces, brothers and sisters!
It is reflected in light over the dull prairies,
It is caught up in the eyes of my people there, who are Polish,
Finnish, Hungarian, men of the Ukraine;
It glows in the gaunt, hard look of my men who are miners
From the hills and forests of Nova Scotia away west to Drumheller!
It is in the cities — your strength and determination!
It shows itself at an eviction struggle, when Zynchuk is shot in the back.
At Stratford it flares up sharply, a sharp row of faces, unyielding—
At Rouyn — fifty below zero — men are marching because of you!

Because of your young faces, children of revolution!
Children broad-shouldered and sturdy, sprung of a lusty seed:
Where love battled with hatred — class against class.

Because of you we have learned that soon "this kind of thing"
Will flower above the ruthlessness
of the bosses' Iron Heel.
We shall see beauty rising from the roofs of factories
We shall see armies marching through new fields of wheat:
We shall be unashamed to face you, comrades!
For our children will have songs, at last
To spur their eager feet!

On my return from Paris, summer of 1932, there was no job in sight; and as I was by now deeply concerned with the plight of the unemployed and the political scene in Canada, I decided to take the new diploma course offered by the School of Social Work at U of T. It was headed by E.J. Urwick, an English professor who had had much experience in London with neighbourhood houses like Toynbee Hall. He was a Platonist, an idealist, a charming and gentle man of the old school. Beside him was Harry Cassidy, who taught us economic and labour history. He was a CCF'er, a mild socialist with whom I had some sharp arguments in class, for by this time I was a confirmed Marxist. At his house he introduced me to Earle Birney, who had not yet become a Trotskyite. As I remember we talked of the relationship between society and literature. Birney made a favourable impression upon me — not for his physical appearance which was spare and spindly, but for his mental vigour and great knowledge of Early English, his intellectual prowess. At that time he had not published poetry (except, as I later discovered, in the Ubyssey) so I did not think of him as a poet (or as a rival, which eventually he became). And in spite of our political differences Earle was very friendly to me all through the war years, writing to me from overseas, and bringing his wife Esther to see me.

But my main friend at the U of T was Maysie Roger, and we both decided to do our second-year field work in Montreal at the Family Service Bureau (earning $60.00 per month) and to share expenses by living together. I think we tried one or two places before settling in the French area, on St Denis. A parallel street was St Laurent, where I soon found communist cronies, all Jewish except the painter Louis Muhlstock. He was such a gentle person — still is, I am sure. I remember listening to a record of Saint-Saens in his parents' tiny sitting room and going with him, come spring, to Caughnawagha Indian Reserve. He had been down there painting Indian people, and I wanted to get the feel of how they lived. I remember being distraught by the flies, which settled all over an old woman's kitchen so that one could not see the ceiling. That was likely my first glimpse, ever, of utter poverty. Muhlstock had great sensitivity to other people's predicaments, though he must have been very poor himself. We appreciated each other, but had no compulsion to join forces. And by this time I was a militant activist, member of a party cell producing leaflets and agit-prop plays and mass chants which we performed in the bleak, cheerless labour halls.

Conditions of the depression in Montreal were at their most terrible; it was worse than the situation in Paris, and the police were even more *vicious. I participated in unemployed demonstrations and political meetings of all kinds, as well as living through the day to day struggle of the unemployed families whom I visited for the agency. The city was giving very inadequate relief, and we had to supplement. We dealt with protestant families, English and French.*

I was active mostly on the cultural front, writing "agit-prop" plays and, by spring, becoming involved in the anti-war movement. I was the secretary of a conference, the first of several I imagine, calling for a united front of youth against war. I learned a great deal about Communist tactics of penetration and camouflage; but I was too committed to be shocked. It was only years later that the false actions and fractional tactics were revealed to me in their real light. This did not cause me to hate the communists, or to red-bait; rather I was disgusted with myself for having been so duped. But I believe I let myself be duped because no one else except the communists seemed to be concerned about the plight of our people, nor to be aware of the threat of Hitler and war. These things they saw clearly and they did extend brotherhood to the down-and-out. Certainly the communist predictions of capitalist depression followed by fascism and war were deadly accurate!

One of the tasks I was given at the time was to help create an ethnic festival of working class plays and songs. This meant contacting Ukranian, Russian, Latvian, Swedish, Finnish and French labour organizations and getting them to send their singers, dancers and actors in competition to the festival. I wish I had kept the programmes! I was entranced with Swedish and Finnish singing, and rather horrified by a Polish play which depicted capitalism as a serpent with a long tail, thrashing about dragging the workers down. This was a bit too much agit-prop for me!

* * *

While I was working in Montreal, my friends in the Progressive Arts Club in Toronto were causing one of the real furors of the thirties' artistic scene. The play Eight Men Speak, *performed by the Workers' Theatre, played only once before authorities had it closed. This was an act of repression we protested and publicized widely.*

PROGRAM

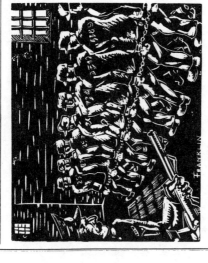

Progressive Arts Club

presents

Workers' Theatre

in

"EIGHT MEN SPEAK"

Standard Theatre

Monday, December 4th, 1933

CAST
In the Order of Their Appearance

MRS. BERKLEY	Lillian Cecil-Smith
MRS. STONE	Jim Watts
MAJOR STONE (WARDEN)	Ed. Smith
DEPUTY - WARDEN	Ben Koza
GUARD X	Max Bloom
TIM BUCK	Al Hershkovitz
MR. DUFRIE	Cecil Greenwold
STENOGRAPHER	Helen Lehrer
SUPERINTENDANT OF PENS	John Haig
EDITOR	H. Francis
SOBSISTER	Mildred Goldberg
CAMERAMAN	Jack Sheppard
COPY BOY	Bruce Ewen
NEWSBOY	Abie Smaltzman
WAITRESS	Kay Phillips
MAN IN CABARET	Chas. Croxford
WOMAN IN CABARET	Helen Lehrer
GIRL ON STREETCAR	Harry Napier
MAN ON STREETCAR	Avrom
OLD MAN	Lon Lawson
CAPITALIST JUDGE	Charles Drinkwater
MOUNTIE	Bruce Ewen
TOM EWEN	Cecil Greenwold
MATTHEW POPOVICH	William Miles
TOM CACIC	J. P. Smith
SAM CARR	Avrom
MALCOLM BRUCE	O. Ryan
JOHN BOYCHUCK	H. Francis
TOM HILL	Lon Lawson
CLERK OF COURT	O. Ryan
WORKERS' JUDGE	Lil Corn
CO - JUDGE	Chas. Croxford
CO - JUDGE	E. Cecil-Smith
MR. CAPITALISM	Toby Gordon
C.L.D.L. ORGANIZER	Ted Broomfield
GUARD SMITH	Fred Gray
CONVICT BROWN	John Haig
GRYSHKO	R. Brown
NARGAN	Ben Koza
MARKUNAS	William Miles
PETER GRABOWSKI	Percy Matthews
NICK ZYNCHUCK	Harry Napier
CONVICT JONES	Joe Burns
GUARD THOMPSON	Saunders
REV. SCRYMGEOUR	J. P. Smith
GUARD HARRIS	Charles Drinkwater
MR. BEDWIN	

NOTE — The Workers' Theatre welcomes new members for its troupe, as well as members for its Supporters' Club. Scripts of plays, sketches, mass recitations, etc., can be obtained at a nominal rate. Performances by Workers' Theatre can be arranged for a small fee. — Persons interested in the work of the Writer's Group, Artists' Group or Photo Group should communicate with the Progressive Arts Club, Box 211, G.P.O., Toronto. — Translations of Eight Men Speak and performances of this play are subject to approval by Workers' Theatre.

"EIGHT MEN SPEAK"
A Play in Six Acts

BY OSCAR RYAN

ED. CECIL-SMITH   MILDRED GOLDBERG
H. FRANCIS

Directed by: Oscar Ryan, Ed. Cecil-Smith, Cecil Greenwold, Toby Gordon.
Stage Management: Lilian Cecil-Smith
Settings: Avrom, Nat Patterson, W. Penny, Helen Nelson, Joy, E. Gray.
Properties: Mildred Goldberg Helen Lehrer, Toby Gordon, Al Hershkovitz.
Music: Standard Theatre Orchestra

ACT I: Scene 1: A terrace on the grounds of the Warden's estate. Evening, late October, 1932, Kingston, Ont.
Scene 2: Tim Buck's cell, Kingston. September 1932.
Scene 3: Office of Minister of Justice. Shortly after. Ottawa.

ACT II: Scene 1: Voices from the prison. Night. October 17, 1932.
Scene 2: Newspaper office. Oct. 17, Toronto.
Scene 3: Cabaret. Oct 17. Montreal.
Scene 4: A street car. Oct. 18. Winnipeg.
Scene 5: A h mc, Oct. 17 Vancouver.
Scene 6: Cross-section.
Scene 7: A scene from the trial of The Eight. Nov. 12, 1931. Toronto. out from the trial of Park, July, 1932, Kingston.

ACT III: Scene 1: The Workers' Court. The present.
Scene 2: A whipping, in prison.
Scene 3: The Estevan miners speak.
Scene 4: Peter Grabowski speaks.
Scene 5: Nick Zynchuck.
Scene 6: Tim Buck's cell.

ACT IV: The Eight Speak
ACT V: The Workers' Court. The present.
ACT VI: The Workers' Court. The present.
CURTAIN.

Canada's Workers' Theatre

The following is taken from a two-part feature on Worker's Theatre in Canada by freelance writer Sandra Souchotte.

. . . It was not until the formation of the Toronto Progressive Arts Club in the Fall of 1931 that criticism of society was unified with a distinct proletarian artistic policy that included theatrical activity.

The awakening proletariat must have a revolutionary culture that will expand with the growing realization of its need and the methods necessary to their fulfillment. They must have songs that will stir them emotionally, that will waken a response in their own subjective suffering, and lead them on to revolt. They must have plays that will depict the drabness and sorrow of their daily lives and resolve the doubts and fears that arise in the minds of the frustrated, into a clarified determination to assert their own strength as a class. In teaching the workers the ways and means by which they can achieve their social salvation the theatre must take its place with the soap box and working class press. . . .

Progressive Arts Clubs eventually became active in six Canadian centres, Halifax, Montreal, London, Toronto, Winnipeg and Vancouver until their gradual demise by 1936. The objective of the thirty-five initial members was to provide the basis for a militant, working-class art and literature and to register popular complaint about the economic crisis of the thirties in Canada. The means came through the publication of a national socialist magazine called *Masses,* which ran twelve issues covering the period from April 1932 to April 1934.

In the first issue editor E. Cecil-Smith strongly rejected any suggestion that art could have nothing in common with politics, while in an article called "Theatre of Actualities" David A. Hogg called for a workers' theatre group which would operate in crude Elizabethan-like surroundings and provide soul-gripping plays. "Plays that would fill a deep need in the hearts of a working class audience, and etch there the fundamental ideas of a revolutionary philosophy of life, in a way no other medium could."

By the winter of 1932 a small amateur troupe of actors had formed the Workers' Experimental Theatre (later abbreviated to the Workers' Theatre) with the intention of using drama to expose and ridicule what was considered to be an exploitive bourgeois society.

Although occasionally indebted to outside sources for scripts, the Workers' Theatre was determined to create its own selection of Canadian plays based on "a drama rooted in the lives and struggles of the toilers of Canada's shops, mines, farms and slave camps." Early attempts to meet these requirements were at least moderately successful and the first performance of a Canadian agit-prop *Deported* was given at the Ukrainian Labour Temple on May 6, 1932. Other short agit-props and mass recitations followed, characterized by a subject matter that focused on social inequalities and the need for increased social consciousness and a style built on collective declamation, tableaux formations and rhythmic movement. Such indigenously produced and descriptive plays as *Solidarity Not Charity, Eviction, Farmers' Fight* and *Labour's Love Lost* soon became part of a standard repertoire. One of the later playwrights for the movement Francis H. Love (who wrote under the pseudonym H. Francis) reported, many years later, on his impressions of the early Workers' Theatre.

> The troupe performed in labour halls, on the backs of trucks, in the parks, any place they could find an audience. Their repertoire consisted mostly of mass recitation advocating change and given with all the fervour of dedicated youth. The first performance I saw shocked me but it also stirred me to the core. I noticed that the audience was also deeply moved. At last I had found people who had the courage to stand up and shout their disapproval of the deplorable conditions under which we were then living. . . .

Toronto Mail, January 1934

THEATRE WARNED TO PREVENT PLAY

Government Acted Upon
Police Board Request,
Official Says.

ARTS CLUB OBJECTS

Proprietor of Standard
Told License Would
be Forfeited.

The Toronto Police Commission is responsible for the warning, issued by the provincial government, to the proprietor of the Standard Theatre that his license would be forfeited if he allowed the play, "Eight Men Speak," to be presented on his stage, according to W.A. Orr, assistant controller of revenue in the Ontario Treasury Department.

Without the slightest hesitation, Mr. Orr admitted yesterday that such a warning had been issued by his department to I.J. Weinrot, proprietor of the theatre, this week. The theatre had been rented for Monday night by the Progressive Arts Club, a workers' movement, for a repeat performance of the play which appeared several weeks ago at the same theatre.

The Progressive Arts Club brands the warning as "the beginning of Fascism" and "an attack on the freedom of the stage."

"What reason did the police commission give for its request?" Mr. Orr was asked.

No Reason Given.

"None," he replied. "They simply said they did not want the play presented. They are privileged to make the request because the censorship of the legitimate stage in Toronto is in the hands of the municipal police."

"Is there no board of censors?" "No, there is for motion pictures, but there is none for the legitimate stage. Just as we do not demand a reason when the board of censors for motion pictures asks us to prevent a picture being shown, so we conform with a request with regard to the legitimate theatre."

Mr. Orr went on to say that censorship involved such matters as the showing of plays and pictures which are not in the public's interest, which are injurious to the maintenance of law and order and so forth. Under the Theatre and Cinematographs Act, the province is permitted to cancel licenses of theatres that present, in the face of warning, plays and pictures which the legal censors, in this case the Toronto police, condemn.

He also explained that if the province, which issues theatre licenses, gives a theatre a license the municipality cannot intervene to prevent the theatre receiving it. The province co-operates in return by meeting reasonable requests advanced by municipalities with regard to cancellations.

Ed Cecil-Smith, a director of the Progressive Arts Club, stated that if there was anything in the play which offended action should have been taken against the club rather than against the theatre. The club was endeavoring to develop a Canadian stage, he said, and as far as the club was concerned it had not broken the law in any way.

"It is worse than an attack on freedom of speech," he said. "It is an attack on the freedom of the stage and such actions are an outrage which smacks of Fascism."

The players had sold out half the house before the warning had been received by the theatre proprietors, he said. Stage properties had been prepared and the play was in readiness for presentation.

Acted After Report

The police commission had acted in the matter after receiving a very full report on the initial presentation of the play several weeks ago, including a stenographic transcript of the bulk of the dialogue, according to Commissioner J.R.L. Starr.

The commission felt that much of the material bordered closely on the classification of seditious matter warranting prosecution, but gave the sponsors the benefit of a degree of doubt in this regard, he intimated. Believing, however, that performance of the drama was of dubious legality, and contained potentialities for disorder in case members of the audience took offence at some of the sentiments expressed, the commission forwarded its data and reports to the provincial treasurer's department.

"I don't recall that we made a definite request or recommendation that the theatre license be cancelled if the presentation was repeated," said Mr. Starr. "There was a suggestion to this effect, I think, but my impression is that final disposition of the problem was left in the hands of the treasury department, which has jurisdiction over theatres.

"Our reaction from the report we received of the play was one of distaste, and I wouldn't blame anyone for stopping it, but I have my doubts whether such a step would be worth while in the long run."

The "Eight Men" alluded to in the title of the drama are the eight Communist leaders imprisoned in Kingston Penitentiary. The play sets forth the alleged injustice of their incarceration and arguments for their release.

The Toronto Star, January 13, 1934

The Banning of a Play Which Gave Distaste

Critics are forever saying that in this country we are over-governed— two Houses of parliament at Ottawa while one would be enough, too many legislatures, county councils, city, town, village and township councils, too many commissions, boards and what not. It would be supposed, then, that we would have laws enough and by-laws and regulations enough to meet every need, so that the Toronto Board of Police Commissioners could, in its performances, keep within the law. It seems not, however.

The proprietor of the Standard theatre in this city has been warned by the provincial government that his theatre license would be forfeited if he allowed the play, "Eight Men Speak," to be presented on his stage. The provincial treasury department issues licenses to theatres and possesses power to cancel them. This power was exercised, that is to say, warning was given that the power would be exercised if the play were staged. An official of the department states that the power was exercised at the request of the Toronto Board of Police Commissioners, who gave no reason for making the request, simply saying they did not want the play presented. The authority of the province was exercised without those who wielded the power knowing why they did what they did.

Mr. J.R.L. Starr, a member of the Police Commission, was interviewed in the matter by a morning paper and is reported as saying:

"I don't recall that we made a definite request or recommendation that the theatre license be cancelled if the presentation was repeated. There was a suggestion to this effect, I think, but my impression is that final disposition of the problem was left in the hands of the treasury department, which has jurisdiction over theatres."

An official of the department makes it clear that all the government had before it was the request from the Police Commission which was acted upon. There was no inquiry into the case by provincial authority. The play had been presented in the same theatre some weeks ago and the Police Commission had a stenographic report covering much of it. Mr. Starr in his interview said.

"Our reaction from the report we received of the play was one of distaste; and wouldn't blame anyone for stopping it, but have my doubts whether such a step would be worth while in the long run."

It is rather late for Mr. Starr to express his doubts about causing the banning of the play because he had a "distaste" for it. Many have a "distaste" for quite a few plays and movies and parts of radio programs, but no law empowers the Police Commission to ban a play because it has received a police report of it which causes a distaste for it. If a play offends, if there is indency in it or sedition in it the police can institute proceedings in the courts against all or any connected with it.

To set up a short-cut method such as this wherein a police request to ban a play will cause the provincial authority to ban it instantly, without asking questions, is indefensible. There is a growing police tendency to adopt plans by which they may evade the courts.

This play about eight men deals with the trial of the eight Communists sent to prison from this city. It does not seem desirable that court trials should be parodied on the stage, but to prevent the undesirable by resorting to unlawful methods on the part of the authorities is more undesirable still because worse results can flow from it. This play, it seems, was produced some time ago and little was heard of it. By banning it in a way that makes a brass band issue of it the Police Commission and Queen's Park take some chance of giving the play the advertising it wants.

RESOLUTION ON THE FREEDOM OF THE STAGE IN CANADA

WHEREAS:

Roy C. Buckley, of the Ontario Provincial Treasurer's Department has threatened to revoke the license of the Standard Theatre, Toronto, if the management permits the second presentation of "Eight Men Speak" by the Workers' Theatre of the Progressive Arts Club; and

WHEREAS:

Authorities of the Provincial government have publicly stated that this action was taken on the request of the Toronto Police Commission, who in turn state that their request came as a result of a report made to them by Detective-Sergeant Wm. Nursey, which places the determining of what shall be presented on the Canadian stage in the hands of a policeman who, by his well-known character and training, is obviously no critic of the drama; and

WHEREAS:

A certain Dickson-Kenwin, unable to make a name for himself legitimately on the Toronto stage, after years of attempts, has sought to bring attention to himself and gain some prestige by attacking the Progressive Arts Club and the Workers' Theatre movement, and has publicly announced that there is an organized campaign being launched against all workers' cultural organizations in Canada; and

WHEREAS:

The packing of the Standard Theatre on December 4th, for the first showing of "Eight Men Speak," by more than fifteen hundred people, while hundreds had to be turned away; and the large advance sale of tickets for the second presentation — many clubs, groups of intellectuals and students, artists, trade unions and shop groups having bought blocks of ten, twenty and more tickets — show conclusively the mass support which the Workers' Theatre group of P.A.C. enjoys among Toronto workers and intellectuals, and the interest which Canadians have in a living stage; and

WHEREAS:

Such actions on the part of the authorities show very clearly how rapidly the development of fascist tendencies is taking place in the repressive machinery of the Canadian "democratic" State; and

WHEREAS:

Such an attack on the freedom of the stage was previously unknown in modern times in English speaking countries, and in fact can hardly be paralleled anywhere in the world, outside of open fascist dictatorships; and

WHEREAS:

If this system of censorship and intimidation is allowed to continue, it cannot but result in a serious warping and stunting of the growth of Canadian Theatre Art.

THEREFORE BE IT RESOLVED THAT:

This .... at ....
consisting of .... people

DEMANDS

The immediate rescinding of the ban against "Eight Men Speak," and the permitting of it to be shown in any theatre the P.A.C. may choose to rent, and also

DEMANDS:

Full freedom of the Canadian stage from censorship and police intimidation, so that a living Theatre Art may be built in the country; and also

DEMANDS:

An immediate end to the campaign to stamp out the workers' cultural movement, so frankly announced by Dickson-Kenwin, the very day that the government ban was known; and full freedom for all workers' cultural groups in Canada to carry on their artistic activities, and specifically

DEMANDS:

Full freedom for the Progressive Arts Clubs in Ontario and throughout Canada, who are particularly threatened as the first victims of this reactionary campaign.

AND BE IT FURTHER RESOLVED:

That this resolution be sent to Attorney-General W.H. Price, Queen's Park, Toronto and copies be sent to the press.

SIGNED   . . . . Chairman
          . . . . Secretary.

Please detach this stub and send it to Progressive Arts Club, P.O. Box 212, Toronto, Canada.

Resolution on the Freedom of the Stage in Canada was passed by our meeting on . . . . 1934; Number of members of organization, or number present at mass meeting . . . . ; Name of organization . . . .
. . . .
Address . . . .
Chairman . . . .   Secretary.   . . . .

PROGRESSIVE ARTS CLUB
3778 St. Denis St., Apt. 9
Montreal

Jan. 16, 1934

Friends:

You have witnessed the result of cultural suppression in Germany. The Theatre, once a living force, is dead.

A new gesture of suppression in Toronto indicates that a similar situation will prevail in Canada unless strenuous efforts are made by all those interested in the Theatre, against the dictatorial conduct of the authorities. A play, "Eight Men Speak," presented by the Progressive Arts Club, Toronto Branch, was banned by the police of that city on January 13th, 1934.

The usual ground for discontinuing a play is that it has offended the modesty of some police officer, but this play is banned for an altogether different reason. The authorities do not wish the public mind to dwell on the vital issue this play presents.

Believing that this play is a sincere effort on the part of the producers to build a living Workers' Theatre in Canada and that it is imperative that the ideas contained in this play be brought to public attention, we are asking you to co-operate with us to re-establish the freedom of the Theatre before this phrase becomes an empty one.

With this aim in view we are calling a meeting of protest, to be held on Sunday evening, January 21st, 1934, at STRATHCONA HALL 772 Sherbrooke St. W. at 8:30 p.m. Participate with us by inviting your membership to attend.

Yours truly,
PROGRESSIVE ARTS CLUB
D. Livesay
Secretary

The unemployed were completely without recourse. They were evicted from their homes, their water and heat was cut off, they were given the meagrest amount for food and so on. That life was one of great despair, and though I myself of course was earning sixty dollars a month and feeling quite safe on that, it was heart-breaking to see people who had nothing. Just at the time when I came to Montreal there had been a very great unemployed demonstration over an eviction, and since I had seen other evictions as well, I wrote a poem about it.

An Immigrant
(Nick Zynchuk)

Spring returns again, soft winds caress
The huddled houses of St Louis Ward.
And you return again, newcomer here,
Unknown and unobserved. Over the sea
They knew you. You were a small boy breathing spring
On a bare farm in Poland.
You grew, and starvation matched you, stride by stride.
On a railway platform, barefooted, you saw
Our golden stretch of wheat, our skyscrapers
Embroidered on the air.
It was too much! The sweetness of far suns
Burned deep and touched your hunger: you broke loose.
And soon the ocean's tossing washed your dreams.

The immigrants come in. Women with shawls
Wide-eyed and silent view the fluted towers
Of granaries. They see the mountain's cross.
So Montreal is real! Its wide shores hum
Its streets stretch into dimmer distances—
Spring is a peasant woman in a shawl
Blowing green mist all along the hills.

Work is spasmodic. Shovel and pick,
One day here and another day there.
Sit on a gravel pile deep in the sun
Munching sandwiches one by one.
"What do you say, Nick? There's a fine girl,
Catch her and snatch her and give her a whirl;
If we can't be millionaires, let's be men!
It's a hell of country — till you kiss her again!"

The immigrants come in; year follows year.
Slower the wheel turns, faster more are thrown
Ruthless against the wall, to sleep in parks
Or at the Refuge face the lice and rats.
Five years of this now, Nick, with just enough
To live on when you worked; for two years now
You've tramped the streets and knocked at factory gates
That only rattled harshly, and relapsed
To rusty silence. On the wall, a sign
"Your opportunity" is blotted out by rain.
Alert, but empty-handed, the refrain
Comes back to you, Nick Zynchuk: "Years of hell!"

Deep in St Louis Ward soft winds caress
The huddled houses, spring returns again.
The winter's gone, and no one's paid their rent:
The couple upstairs went to jail, and Nick
Here's Nick again, his pockets empty still.
We've appealed to the landlord, then to the City Hall;
We've appealed to our candidate for alderman.
Tomorrow the day is set, out we go, wife—
Unless the neighbours help us fight it through.

Click click click. "Attention, men!"
The sergeant's at his words again.
"All right, Zappa — take this whiskey,
Use your billies if they're frisky,
See? They're bastards, not fit to live,
Give 'em all you've got to give."
The crowd held firm. Then a single cry went up
As the furniture came out. Now working-men
Stood shoulder close to shoulder; silent, tense—
Until policemen charged, beat back, and struck.

Then you returned again, newcomer here,
Unknown and unobserved. What you had left,
A few possessions — trousers, and a hat,
Were still upstairs in an old travelling bag.
You moved towards the door, towards the stair
And scarcely noticed Zappa standing there.
The crowd stirred restlessly. You passed—
There was a roar and pistol crack.
Nothing had happened in the street—
Only a worker was shot in the back.

* * * *

When spring returns again each widening year
Blue loft of sky, scent of sweet grass hay
Still penetrate the asphalt: wider cracks appear.
Deeper the fissures by the window-sill
And more the feet, parading now, sound out
In wider unison. Alert and quick,
New voices take command; thin children grow:
As willows stiffen in the sun their arms
Stretch out to life; and Zynchuk, smiling quietly
Is part of moving green along the hills;
Is garden for their seed. His breath is blown
Stronger than this March wind upon their lungs.

Longshoremen (1940), Miller Brittain. Collection of the National Gallery of Canada, Ottawa.

Zynchuk's Funeral

It was idle curiosity brought me to my senses. That day when the news bills splurged the story that a guy was killed at an eviction — by a cop — I bought a paper for the first time in weeks. Funeral was around where I lived, so I went.

It was queer. People streaming out of houses like going to a ball game, but low voiced. "Keep close to me Minnie." The same streams as to a ball game but different, no gladness in the way they moved — heavily, slowly forward. People lined the streets where the parade was to come, so close together you began to feel you had never felt people before — the powerful, still waiting of bodies with the breath held back.

It was funny, too, seeing so many policemen. Regular as telephone poles, their arms wiring us back, dumb, but with one message running silently between them. And in the background, horses twitching.

The parade came along. Nobody had any greetings, the men marching, silent — lowered heads, hatless. They were workers just like I saw every day in the shop. High cheek bones, skin light, eyes straight ahead, burning. Some women — broad beamed, hair cut roughly — seemed more masculine with more fight than the men with that belaboured feel (I knew it) down the spine.

Marching, marching . . . clamp, scuffle, clamp, scuffle . . . on.

A cop pushed a man from the curb and the crowd raised itself like a cat's back, remembering.

Clamp, scuffle, clamp. Now the coffin. One moment it is bare and black, the next — a flash of red. A surge of banners, slogans, cries, flags and the mass has loosed its voice . . is cheering . . is shouting . . is challenging the slogans, the battle cries, the BREAD NOT LEAD!

Then they must have charged. The hot pressure of bodies was pushed back like water. We were fighting each other to be free, to have our feet, to push our arms, to raise our voice from the smothered mouth. We were fighting not to run, to carry on, to wave the banner, hurl the slogan, raise the coffin shoulder-high on our long, burdened arms. To be released we fought.

I remember nothing much till wham across my mouth the black jack smacking; and I struck out. Others followed then. But the blue posts, the brass buttons, were moving fast, were beating fast, beating us back and back into doorways, sideways, streets and alleys; horses pushing, kicking, kneading, till we could only duck and gasp and run.

That was that. And the drug store where I bleeding went, refused to bind. I saw the man, lean — lean lipped, white faced, sheltering the door against us. And I came to my senses.

Comrades by Y. Kaplansky   (from *New Frontier*)

In order to support the growing anti-fascist anti-war movement in Europe which climaxed in the First World Congress for Peace, the Canadian League Against War and Fascism *planned a national congress to promote this movement. It was held in Toronto, October 6th and 7th, 1934. At that time I was in Montreal beginning my social work, but I had earlier made a trip to Halifax to feel out the peace movement there and urge that delegates be sent from the Maritimes. My efforts failed (because, I think, that the left line to which I adhered firmly was too alarming for the gentle pacifist group in Halifax). At any rate, I am listed in the published programme as being the Halifax delegate!*

GREETINGS TO THE CONGRESS FROM THE WORLD COMMITTEE AGAINST WAR AND FASCISM, PARIS.

Cablegram

Via Marconi
PARIS 1040 OCT 4
Canadian Congress Against War and Fascism
Toronto

BEST WISHES FOR GREAT MOVEMENT AGAINST WAR AND FASCISM ON NEW CONTINENT STOP WE ARE READY TO ACT VIGOROUSLY IN OLD WORLD STOP CALL ON YOU TO ERECT UNCONQUERABLE WORLD BARRIER AGAINST FASCISM DESTROYER OF ALL LIBERTIES AND FOMENTOR OF WAR
  SIGNED
    HENRI BARBUSSE, ROMAIN ROLLAND, FRANCIS JOURDAIN, GABRIEL CUDENET, JULES MALLARTE, GABRIELLE DUCHENE, GUY JERRAM, JOHN STRACHEY, MARCEL ROUFFIANGES RACAMOND.

Message from Pierre Van Paassen, Paris, Sept. 21, 1934:

"I endorse and greet the First Canadian Congress Against War and Fascism with all my heart, because I believe that together will all the humanizing forces in the world, we can still bring to a standstill what now appears to be the victorious march of fascism, and in that way prevent the outbreak of a war which would be the greatest and the most ghastly disaster the world has ever seen.

"I have seen the rise of fascism in Italy and in Germany. Today the lot of the masses in these countries is a hundred times worse than it was before. In Italy there have been seven general wage reductions. An eighth reduction stands before the door. Yet these two countries teem with armies. The wealth of those peoples is poured into war preparations. Do you think those preparations are made to safeguard peace? If you do you ought to have your mind examined.

"No, the capitalist regimes are pinning their last hopes on fascist dictatorships because these dictatorships can reduce wages so nicely to a bare subsistence level and in addition put huge profits in the pockets of the manufacturers of armaments and all the other by-products of a perfect war machinery. They consciously drive for war machinery. They consciously drive for war, because war will mean even more profits. What happens to you and me, to your children and mine does not worry them. After us the deluge, said a French king, so long as we have a good time.

"But the deluge came. And it swept away the old feudal society in a frightful sea of blood. Another deluge, but infinitely more ghastly than the French Revolution, stands before the door.

"What is the remedy? Must we go down then before the onslaught of organized barbarism? Are we really going to plunge back into the middle ages? Must we give up our dearest possessions, the glimmer of freedom we have yet? It depends on ourselves to a large extent!

"Together we can still beat them off and forestall their gruesome plot to plunge humanity into a sea of blood. But be sure of it; time is pressing. There is not a moment to lose. Let us stand together in the widest possible united front. From this moment onward let there be no enemies on the left.

"The bourgeois intellectuals must not be left out. At least some of them will not want to stand by idly while the things they prize highest are trampled underfoot.

"Together! Together! Together!

"It can be done! Let us do it!"

REPORT OF THE WOMEN'S COMMITTEE
Elizabeth Morton, Chairman

The Women's Meeting was held on the first night of the Congress Sessions. Forty-five women attended, representing every province in Canada. A representative of each large city or province was asked to outline the situation in her locality, the type of women's organizations in existence, and the possibility of uniting them in our cause. This brought out some valuable and instructive data that will be used to build up the movement. The meeting then proceeded to discuss a tentative structure suitable for the setting up of a woman's movement in Canada and the outline of a plan of action.

It was recommended:

That the work of these Councils will be to enlist and unite all women's organizations in the fight against War and Fascism. To expose the real nature of Fascism and to explain the real causes of war and to enlist their mass participation in our program of resistance against War and Fascism.

That in order to draw into the movement thousands of housewives, professional women, farm women, women in industry, now unattached to any organization, that special efforts be made to organize them into groups for the specific task of educating themselves as to the causes of War and Fascism and the effects of these evils upon their living standards and rights and to rally them into the fight against the present preparation for war, against Fascist organization, and to carry out mass action against them.

That special efforts be made to penetrate the Women's Auxiliaries of Trade Unions and Women's Unions, and link them up with our movement because of the important part they play in the manufacture of war materials.

That a Women's Conference be called as soon as possible to affiliate the Canadian Movement to the International Women's Congress at Paris, thereby making it part of the World Movement against War and Fascism.

A provisional National Committee to further the Women's Work was elected by the Congress as follows:

Mrs. W. Wilson, Vancouver	Octavia Millar, Regina
Margaret Crang, Edmonton	Miss Rose, Winnipeg
Mona Weiss, Montreal	Mrs. Mendelssohn, Montreal
Dorothy Livesay, Halifax	Betty Hodgson, London, Ont.
Mrs. Baxter, Kitchener	Mrs. Farquhar, Brantford

The following from Toronto to act as a National Bureau:

Alice Loeb	Rose Henderson
Mrs. Geizke	Mrs. Buhay Ewen
Julia Collins	Eve Cunningham
Mrs. Bain	Mrs. Berizanke
Ann Cowan	Henrietta Beder
Mrs. Jean Laing	Mrs. I. Siegel
Miss Alice Chown	Dorothy Livesay

Elizabeth Morton, Secretary
146 King St. West,
Toronto

Fascism in Quebec
By Katherine Bligh*

Santa Claus, parading the streets of Montreal in November, met with an unusual reception. Not only was his procession held up by a mass of demonstrators, but his usual urbanity was somewhat shaken by repeated boos. The French Canadian fascists were protesting against the large department stores, and crying that they did not want their children to see luxurious toys which could never be theirs.

Take another scene, from Verdun, last winter. Fascists descended upon a meeting of unemployed workers, assailing them with rotten vegetables. Before the police came the workers had ousted the enemy, but the affair gave adequate grounds for the social-democratic mayor to decide that all

*Pseudonym for Dorothy Livesay.

meeting halls must be closed.

Walk down St Denis Street, in Montreal, the heart of the working-class section. Painted on many shop windows you will see a bluebird. The merchant inside will tell you that this sign is a guarantee that none of his goods have been bought from Jews. In one window on St Denis Street there is a strange display of helmets, brass hats, small daggers, all flanking a large picture of King George of England. Pamphlets and swastikas will inform you that this is the headquarters of the National Christian Socialist Party — a party which openly admits its fascist character. Adrian Arcand, former journalist and politician, was one of its founders. Programs for unemployment, social insurance and housing are put forward in revolutionary language as the platform of the party, in addition to anti-trust slogans. At the same time there is a consistent attack against Jews and communists, who are linked together as the enemies of all Christians.

In that same window, as on all news stands, you will find *Le Patroite:* a paper whose vicious attacks on "International Jewry" could scarcely be outdone in Germany. "Throw the Jews down the gutters," is a frequent headline. Recently this paper has concentrated on smaller merchants of Montreal and the staunch Roman Catholic groups. Under the guise of sympathy for those who have suffered under the crisis, the paper directs the attention of its readers to the flourishing concerns, headed by Jews, which are still making huge profits. At the same time there is no hesitation in attacking the fascist mayor of Montreal, Houde, for proposing a direct tax on wage-earners as well as a tax on commerce, in order to balance the budget. They deplore the fact that the middle-class is not yet organized in a party strong enough to oppose such moves. Then they attack organizations of the working-class. Their editorials, without exception, end on the note: "We will struggle against communism in all its forms. Our society is sick enough without this further monstrosity being inflicted upon it. We seek a return to Christian principles, and not to revolution, which would lead us to complete chaos."

Le Patroite has a strong appeal for the various religious organizations in Quebec — semi-fascist in nature — such as "L'Union Catholique des Cultivateurs" and the "A.C.J.C.-Roman Catholic Youth." This organization, which corresponds generally to the Y.M.C.A., instils political ideas through its group life, parades and songs. Here is an example:

Be brave, young worker,
Toiling in the factory:
Have hope as you toil,
Jesus will lead you.

The stand taken by Mayor Houde, after one year in office following an election campaign filled with promises for the unemployed, is of considerable significance at the present time. His means of liquidating the city's debt compare with those of LaGuardia — but he has gone further, by being chairman at a fascist meeting and admitting that he is in favour of fascism. Further, he has under his jurisdiction some twenty workers' clubs — the "Federation des Clubs Ouvriere de Quebec" — situated at strategic points in the French sections of the city. Through sheer demagogy he hopes to win the mass of French workers over to his fascist program. However, he is not alone in his demagogy. Equally important organizations are "The Federation Ouvriere du Canada" (Workers' Federation), with Bancour in the lead, and Chalifoux workers' clubs, the "Federation Populaire." Backed and developed by capital in the face of the growing unrest of the unemployed, these clubs have an insidious appeal because they stress the fight for economic demands. They have been known to resist evictions and to demonstrate before the city hall. At the same time, each group is cleverly divided from the other and concerted action is thus made impossible. The members of Chalifoux clubs, where hooliganism is most in evidence, wear the regulation fascist uniform with brown shirts and brass hats. Needless to say, the organizational structure of these clubs does not smell of democracy. In the "Federation Populaire" all the leading positions are filled by men appointed from above (i.e. by leading capitalists), while the rank and file member is silenced by parades.

Two other organizations should be mentioned, although they are not linked with the fascists. The "Association Humanitaire," one of the earliest of the unemployed organizations (6000 members) was in the hands, until less than a year ago, of an anarchist group headed by Saint-Martin. The meetings were dreary and the main activity consisted of protests by correspondence. Due to the good work from within, this organization has been swung over to a militant stand, its bureaucracy disbanded and its programme revolutionized. Another organization, the "Espirits Saints" (Holy Spirits), numbering some 4000 protestant workers, is gradually being turned away from a highly mystical "communism" to participation in the daily struggles. These are worthy of mention because they are organizations which might have gone over to the fascists had not correct work been done.

Such is one side of the fascist picture in Montreal. These aspects seem superficial, however, in comparison with the attacks of the government itself on workers and workers' organizations. To understand the problem, it is necessary to have some knowledge of the historic isolation of Quebec province from the rest of Canada.

Whereas the first comers to Canada were the French merchant traders, those that followed in the seventeenth and eighteenth centuries were peasants mainly from the north and west of France. A peasant economy grew up, in the midst of which the Church was enthroned. At first the conquering British suppressed all rights of freedom and worship, but their tactic changed to cope with the new problems presented by the American Revolution. In order to save French Canada for Britain, Quebec was given a free hand in its own internal and religious affairs. The Church thenceforth assumed a mediaeval control over the lives of the people in agricultural areas. As industrialization advanced, the Church, one of the largest landowners, worked hand in hand with the government. Among the workers the illusion was spread, and still holds, that the capitalists were "foreigners" — that is to say, English and Jewish. They were distrustful of, and indeed had no fellow feeling for, English and European workers yet since 1890 French capitalists have made a steady advance towards control in industry and finance. The Church subtly aided this distinction by stressing the religious issue, and by forming Catholic trade unions where the priest is the presiding officer. All efforts of the revolutionary movement to penetrate into the French Canadian population (which comprises one-third of the entire population of Canada) were without result — until the depression.

When unemployment hit Quebec, where the standard of living is in any case very low owing to the miserable wage rates prevailing, the quickwitted, emotional French Canadian worker was at a loss. On the one hand he listened to the attacks on Jews, English Canadians and "trusts" as explanations for the trouble; and on the other hand he joined with these "foreigners," his neighbors, in protesting evictions.

The culmination of this first stage of struggle took place in March, 1933, when an unemployed worker, Nick Zynchuk, entered a house where an eviction was taking place, to obtain his few belongings. He was shot in the back, killed outright, by a policeman. The storm of protest at this action brought 20,000 workers to his funeral. Then the police attacked, on horseback and on foot, tearing down the banners, slugging men, women and children, following wounded workers to the hospital to arrest them. As a follow-up of this brutality, fear halted the progressive movement. The "Canadian Labor Defense League," as well as the underground "Communist Party," were too weak to go forward. Reaction set in. For a year it was impossible to hold demonstrations of more than a handful of unemployed; and always the police attacked viciously. This was the year in which fascist organizations, appealing to the veterans, the unemployed and the small traders, advanced by leaps and bounds.

In the winter of 1934 three bills were passed by the Quebec legislature. The "David Bill" forbade any public meetings, or notices thereof, without the consent of the police (educational and religious meetings excluded). A "Bill of Search" was passed which gave the police permission to search any man's dwelling without a warrant. Lastly, the "Arcand Bill" laid a restraining hand on labour, claiming that any agreement between employers and employees submitted to the government would be binding for the whole industry. During the same year offices of the "Canadian Labour Defense League" were attacked and searched, arrests were made of anyone found distributing leaflets, and finally the only French working-class paper, *La Vie Ouvriere*, was denied entry to the news stands. One bookseller, for selling this paper and the magazine *Soviet Russia Today* was recently sentenced to two months in jail.

Probably the most organized and brutal form of suppression in Quebec has been centred far away from the industrial centres in the lumber camps and coal mines. Last winter, the lumbermen fought a heroic battle for higher wages and improved conditions, with picket lines fifty miles long and the weather forty degrees below zero. The R.C.M.P. and local police made a concerted attack, using airplanes and tear-gas. They arrested eighty-seven men, nearly all French-Canadians, many of whom are now in the penitentiary. Recently, a Quebec judge selected eighteen foreign-born striking miners from Noranda. In sentencing them to two years and deportation, he remarked: "Your union gave you bad advice. In this beautiful country, where there is good work and good wages, we have no room for agitators." In this same beautiful country this Sunday is "Anti-Red Day" — a new addition to the calendar.

What is the meaning of this great wave of attack on the working-class? Fear in the ruling class is evident. Each attack on an organization which is struggling for better conditions is strengthening the resistance of the workers, is teaching them to know their real enemy. The struggle, led first by the "Canadian Labour Defense League," has been considerably broadened within the last few months by the "League Against War and Fascism." This summer, freedom of speech was won in the parks. Even more important, a few weeks ago one of Mayor Houde's supposedly fascist clubs became affiliated with the "League against War and Fascism" as a protest against his refusal to grant their demands. Some of his clubs, realizing the fascist structure of the organization as a result of education by militant workers, have openly renounced Houde and become independent. They are not openly communist, nor do they have much understanding of the political situation in Europe and its resemblance to their own, still, they are organizing on the basis of democracy from below. Some of their members participated in the campaign to send French-Canadian workers on a delegation to the Soviet Union, still others are active in the "Friends of the Soviet Union" which has its own French branch.

In November of 1934, the largest unemployed rally ever held in Montreal resounded with the song of the Internationale and cries of "Vive le Parti Communiste!" Organizationally the unemployed are going forward, turning their backs on the fake workers clubs and joining the "Conseil des Chomeurs de Montreal" (Unemployed Council), where the open forum, free expression of opinion, and democratic elections are the rule. On December 16, this organization called a conference for non-contributory unemployment insurance, with delegates representing nineteen organizations and a total membership of 16,360 members. Two of these were trade unions, eager to show their solidarity with the unemployed and to help forward the demands for insurance and hospital care. Moreover, the trade unions themselves are moving forward from their reactionary position, French Canadian workers appear on the picket lines with Jewish and English and European workers. Others, who have been kept inactive by anarchist leaders, have come into the movement and are putting all their native vivacity and courage into the fight against fascism and fascist measures. Sleepy, mediaeval Quebec is awake.

Munich, 1934

Dee Dear,

So glad to get your letter when I was in Weingarten. It was a swell letter. Write more like it. I *am* interested in the P.A.C. (Progressive Arts Club) etc. more here than anywhere but I can find out nothing till I learn more German. Even then I probably won't know anything. As it is I cannot even read the paper so I have no idea what is going on. There's nothing about America anyway. Here it is all "Deutschland" nothing but. Vienna is very unpopular and they hate Dolfuss. Everywhere pictures of Hitler and Swastikas.

Last night Hitler spoke over the radio. Of course I couldn't understand it so finally I went to sleep. I don't think it is so noticeable in Muenchen as in Weingarten. Communists are sent to concentration camps for a couple of months or so, after that they are said to be released. I think I saw some being taken from the train at Ulm.

One can find out nothing here, so I'm giving in: that is, I'm friendly to the few Nazis I meet. On Wednesday night three of us went to a charity (Winterhalfe) concert given by the S.S., sworn to death Nazis in black uniforms.

All very young and innocent. One of our middle-aged friends told us he was not such a strong Nazi because he was too busy. It's mainly the students and the unemployed. In some ways it's astonishingly like Russia — a tremendous youth movement, and organized recreations etc. There is something rather terrible about their passion over their "Fuhrer", sentimental but even more than that. And the hatred of Jews is very real — God, the man we met in the Beer Cellar — he was a fanatic and a dangerous one. They feel toward Jews as the Southern States feel toward Negroes. One girl told me she'd sooner marry a Negro than a Jew. We thought we had a Jew in the Schule, very dark, but he turns out to be a Catholic. He's quite nice and a German, thank God, not an American.

Your loving sister,
Sophie

Struggle

A mass chant. Two groups are needed, one on each side of stage.

Group I
    1 Listen, comrades.
  All Under the threat of the swastika,
         Under the terror of Hitler,
    1 Listen, comrades,
  All To our voices.

    2 Hitler has fine words and slogans
    3 Hitler has storm troops and bullets
    4 But Hitler has no bread for us
  All Bread! Bread! BREAD!

    2 Fascism destroys our culture
    3 Fascism jails our comrades
 2, 4 Fascism poisons our children
3, 4, 5 Fascism tortures our leaders!

    1 Listen, comrades.
  All Under the threat of the swastika
         Under the terror of Hitler
    1 Listen!

    2 Though Nazi spies dog us at every step
    3 And torture chambers await us
    4 We have a call that cannot be silenced:
  All THE GERMAN WORKING CLASS LIVES

Group II
    6 We hear your voices!
    7 We too know oppression.
    8 There is struggle in Canada!

    9 Because three miners of Estevan, striking, were
         murdered in cold blood
    6 By the yellow dogs, their bosses.
    9 Because eight of our leaders
         Who fought to save us from unemployment
    8 From wage cuts and starvation
    7 Were jailed and sentenced to five years
         Smothered in Kingston Pen—
    6 Tim Buck forced to be silent!
    9 Because at an eviction struggle
    8 Nick Zynchuk was shot in the back

9 Because the Saskatoon jobless were savagely attacked
7 Twenty-seven arrested!
9 Because of one year's imprisonment
6 For fourteen of Calgary's unemployed
9 Because in Verdun the fascists
8 Invaded our halls
6, 7 Because we fought back

9 Because they met our resistance with the iron heel of ruthlessness

7, 8 Because of this terror, comrades,
6, 7, 8, 9 THERE IS STRUGGLE IN CANADA!

Group I

2 Hitler has tried to turn us back,
3 To force us into line
2, 4 Shouting with his mimics
3, 4, 5 Hail, Hitler, hail!

1 But are we not WORKERS?
2 Have we too not spent a lifetime
3 In struggle against wage-cuts and unemployment?
1 Can there be greater terror
2 Than seeing our children starving?
1 No!
2, 3, 4, 5 NO!
4 Here is the final test of our strength
5 Here is the last blood squeezed by the boss.

Group II

6, 7, 8 Workers of the world, we listen!
9 Workers of the world together face
The brownshirt and swastika—
6 Arbitrary bonds
7 Are made by the swastika
9 But the workers have a bond
8 More strong, more deep
6 Of labour in the mines,
7 Of labour at machines,
8 Of labour in the smelting furnaces!

Group I

2 In the factories and labour camps
Struggle is going on
3 In the street and in secret
All Workers fight!

1 By leaflets

2 Scattered from roof gardens
3 Smuggled in labour camps
4 Thrown from street-cars.

1 By newspapers
5 Printed in secrecy
4 Disguised as advertising
3 Hidden in newsboys bundles;

1 By slogans
2 Chalked upon railway bridges
3 Factory chimneys
4 Walls, roofs, canal embankments!
1 On the street corner a musician
5 Thumps his innocent jazz
4 Then suddenly everyone's singing,
All "RED FRONT"

1 Who leads strikes in Germany?
2 The communists.
1 Who demands work for the jobless?
3, 4 The communists.
1 Who fights against fascism?
2, 3, 4, 5 The COMMUNISTS!

Group II
All We, workers of Canada,
Workers of the world
Salute you!
9 We hear your call
8 In our own factories and flophouses
9 Our cry is: "Struggle"

Group I
1 There is hunger in Germany

Group II
All Hunger in Canada

Group I
2, 3 Terror in Germany

Group II
All Terror in Canada

Group I
All POWER in Germany

Group II
All POWER in Canada

Group I
    1 Against the bosses

Group II
    9 Against the system

Groups I and II
    All Against FASCISM!

Group I
    1 If we struggle for our class in Germany
    All Will you too struggle?

Group II
    All Yes!

Group I
    3 If we conquer for our class in Germany
    All Will you too conquer?

Group II
    All Yes!

Groups I and II
    All United the workers of the world
    9, 2 Will destroy fascism

Group I
    5 By raising our voices

Group II
    8 By clenching our fists   (red front salute)

Groups I and II
    All By struggle, comrades!

Group I
    All Stronger than Hitler's bloody arm

Group II
    All Stronger than Bennet's iron heel

Groups I and II
    All Strong and mighty building a world for workers!

 *It was this activity, and these incidents that brought me closer to Louis Kon. "What are you, a poet, doing in politics?" he would say. I had met Louis Kon under rather unusual and amusing circum-*stances. *He had come from Russia to Canada, to Winnipeg, along about*

1918, on behalf of the new Soviet government, to arrange trading horses for wheat. Later he led a group of Canadian businessmen and politicians to Russia on a peace mission — an event which he has written about himself with his usual wit and perspicacity. At any rate, he lived in Winnipeg with his French wife and small children on Lipton Street, not far from our house. He must have got to know my father, J.F.B. Livesay, through newspaper interviews. And they often talked over the fence — Louis with his black moustachios, his Russian accent, his twinkling eyes. I am sure I remember seeing him in those Winnipeg times. Nearly fifteen years later, when I was in Montreal doing social work, I had contracted a severe case of grippe, as we called such sufferings then. I was at home alone in the flat when the buzzer rang. I got up out of bed to push the upstairs buzzer, leaving the door ajar for the visitor, whoever she might be. Suddenly a large bear of a man stood in the doorway, saying: "Is it Dorothy? I knew your father." He came into the room, full of sympathy, for my fearful cold — "you must take care of yourself" — and talked about his life, and mine.

"You are a poet. I have read your book, Signpost.*"*

"But why. . . ? How. . . ?"

"Well, I heard about you being active in the peace movement. My job here is with the "Friends of the Soviet Union." You must come to our meetings. But I won't give you a job to do. You've taken on too much already."

"How do you know?"

"Why aren't you writing poems? You have the lyric gift and you are wasting yourself writing propaganda?"

"But my poem Nick Zynchuk is not just propaganda!" Could Louis Kon be bourgeois revisionist? Is that what he was? I told him I did not want to write lyric poetry anymore. All that was finished. My guide was Lenin.

"Lenin? Gorki? Have you not seen what they wrote about literature? I knew them! I knew their humanity. If an artist is given the power to create, he must do so. In that way he will be helping humanity. There are plenty of other able people who can go out on the picket-line. Your job is to write."

"We carried on this argument all year and the next — when I went to New Jersey as a community worker in Englewood, and discovered apartheid, and discovered the English poets who were, with Cecil Day Lewis, writing about "A Hope for Poetry" namely, alignment with revolutionary forces for change. I linked these ideas with those I had heard from Louis, and came back to Canada to write my documentary poems: "The Outrider" and "Day and Night."

101

*Until moving west in 1936 I continued to be in touch with Louis Kon.
For some reason I never remember meeting his daughter, Irene Kon,
who was soon to become involved in the movement in aid of Spanish
Democracy, and to become an associate of Dr Norman Bethune. (I had
not met him either, as I left Montreal just at the point where all Bethune's
activities started.) But in memory of those days, and of the support Louis
Kon had given me, I dedicated my* Selected Poems *to him. Alas, he did not
know it, having died a month before its publication in 1956. Strangely, I
heard that his funeral was unattended, his work unsung and all I have to
remember him by is this letter, which reached me soon after the publication of "Day and Night." I am glad he was pleased!*

Louis Kon
P.O. Box 123 - Station "G"
Montreal

2 September 1944

(Second day of the Second Reign of Maurice Duplessis in Quebec.)

Dear Dorothy,

It is a long time since I am trying to find a way of hearing from you
direct — indirect scraps of information about you and your work, I don't
know how reliable, I was getting here and there. Some time ago, after
having read your "Night and Day" in one of the privately circulating
mimeographed publications, I wished to write to you expressing my very
great delight at and after having read it. I admit that my literary taste is
barbarically crude, and especially a great deal of super-modern poetry —
for me just a throwing together of words with a motive and ultimate aim
for doing so concealed deeply in the brain cells of the writer — did not
help me to appreciate poetry. I can also frankly admit that your work is
like Langston Hughes', about the only poetical creations I derive a real
pleasure to read and re-read many times.

Some months ago, when seeing in the press of your father's death, I hoped
for an opportunity to see you, but either you did not come as far as Montreal
or I might have been out of the city at the time.

Last night, reading a queer review of your new volume by Beth Paterson in
the Gazette, I've decided to try to reach you through your publishers in
Toronto: to find out how you are, how happy you are, how are your children
and if now you agree with me that a person like you is of an immensely greater
value to the cause of pushing humanity on the right track of just, peaceful, full
life by writing and thus influencing others, than by running around with
leaflets and posters edited in a language which makes the same effect on those
few reading them as twenty odd years of efforts by Bolsheviks on Churchill
and countless others, and as little understood by them as Marx is understood
by the rabbis, priests or ministers of gospel or crown.

Especially now, when grace to the Soviet turntable all the engines of the world were put on the right track, the very few of our ideology — or have you changed your beliefs and aims? — are so badly needed to educate intellectually and ethically ourselves and the rest with us by their inspiring writings, because so far we were doing only the foundation digging and more to the plans and specifications of engineers and architects who never did see either our type of soil, nor the material with which we have to build, than of our own. The present calls for a great effort to keep step with the world which was immunized against ills of society by this war we were not, and it will have to be done in a great measure by forceful writers and poets and painters and sculptors, who understand well what the Russians were learning theoretically and practically for 27 years. . . .

Best regards and wishes, faithfully
Louis Kon

Case Supervisor

Last night she had escaped to a movie. But it was no escape. The news reels flashed by as if unrolling from her own mind: war, breadlines, crisis, drought — and yet again those letters in thundering black type — CRISIS.

After that she laughed hysterically at Popeye. And the comedy, which should have lifted her into ease, into deep-sofaed and luxuriant rooms, remote as an aquarium — the comedy began where she had left off. A girl was climbing Mrs. Rooney's rickety stairs, turning a door-handle slowly, afraid to protrude herself into the threadbare room. A girl was hot and angry after standing all day long behind a counter. This was to be department store love, just above the landlord's dispossess, just above the breadline. . . .

As quivering scenes melted and were speeded up, held still and shot across the eyes, she found herself tensely clutching the chair seat. It could not end the same way — it must not. With Mrs. Rooney fighting her daughter for the rent. And "I'm going to have fun when I'm young — see? I'm going to live in spite of the landlord!"

No! It couldn't be like that. Love on the screen was different, it spread a film across the truth. Thank God, love was happy there, balancing itself above the dole. . . .

She went into the chill, wet air with face prickly and dry, her head aching. Thoughts must be pushed aside, and a furrow driven straight home to bed. There would be a long enough fight for sleep.

Now it was morning. She was sitting at her desk, absently opening mail, heedless of the telephone which went on and on like the ringing in her head.

"Oh, Miss Chilton?" A round curly head was in the doorway. "May I see you before I go out?"

"But we have a conference at two o'clock."

"I know. It's terribly important, Miss Chilton."

"One moment then. Sit down while I answer this." Then crisp and cool came her business voice: "Miss Chilton speaking." In a moment a pucker gathered above the clear eyes. "Oh yes. Yes Mr. Jones. . . . No, I really can't do anything further about it, Mr. Jones. What we said yesterday closed the matter as far as I am concerned. . . . Well, Mr. Jones, I gave you one hour and a half of my time, if you don't think that fair. I have to think of other people too. . . . No, I am busy with conferences all day. I wouldn't be able to see you. . . . If your wife feels so badly about it why didn't she say something? I understood that she was perfectly satisfied. . . . Well, we won't discuss that over the telephone. I would rather see your wife alone. Yes. Yes. I will call on her tomorrow afternoon. . . . No. . . . Goodbye."

Cowardice, she was thinking. Pure cowardice to say I'd go in there again.

The girl was squirming in her seat, pretending not to listen. She probably thought things boded ill for her case. But she gathered her courage in her hands, her cheeks flushing, her candid brown eyes staring out under the shock of hair.

"Miss Chilton. It's about the Caporetti's again." She was apologetic at first, as if their misfortunes were her own fault. But as she went on she seemed to become unselfconscious, as if she was Mrs. Caporetti herself talking, stout and solid and determined, but perilously near the danger-line of lost control. When the worker had called yesterday Mrs. Caporetti had been like that, for the baby was sick again, Dr. Hart refused to come because he hadn't been paid for the last three times: Mr. Caporetti was off work again on account of his neuritis. He had had to keep the stove low to make the fuel last, but anyway his bedroom was simply freezing (I was in it Miss Chilton, and I know: what can you expect when the bedroom is so far from the kitchen, and no stove in the hall?) And now they were entirely out of fuel (I went out to the back porch and there was only a shovelful. It would not last the night). Here it was morning, and all Mr. Caporetti's available cash had to go for food and milk. (That's if we budget it like you said, Miss Chilton). So the girls wanted fuel ordered, and a doctor sent in from the Welfare Dispensary (because it's not a city case and we can't send a relief doctor).

Miss Chilton was fumbling with the leaves of a calendar on her desk. "But Miss Cherry. I see that coal was sent to the Caporetti's only two weeks ago. It is supposed to last a month."

"I know. But it never does. Not anywhere. Three weeks at the most. And the Caporetti's use their stove for cooking and everything. They have to keep it going all night so it won't be too cold in the morning for Mr. Caporetti's leg. Anyway, they have no matches in the house, Miss

Litho by Ellen Simon   (from *New Frontier*)

Chilton. They can't afford to buy matches."

"Did you put them in the budget?"

"Oh yes. But now the budget is all thrown out of kilter, with the baby sick and Mr. Caporetti not working."

"Tell me, Miss Cherry. Have you ever really investigated whether the relatives could not help in this case? I mean her relatives? I know his are on relief."

The girl flushed a little, biting her lip. "But Mrs. Caporetti doesn't want me to see her relatives. She hasn't had anything to do with them since she married an Italian. They were so mean about it before."

"I realize that. But now that times are so hard all around, do you really think they would blame her, if they were approached the right way? Don't you think they might be willing to help a little, in times of stress, like this one?"

The girl would not answer her, but sat silently looking at her lap. For all the world like Mrs. Caporetti herself. Really, Miss Cherry was too emotional. She was undoubtedly letting her clients become too dependent on her. All Mrs. Caporetti had to do was tell a hard luck story and Miss Cherry flashed back to the office like a telephone message. She had no sense of proportion. She wasn't letting her clients develop any self-reliance. It would do no harm to pull her up sharp, right now.

"Isn't it just possible, Miss Cherry, that Mrs. Caporetti has been in touch with her people all along? I mean" (as the girl shook her head stubbornly) "that if she were left to her own devices now she might quite naturally turn to her mother? I am sure they would help her out with a little fuel; or certainly they would send their family doctor. After all, if you were to tell them that their grandchild was ill, can you believe that they would be hard-hearted?"

"There are plenty of hard-hearted people in the world," the girl said.

"Well, Miss Cherry, I am not insisting that you see the relatives right now, in this emergency. But I would feel, would you not, that it might be well to carry on with the case with that step in mind?"

"Oh yes."

"Well then. Visit the family, and if the child is not better, send a doctor from the centre. But I certainly do not believe we can afford to send in fuel again. We've done it too often every two weeks. We have to think of other families."

"Yes Miss Chilton."

"Ask them what sources they have. Find out if they couldn't borrow from neighbors until next week. Or perhaps the store would give a little charcoal on credit."

"All right, Miss Chilton. Thank you." In a whisk, the girl was gone. Miss Chilton opened the window wider, then plunged into her mail.

Automatically she slipped the letters into files, or made notes on little cards. She would have to telephone the city relief and report that new family, before Miss McQueen called her in for conference. Ten o'clock that was to be. But Miss McQueen had an erratic sense of time. It happened that she was just in the middle of her report when a secretary came to the door and told her: "Miss McQueen is waiting."

So be it. She arose, gathering pencil and paper and two files, and walked through the noisy stenographer's office down the hall to the big end room. "Come in." Miss McQueen, heavy and imposing, with white hair plastered neatly over one side of her forehead, was talking to Miss Dogherty, the other case supervisor. She was a big-boned woman, with a dour face and sallow complexion, her straight black hair as usual falling down over her eyes. Sometimes Dogherty seemed to be aware that she was a failure; at other times she was indifferent to that and to everything. Trouble just slid away from her as she stalked through the office with her mind somewhere far off.

Today Chilton could see she was flustered. And when Kay Dogherty was flustered the whole office could be counted onto get into a panic — especially her particular flock of workers and students.

Miss McQueen was speaking in her heavy, emphatic way. "We had a Board meeting last night, as I expect you know. I had to report that the budget in this district had exceeded the quota by almost one-third. One-third. And we haven't reached Christmas yet or the first of the year. Fortunately the other districts were almost as bad. But not quite. Still, those business men were quite stunned. Mr. Farrow said that if he ran his business that way, he would have been bankrupt years ago. Mr. Tuthill mentioned that in his opinion the only solution was to put a business man in as head of each office. You know what that would mean: the end of our case work approach, our professional standards. . . . Just imagine, for instance, Mr. Tuthill or Mr. Augustus Brown sitting here in my place! Just how far would you get? No my friends, we have to maintain our standards, even at the expense of being more severe in our distributions. Every source of saving must be checked up once again, in particular I think the emergency fund must be watched carefully; and wherever a client can be turned over to a religious organization or an institution, it should be done. We have to catch up on that budget."

"But we are not a business organization." Dogerty was speaking as if she had only heard Miss McQueen's first sentence.

"We would be nowhere without the help of business, Miss Dogherty. Please remember that. You owe your position to it. I am not concerned here with what we are, but with what we can do. We have a vital function to perform and it must be performed with the least possible sacrifice — on all sides. . . . Miss Chilton, have you any suggestions?"

She remembered Miss Cherry's silence. "Now that winter is here, Miss McQueen, I was thinking we would need *more* money for fuel and medicine — not less."

"Well, we can't have it. And you must convince your workers of that.

107

These young ones must be pulled up sharply. It is they who are putting in a little extra, here and there — perhaps without your noticing it, Miss Dogherty. I think we will have to call a staff meeting on the subject. Now concretely, let us come to the point, where can we cut down? On service or relief?"

Service is relief, Chilton was thinking, nearly all the time. But she must not say that. Neither of them were expected to say anything. As long as they listened meekly to Miss McQueen, carried out her suggestions, they were safe. So she went on talking, planning, for upwards of an hour. Dogherty was getting restless, she probably had an appointment. Dear knows what she might not say. . . .

Finally it was over. Dogherty pounded her way out. At the door Chilton was recalled. "One moment." The small glassy blue eyes were inscrutable. "I noticed that your expenditures were lower than Miss Dogherty's, Miss Chilton. I am glad to observe that you are aware of your responsibilities."

She smiled in a faded way, and hurried out. Damn! So they were being compared like two mice. And good old Dogherty was in danger again, Dogherty whose heart was like a sieve, anyone could flow through it, even though she hadn't had any scientific training. . . . She would have to get together with Dogherty, — they could sign each other's slips, if necessary. She would do anything for Dogherty . . . but not for Mrs. Caporetti? Dogherty herself would only be interested in Mrs. Caporetti. She wouldn't care about her job.

Damn. She must stop thinking. Her mind was getting fuzzy again. Crisis. Crisis. Hang onto yourself, old girl. Watch out. Now. At your desk. Turn around. Smile. "Goodmorning Miss Svenson. Yes, I can see you now." (Even though she lies to me and swears she isn't pregnant, I can still smile.)

At noon she came down late for lunch. Miss McQueen must have gone out for lunch, if the sound of laughter and the sense of relaxation had any meaning. But when Chilton entered the girls stiffened up perceptibly: and this, although Dogherty was present. It was like a school room, this restraint which Miss McQueen had so carefully built up between supervisors and juniors. Only Dogherty ignored it.

Food was passed politely, coffee gulped in a hurry. An hour and fifteen minutes was their right, according to regulations; but Chilton couldn't remember when they had more than three-quarters of an hour. Today she wanted to sit and sit, to gossip with Black and Dogherty. Young Cherry, as they called her, had not come in. So she felt relaxed, puffing at a cigarette. Then there came an urgent telephone call, and it was all over.

Conferences. Two full hours of conference with different workers. She wouldn't be able to make a single call that day. And Mrs. Harris had to have. . . . Stop getting like this, she told herself. Mrs. Harris can wait. Everybody can wait. Everything can be done tomorrow. Nobody can

(Public Archives Canada PA-87384)

Men hunt for coins at the foot of York Street, Toronto.

starve in a day. "It takes weeks to starve," Black had said, or was it Dogherty? "But one night can cause pneumonia."

She felt the workers lined up outside her door, as at a lavatory. "I've got to get in there first" someone was saying in a fierce whisper. "I'm taking the trolley out to Greenfields, and you know it takes all day." "But I have an appointment downtown at 2.30 and it's nearly that now. I'm first on the list, you know it Dolly."

Supposing she called it off, let them scatter? But no, they had things to ask her, they might make mistakes. She opened the door, looked surprised to see them there in the hall, and asked them all in together. "Unless there is something specially important, we will just discuss finances," she explained.

It had seemed easier to cope with them all at once. Now, with four pair of eyes staring at hers, it was more difficult to sound convincing. "You must cut your budgets, cut your extras, cut your coal orders." They couldn't accept it.

"But Miss Chilton—"

"What about Dora O'Brien's arch support?"

"And the Brown baby?"

"And Mrs. Saunder's convalescent care?"

"Miss Dogherty said—"

She pounced on that one. "What did Miss Dogherty say?"

"I don't remember."

"I do. She said we couldn't really make any big changes in our plans or it wouldn't be social work we were doing, but police work."

Chilton flushed. Dogherty had reached them first, Dogherty has sowed rebellion. She was right, oh yes, but this wasn't a question of right and wrong. This was a practical question, a "business proposition." She would have to make them see it that way. She began talking, coldly and sensibly.

She could feel their chill growing, their distrust. Fortunately Miss Cherry wasn't there (where could she be?). But there was someone to take her place: Jean Vronsky.

"That is quite understandable, Miss Chilton. But what we would like to know is this: who are *you* for? For the people we are trying to help, or for the Board?" There was a gasp and a silence after it had been said.

Chilton was angry this time. "There is no question where my sympathy lies," she said. "As a social worker of some years' standing I do not have to explain myself to you."

There! She had done it. Lost her temper — and isolated them for her, forever. She watched them filing out miserably, her face set. A fine social worker who could not stand criticism. . . . A fine example.

She called a stenographer and began to dictate, so fast that the girl protested. "Sorry. Just mention it and I'll slow up. Where was I? — 'Mrs. Jones then said that Mr. Jones'. Yes. Paragraph."

When the afternoon was finally over, when the new case had been attended to, when Mrs. O'Hara had been given sewing materials and Miss Mickle had received her food order in advance — when everyone was getting ready for five o'clock with a sudden quickening of tempo — then she knew that she couldn't go home to the apartment for a long, long time. She would just sit here after it was quiet and smoke cigarette after cigarette. For a second now she folded her arms on the table and laid her head down.

She scarcely heard the timid knock on the door, and only raised her eyes in time to see Miss Cherry slip through the door and close it.

"I'm sorry to bother you, Miss Chilton."

"It's what I'm here for. I just happen to forget it sometimes, that's all."

Cherry should have been warned by the ironic tone. She was too full of her story to notice.

"I could only get there this afternoon. . . ."

"There?"

"The Caporetti's, you know."

"Oh yes. There are so many Caporetti's."

"Well, these ones especially. The baby was awful sick. But luckily I was able to phone next door and got him to come right away — the Welfare doctor. The baby has pneumonia, Miss Chilton. . . . And all they had been burning in the stove since last night was wooden boxes. There were no more left when I got there. . . . I just couldn't ask Mrs. Caporetti any questions, Miss Chilton. . . ."

"So you telephoned the coal company?"

"Yes. But it's all right, Miss Chilton. It's all right. I paid for it out of my own money. Luckily I had just had my cheque cashed."

"You paid for it. . . !" Chilton set back in her chair. "But you have to live too, child."

"I can live. I can easily live. It's they who can't live."

Then Chilton's head turned away, her elbows fell upon the desk. "Go away. Go away child. . . . Leave me, I say!"

Indians at Caughnawaugha
By Dorothy Livesay

"Hi, mister! Throw a nickel." The brown Indian boys shout and gesticulate, then dive from the rowboats into the green water. One of them, victorious, comes up with a shining nickel between his teeth.

This is on the shore of Caughnawaugha, Montreal's Indian Reserve. A mile across the water is Lachine, where the great iron foundries are mud-smeared and silent. The Indians used to go across daily to enter the factories as strong, cheap labour. Caughnawaugha at that time was a great asset to Montreal's business men. The Indians can subsist on little. Although many of them develop consumption, these can easily be replaced by younger boys. Anyway it would be dangerous to pay high wages, for then the Indians would get drunk. To prevent this from happening, the government has placed a ban on all liquor selling on the island. No Indian found intoxicated in Lachine is allowed to go home at night.

He hasn't much to go home to. The island has a dilapidated, graveyard appearance. Many of the grey stone houses are several hundreds of years old. Outside, they have a solid look, but inside they are falling to pieces, worn and cracked. There is no water system, no electricity or gas, only a few ancient stoves where wood is burnt summer and winter. The streets are unpaved, narrow mud alleys where a few chickens regale themselves.

One or two houses are decked out to attract tourists. Old, old women sit over their basketwork and beads, but only a few articles are sold. And the beads cost them 70 cents a pound. Most houses are small one-room affairs, where the whole family cooks and eats and sleeps.

Nearly the whole island is on relief. Indians live cheaper than other people, so the government allots them sixty cents a week per person. The older men fish in summer, haul wood, and in the winter they make sledge-hammers which they sell sometimes at $2.50 the dozen. The women sit at home restlessly, the children grow up anyhow, taught "all they need to know" by the Roman Catholic sisters. Of course education in Quebec is not compulsory, and even if there were a high school on the island, no one could afford to go because the fees are so high. And what of the youth? In the winter they face complete idleness. In the summer, the canning factories at St Hilaire, twenty miles away, open their doors to Caughnawaugha. The bus fare there and back takes twenty-five cents out of the day's pay. The girls arrive in the morning at seven. They are paid seventy-five cents for every hundred pounds of vegetables, but two hundred pounds is the limit for a good day. Most days are much poorer and involve a great deal of waiting which goes unpaid for. It is a common thing for a girl to come home at six at night with only thirty-five cents in her pocket — the rest of her day's earnings having been paid out in bus fare.

112

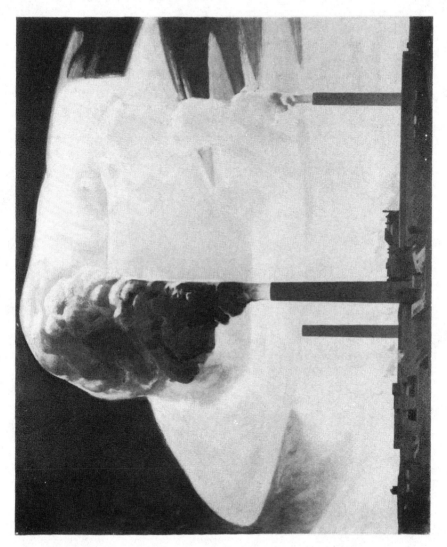

Smelter Stacks, Copper Cliff (1936), Charles Comfort, O.C., R.C.A. Collection of the National Gallery of Canada, Ottawa.

Under conditions like these, the youth is called "degenerate." Many of them are tubercular, and are promptly packed off to the Indian Church hospital on the island, there to end their days. Dental and general medical aid is given out at a minimum, and the Indians have no access to the free city hospital clinics.

Now that their labour is not needed, the government of Quebec has no interest in maintaining the living standards of the Indians. They are allowed to rot away, to be exploited by tourists, to live on a relief system that no other workers could exist on. Finally, the whole power to think for themselves, to resist, is taken away from them by the priest, who owns the biggest house on the island (with a fine secluded garden). Not until the working-class as a whole fights for these, their fellow-workers, and helps them to organize, not until the rising struggle and triumph forces the bosses to retreat, will the Indians be released from slavery. Every victory of the working-class is a victory for all oppressed peoples.

Toronto 1934

"Such were the dichotomies I found in male-female relationships in the thirties. In theory, we were free and equal as comrades on the left. In practice, our right hand was tied to the kitchen sink!"

 *On my return from Montreal, about May 1934, I was recruited by J.B. Salsberg of the Worker's Unity League to help organize the unorganized white collar workers. This account of my first trade union organizational meeting was written by Ed Jolliffe of the Canadian Press — my father's news co-operative. I had to beg Ed to use the pseudonym "Dorothy Randal" for me.*

Toronto Star, 1934

Store and Office Workers unite to form new union

Must Band Together to Protect Themselves, Meeting Told— Seen as Opportunity to Make Employers Pay Deserved Wages — Provisional Committee Elected

By Ed Jolliffe

"Office workers are the victims of the worst discrimination now being practised," declared Miss Dorothy Randall last night to a group of men and women who had gathered to form a union of office and store employees.

"The time has come for them to band together and protect themselves. They work under conditions that were long ago wiped out in factories. Office girls and men are ever haunted by the need to "speed-up", they are forced to work overtime without remuneration, forced to accept under wages, and are afraid to protest for higher wages lest they be discharged. This union will do away with all that." With this declaration, the first union of office workers and store employees was given its initial start.

Wide-spread Movement

"Last night's meeting laid the basis for a wide-spread movement. Never before in Ontario has such a union been attempted. Now that the Ontario government is planning to set up codes for all industries," said Miss Randall, "office and store employees should band together and be able to express what is needed to improve conditions. Only by being ready to do this, and by being ready to push out any effort to diminish the code, can a union hope to have strength."

Distribute Leaflets

Miss Randall outlined the origin of the movement, from the discussion of two office workers, who felt the need of some organization, to last night's meeting. The two instigators met with eight others from stores and offices and planned to have leaflets distributed and arranged for telephone service. On October 8 25 people met and discussed the setting up of a definite union with the name Office and Store Employees' Union. The union is to be independent for the time being.

Dragged To Lowest Level

The speaker of the evening was Mr. J.B. Salsberg of the Workers' Unity League. "Alone you are unable to gain one penny on your hour," Mr. Salsberg told the meeting. "Only when you are united are you capable of demanding better wages and improvements in the conditions under which you work," he said, emphasizing the need of a united front. "Not until the past few years have large numbers of office workers been gathered under the same roof," he continued. "Office workers have remained aloof, considering themselves the aristocracy of labor. If you are that, why are you not paid as aristocrats? Your wages drag

you down to the lowest level; now you have the opportunity to make your employers pay you the wages you deserve and to earn the livelihood to which you are entitled. Organize, join hands with other workers and rise to higher standards."

"Organize At Once"

Mr. Salsberg urged them to organize at once, declaring that it will not be the established law of minimum wages that will count but the force of workers at the negotiation table when the code is being discussed.

An open discussion followed Mr. Salsberg's address, and speakers from the floor told of some of the conditions under which they were forced to work. One young man told of one organization that is open for a period of 70 to 75 hours per week for business. "As the employees are allowed only 48 hours a week, by legislation, this organization twists the hours around to its own advantage. A girl may be told to work Monday afternoon and evening, and take Tuesday off. She may be told to work any time of day or evening, for half a day or any evening of the week. In this way she is on call 72 hours of the week, and is receiving wages for but 48 hours. Hours should be conservative."

Not Paid Overtime

A bank worker next told of her hours. "Our work really begins at 3 in the afternoon, when the bank is closed to the public," she said. "We work until 7 in the evening, or until we have finished our allotted amount. We are not given wages for this overtime, nor are we paid supper money. Twice a month, the first and the fifteenth, we work later, under the same conditions."

The complications of making a living on the commission basis was explained by a saleswoman. "We must make $12.50 a week, or we are subject to discharge. On rainy days there are few customers and, through no fault of ours, we are unable to make the wage, and so find ourselves without a position. A union would make it easier for us."

Union meetings often ended in a mass signing of a list of demands or a pledge of support for leaders. (Public Archives Canada C-27903)

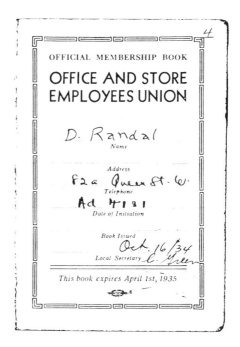

Two Women

"Are you being waited on?"

The day seemed suddenly endless as Bertha asked that question for the twentieth time. *Are you being waited on?* She used to say it in her sleep, sometimes, so Laura said. Laura, sleeping too lightly, as she often did, at the far side of the double bed, would hear Bertha talking in the darkness; she would remember to wake her in the morning with the words: "Are you being waited on! Hurry up, Bert, we're late . . . Get up!" And by the time Bertha struggled out of bed Laura was already dressed, neat as a pin. Her soft black hair tucked in at the shoulder, adding to her small-boyish appearance.

"Do I have to punch the clock late, because of you?" Laura would demand — half in earnest.

"N-no." Bertha yawned. "I'll be ready." And then she had a bird's eye view of the day ahead: a day of feet, feet, feet, trying on other people's shoes. "Gee, I'm glad night comes in between," she muttered. "Aren't you, Laura? We'll have a good time in the evenings this summer — we'll go to High Park, and Sunnyside. . . ."

"Uh-huh." Laura was putting on her make-up. "But hurry up now, Bert. You really are late."

Bertha pulled her big frame out of bed, stared distastefully at the cold linoleum floor. "Think that salesman's out of the bathroom yet?"

"How should I know?"

"Oh well." Bertha plunged out into the rooming-house hall, just squeezed in before Miss Pope got there. "Gee" she thought, scrubbing her teeth, staring at her bony face in the mirror: "Gee, Laura's snappy these days. The slow spring maybe, made her feel tight, all tied up in knots — and everything always the same, day after day . . . wait till summer comes, she promised herself. She'd give Laura a good time then.

"Are you being waited on?" With a jerk, Bertha heard her own voice saying it. She was looking down brightly into the face of the small, fluttering old lady.

"We want a pair of shoes, if you please." That gentle, precise voice came from the old lady's husband. Round-faced and brisk, with a small white goatee which quite tickled Bertha, he was holding tight to the old lady's arm, pointing to her foot with his.

"Certainly sir. Will you sit down here?" And Bertha squatted on her heels, holding the footrule, looking enquiringly from one to the other as they sat down. "What sort of shoes?"

The old lady looked frightened at the question, turned helplessly to her husband.

"Black brogues" he told Bertha. "Strong, with a low heel. Size five-and-a-half," he remembered, repeating it slowly, "five-and-a-half."

"Bertha held out her foot rule, drew off the old lady's tough black boot. She adjusted the rule. "Five-and-a-half is right!" She nodded back at him. But the old lady burst into peals of laughter.

"Five-and-a-half," she repeated, in a shrill quaver.

Like a parrot, Bertha thought, sinking instinctively backwards on her heels. The old gentleman was so embarrassed!

"There, there, my dear." He patted the old lady's skirt. Then, abruptly, to Bertha: "Black brogues," he ordered.

She left them, puzzled. Would they be fussy? And remembering the last three women she had fitted, hard, metallic young women who never knew what they wanted until she had shown them all the stock, Bertha decided that this couple would be easy. "She's scared — a bit queer. He don't like taking her out." Bertha thought this, then her mind was a blank again. She was looking for shoe number 986.

Bertha had a sudden fear that the old lady was going to start laughing again. It made her feel scared, somehow. But no, the old lady seemed suddenly to shrivel up, like a chastised child. She stood, docile, while he took off the brogue and adjusted the boot.

"There!" He stood up with a sigh. Catching Bertha's eye he bowed slightly. "Thank you," he said.

"Here's your change, sir. I hope the shoes suit."

He nodded, seized his wife's arm, and trudged away fast towards the elevator. Bertha watched them, fascinated. Then she became aware of a raw, harsh voice in her ear.

"I've been waiting to be served for fifteen mintues" a woman was saying.

"Certainly. Sit down, please." Bertha's face was self-possessed, polite. Her back had begun to ache, she was conscious of the pucker in her forehead. But after all, it was getting near to closing-time — and this was Friday.

Bertha automatically fitted the customer, but in her mind the word Friday was flowing like a cool draught of air. Friday, the day of going home without a feeling of rush, of meeting Laura in their room, of going out, leisurely and gay, to have dinner at Hunt's, and then go to a show — the weekly treat she always gave Laura.

Suddenly feeling alive again, she straightened up; went to the stacks in search of the next pair of shoes.

At 5:30, as the sales-girls were leaving the department, taking off their smocks, hurrying to the cloakroom, Bertha met Mr. Brace. He crinkled up his round eyes, took a pencil from behind his ear, and pointed it at her accusingly.

"I wonder who
Nearly let someone
Run off with a shoe?" he chanted.

Bertha flushed, then guffawed. "Oh, did you see that, Mr. Brace? Say, wasn't she a queer one!"

He laughed in return. "I'm wondering how she ever escaped!" And tapping his head, rolling his eyes, he passed on.

Bertha went down on the elevator smiling to herself. What a good joke it was . . . and fancy him seeing it. She would tell Laura about it in the restaurant, at dinner. Laura would just know something had happened, because Bertha could never keep that wide grin off her face when she had something to tell. But Laura would sit there demurely, saying nothing; just waiting. Then, at the right time, she would say, "Come on now, Bert. Spill the beans." And while Laura's eyes roved around the restaurant, watching to see the latest hats and styles and staring at other office girls like herself, coming in with their boy friends, Laura would be saying to Bert: "That's a good one. There's always something funny happens to you, Bert." And her eyes would flutter back and forth, like. Not settling anywhere. Laura sure was restless these days, Bertha knew it. Jumpy and sometimes too excited and sometimes very low. She needed to get out more often, maybe they could even afford to go out Saturday night, too.

Bertha was thinking and planning all this on the way home, as soon as she got a seat on the street-car. If she had to stand up, in that awful crush, stretching her arm-socket by hanging onto the strap, she could never think at all. But tonight the car seemed less crowded. She found a seat at the back and let her heavy bones ease into the wooden seat. She smiled a little, thinking of Laura. Happy, suddenly.

"Euclid and Manning," the conductor called, above the roar of the streetcar. Bertha jumped up in a rush, almost too late, elbowed her way to the door.

"At last." She stepped onto the pavement, saw above her the long branches of chestnut buds beginning to uncurl, and smiled, at her own corner, as she heard the organ-grinder with his gurgling tune. Kids ceased their shrieking, listening to the music, the evening came down softly. It was spring!

Running up the steps of the narrow brick rooming-house, Bertha was smiling, ready even to be friendly with the landlady. She unlocked the door, humming a little.

Inside the hallway it was dark, as always, with that stale, greasy smell. She had her hand on the bannister, to go upstairs, when the landlady's door, to her left, opened suddenly.

"Oh-h. It's you, Miss Boyd. I've been trying to get you since five o'clock."

"What's the matter?"

"I've had to get the doctor for your friend."

"Laura!"

Mrs. Duggan nodded, fat and impressive in the doorway. "They brung her home from the office in a taxi. Said to call a doctor. They didn't seem to know what was the matter."

Bertha turned, ploughed up the two flights of stairs. "Laura," she was panting, "Laura." At the door to their room she paused, for it was open, propped by a chair with the doctor sitting in it. She looked past him, towards the window. Laura was standing there, looking out, twisting the curtain in her hands.

"Why Laura," Bertha began. The other stiffened, yanked at the curtain.

"That's my name," she said. "Yes . . . yes." Her eyes wavered, then turned back to the curtain, where her hands were clenched tight.

"Laura" she said. "Laura. LAURA!" And she began to laugh.

Bertha fell back, her heart pounding. The doctor was standing up now, very grave. As she looked round he beckoned to her, he drew her through the doorway.

Laura's laugh followed them down the hall, like a parrot's.

 *My first concept of the role of women in our society was determined by the ideal held up to me by my father who made sure that I read the 18th century women writers, Fanny Burney, Jane Austin; the 19th century women, George Eliot and the Bronte sisters; and those delightful women of our age, Virginia Woolf, Dorothy Richardson and*

*Katherine Mansfield — not women's libbers, any of them, but creative
women who dared to live by their own standards. Perhaps* The Mill on
the Floss, *Maggie Tulliver's trials in relation to her brother, roused me
against the injustices of family life, so male-dominated. Then at the
University of Toronto, I joined the Women's Press club and a sorority for
women journalists, Sigma Phi. In those days even the Students Admin-
istrative Council had two sections, like the washrooms — male and female. The only time we saw the inside of Hart House was at a ball. In
the all-male Writers Club "discussion began with a battle royal as to
whether women could ever be great artists." The clearest expression of
this alignment is to be found in interviews in the University of Toronto
student newspaper the* Varsity *for 1929:*

WOMEN IN POLITICS
MATTER OF OPINION

Woman Claims They Have All
the Brains so Why
Worry?

Men are justified in thinking wom-
en should not be in political clubs
because large percentages of women
have not availed themselves of their
right to vote," said Connie Nelson, III
Vic, when questioned about men not
wanting women in their political clubs.

Another co-ed said. "We don't want
to be in their political clubs. We can
form our own."

Women should not be in the same
political clubs as men, for they have
not the same point of view," thought
Alliston Shiel, II U.C.

But the general opinion is that
women ought to be able to do what
they want. "We've been down-trodden
long enough now, and women repre-
sent the nation as well as men."

As for men not wanting women in
the university at all, one strong feminist protested violently. Women have
all the brains and they pay their
tuition and get high standing so why
not? Anyway men themselves should
be in the business world not sticking
around in Arts.

Another was of the opinion that
"Men who think women should not be
allowed in college, don't really. They
wouldn't be able to get along.

Almost imperceptibly, by 1931 when I graduated, the climate had changed. Women were taking a marked interest in politics, in the arts, in the fight for freedom of religious belief led so bravely by Andrew Allan. (The Varsity *was banned because he had made the statement, editorially on Feb. 24, 1931 that "the students of the University and the majority of the graduates are largely atheists and that the professors and staff are teaching atheism to the students.")*

Although women were still coralled in separate colleges and separate organizations, a liberated group of free thinking men and women were meeting informally with professors such as E.K. Brown to discuss literature; and with the economist Otto Van der Sprenkel to discuss the state of the world: capitalism, socialism, communism. The final hurdle for the young women in those groups was that of "losing your virginity." Quite a few managed it. But so clandestine did the taking on of a lover have to be (on account of parental and religous disapproval) that the relationships were fraught with anxiety. We learned of only two methods of birthcontrol; the French safe and the chemical pessary. Becoming pregnant would be out of the question financially and socially. However, by 1934, when I was doing field work at the Infants Home for unmarried mothers in Toronto, I knew the full story on abortion, illegitimacy, unwanted children, parental disinheritance. This I wrote about in the poem "In Green Solariums." I saw that only in a society where men and women struggled together for equal opportunity and equal responsibility would the illegitimate child be accepted, and with no black-listing of his mother. Liberal attitudes, egalitarianism between the sexes were certainly practiced amongst intellectuals. The story is told by Grace MacInnis that when J.S. Woodsworth, her father, needed his wife's advice on a speech he was giving, he tried to read it to her as she put the clothes through the wringer. "I can't hear you," she said. "Here," he replied, "I'll finish the washing and you read this." Such scenes took place in these middle class intellectual families committed to "the movement."

Probably the most severe restriction against pre-marital sex and illegitimate births occurred not in the middle class (where they were secretly acknowledged or condoned) but amongst the working and farm people. These I came to meet in Ontario when I was in the young Communist League and contacting unemployed families to encourage organization against low relief rates and against the shabby treatment of the single unemployed. The young organizer for whom I wrote pamphlets had two children; and a wife who was "unpoliticized" and left behind in the kitchen whilst we were at meetings. Naturally, she resented the fact that I would spend evenings with her husband, typing up his leaflets. My story

"Six Years" illustrates my sympathy for those thousands of women who were unable to play an active role in politics, often because their politicized husbands still regarded them as property — "I married her to raise my children."

Such were the dichotomies I found in male-female relationships in the thirties. In theory, we were free and equal as comrades on the left. In practice, our right hand was tied to the kitchen sink!

The topless thirties; Dorothy Livesay (lying down) with Jinnie Morton (right) and a friend.

New Frontier, 1936

Women:
Bound or Free

Margaret Gould

The placid acceptance of a "woman problem" should be spiritedly resented by those it is supposed to concern. In a civilized society there is no longer any excuse for such a habit of thought. There should be, of course, provision for protecting the child-bearing function: but when this is rightly regarded as a function rather than a personal disability, it is a problem not of woman but of all society.

But, undoubtedly, under conditions similar to our own in Canada, there is much to worry about in this direction. . . "Women are inhibited," said Dr.

Karen Horney, psycho-analyst, addressing a convention of women's clubs in Seattle, "inhibited by their feeling of insecurity, dependence on men, and their over-emphasis on emotional values. A woman is inclined to place love on a pedestal as the only real value in life. She limits her interest to husband, home and children. She would rather endure things as they are than fight to change them.

"But these inhibitions are not innate in woman's nature. They have been developed through social influences. . . ." This indicates the real root of the matter. Women are held back by various social and economic considerations from doing what they might do and becoming what they might become. We have, in effect, by exaggerating the disabilities imposed by child-bearing and its allied functions, bred an inferior sex. Inferior to what? Inferior, in the case of each individual, to what she might be: that is the point to be remembered.

Fortunately, it is not true that all women "rather endure things as they are than fight to change them," for they have fought to secure something they used to call "the emancipation of women." Their efforts have often been misdirected, often silly to the point of ludicrousness, but on the whole, heroic. And the defeats and victories of that battle up to the present have helped to define the aims and tactics which must be used in the future. . . .

New Frontier, 1936

Women Are Mugs

Marjorie King

Women are trying. They don't think much of themselves. Their husbands have no great opinion of them. To their grown children they are a pain in the neck. Women's conversations with each other are about trivial subjects, persons, clothes, or repairs. They skip the news stories and editorials in the papers and read the society pages, the gossip sections and the cookery columns. Where women gather in numbers they shriek and exclaim. Their speech is full of over-emphasis and blanket adjectives. In mixed groups even among the serious-minded, the women are apt to be silent and ineffective when the talk turns to science, politics and other non-personal matters. They get round their children by underhand appeals to their softer feelings. They spoil discussions by dragging in the personal element all the time. They give way to tempermental outbursts.

But that is not all that can be said. Women are not essentially mugs. They have been made into mugs by social conditioning. How, precisely, does this come about? How does the kind of life we consider normal for a woman make a mug out of her? But remember that for the moment it is middle-class women we are discussing. The case for working class women is quite different.

The National Council of Women, Moncton, New Brunswick, 1931.

(Public Archives Canada PA-51605)

Women are mugs: *Because* they are brought up to believe they must marry and keep house for a living. They are taught to expect less of themselves than men and to fear and distrust "working" for a living as a permanent prospect. The economic system makes this inevitable of course. But what a ridiculous situation! It means that myriads of intelligent women, with extremely varied capabilities and interests, find that if they wish to live a full emotional life, to which mating and parenthood are necessary, they are automatically doomed to one kind of occupation, whether they like it or not. A few can and do carry on their chosen work and bear and rear children as well, but in the face of our social customs they must have almost superhuman strength, and luck as well, to do it successfully. All very well to say a woman can use every bit of talent she possesses in the task of homemaking. The fact is that in our inefficient and antiquated housekeeping plants too much energy goes to laundry work and dishwashing, and not enough to the human life that goes on within the home, especially when it is assumed that child-rearing is unskilled labor.

Because following on this, women are cut off from the conditions of the world in which their children are to live. They are expected to be heavily responsible for moulding their offspring's characters, but must live in such a way that they can neither know from experience the nature of the productive world nor have any adequate opportunity of shaping that world. People imply this when they complain that married women lack discipline. A few years of marriage and motherhood almost completely unfits a woman to go back to a job again. Housekeepers have plenty of discipline, but it is not the dicipline of co-operative social labour and indeed, militates against co-operation. Hence the common complaint that women do not co-operate well. It is true, but only partially and not because of any innate deficiency. . . .

Because women's personalities are warped by unsatisfactory sexual life. The need to marry to be assured of a living makes it necessary for women to resort to all sorts of tricks of dress, make-up, deportment and speech to attract the male. See the advertisements in any popular magazine for proof of this. But after marriage, full, free expression of love is inhibited by many things, fatique, discontent, conflicting routine of husband and wife, worry over money, fear of pregnancy. A deal of nonsense has been written about the frigid wife, the impotent husband, faulty marriage technique and the like, and we are led to believe that marriage would be heaven if all followed the directions of this or that sexologist. The abnormal interest in the subject is in itself a confession. As a matter of pride, pride born of the whole social complex, women pretend that their marriage — which is their life — is a success. Because they live isolated from each other there is little opportunity for comparison of the real facts, except by discussion. And who will take the first steps in a discussion which may reveal disappointment, disillusionment, and worst of all, apparent failure? Only a handful of intellectuals can keep discussions of personal affairs and private lives on an impersonal level, in any case. But a thousand chance confidences and catch phrases reveal that most women harbour a strain of bitterness in their married lives. This breeds a cold and cynical attitude towards sex. And this attitude, combined with the low grade of physical health we tolerate, makes a poor neurotic thing of love. We are not likely to know how glorious and lasting a thing it can be until men and women come together in the zest of exuberant health and happy work and play together, as economic equals and not as pursuer and pursued, supporter and dependent breadwinner and cook. . . .

Because by the time her children are grown up the mother has lost touch with friends and activities which formerly stimulated and developed her and has hardened into the habits of housekeeping and motherhood. When at last she might seem to be free of her handicaps she is more than ever in their grip. She has performed the only function society recognizes, and now when she looks about for serious occupation she finds herself at a loose end. This is no imaginary problem. Several times a year one woman's magazine or another comes forth with an article on the woman of forty-five. They prescribe activities for her, clubs, books, gardening, music, but she knows, if she is honest, that these are just time-fillers. Whatever unaccustomed outside activities she may undertake, her husband and children will look upon them with some amusement. No one thinks they are really and truly important. She pathetically tries to keep the family together and organizes Thanksgiving dinners and Sunday teas, and everyone tries to co-operate because they are fond of her and rather sorry for her — her health is never what it might be. But they know in their hearts that all this is a little false. Actually the children have gone their own way, far from the mother.

This is a picture of what middle class women may well fear as their lot in life. They are mugs, and if they allow themselves to be submerged they are likely to be just like the older women they see around them. The only ultimate escape is economic equality. But in the meantime what? Not an attempt to make the best of a bad job surely. That is just defeat. There is another way for the woman who rebels against a life like this. She can illuminate it with a healthy realism and get rid of a lot of the lumber which a bourgeois tradition has imposed on her. She can sort out the real from the false in her relationships with other people and in her material life, and get rid of the claptrap of stereotyped, meaningless social obligations and conventions in house-furnishing and table-setting and food. It is only when she has done this that she is free to work toward the real goal of economic freedom for women.

New Jersey 1935

"At that time the United States represented for Canadians what Canada represents for Americans today — a place to breathe in."

The comradeship of communist friends continued when I went to find a job in New Jersey, in the fall of 1934. After some penniless waiting, living with friends, I took the first offer I got — in Englewood New Jersey, just across the Hudson from New York City. I was to be the only case worker in a recreation agency which served the Negro population of the town and also middle class white families who were on relief, or having a psychological struggle coping with a lowered standard of living. The dichotomy was startling. My only relationship with Negros had been on trains — with friendly coloured porters — and in Canada; even in Montreal, I had not encountered the racial antagonisms or thought they existed. I knew all about the Jewish problem of course and was always out in defence of the Jew as underdog.

The double standard which I found amongst social workers and of course the townsfolk, the social taboos against mixing even at a party, the segregation and the lower standard of education — all this opened a new area of identification.

One friend I met there was a young Negro named Fred Morrow who had done an amazing thing. He was very brilliant and wanted to go into law and his name was the same as that of Charles Lindberg's wife, Anne Morrow. He applied to Harvard without in any way setting down the fact that he was Negro. He was just Fred Morrow from Englewood. They

129

thought Anne Morrow came from that area and simply assumed he was one of the family. He was the first black person at Harvard I think. And he would sit and tell me how he stuck it out and got through but couldn't get a job as a lawyer so he was working with the agency.

Within the community centre we were all as one, but out in the street, in a car, or even, as I found, in my own rooms, it was not permitted to be seen with a Negro.

Also in this town I met some fine Jewish people, a Polish tailor, a Hebrew Scottish carpenter who all amazed me with their sense of freedom, their belief in liberty. For I had come from Bennett's "Iron Heel" country and Roosevelt's NRA with its policies of making work — building cultural projects and encouraging free discussion and meetings — made me start believing in democracy again. At that time the United States represented for Canadians what Canada represents for Americans today — a place to breathe in.

Roosevelt established the Civil Works Administration. The CWA workers were on the federal payrolls. The agency took half its workers from relief rolls. The other half were people who needed jobs, but didn't have to demonstrate their poverty by submitting to a means test. CWA did not give relief stipends, but paid minimum wages. They mobilized in one winter almost as many men as had served in the armed forces in the war. They had to invent jobs for four million men and women in thirty days and put them to work. So in this brief span the CWA built or improved some 500,000 miles of road, 40,000 schools, 3,500 playgrounds and 1,000 airports. Workmen renovated Montana's state capitol building, Pittsburgh's Cathedral of Learning. The CWA employed 50,000 teachers to keep rural schools open and to teach adult education classes. It provided enough money to put back to work every teacher on Boston's unemployed rolls. And this is the point that of course interested me: it hired 3,000 artists and writers.

The writers' project interested me, and I got to know some of the people in it. Some of the leading writers of the thirties were employed to do research work on the history of areas, and the literary development in certain places. There was almost an army of them doing this. There were of course artists painting murals for public buildings, and there were musicians exploring the past folksong life so it was an extraordinarily stimulating experience to be there.

But I came back and found the opposite situation, of course, in Canada. That is to say, all they offered the unemployed was relief camps for the men — men selected through the Employment Service of Canada. Candidates were required to be single, homeless, in need of relief, free from communicable disease, and physically fit for ordinary manual labour.

130

They were issued clothing and razors and mending kits, a toothbrush, and were issued 1.3 cents' worth of tobacco a day. In 1935 this was raised to two cents' worth per day. Transient life left many men undernourished.

*   *   *

I had been transferred to the communist party in the United States and had planned to end my sojourn in a tourist's trip to Russia (such as a number of American professionals had taken). But I developed what was thought to be an ulcer and was advised not to venture to Moscow but to return to the quiet woods of Clarkson.

The true story of my year in New Jersey is told in the retrospective poem herewith, "New Jersey: 1935." The fictionalized play "The Times Were Different" and the story "Herbie" are true also but in a wider sense. If I had the time and space really to record the facts of belonging to an underground movement in the U.S. — across the river from New York's Worker's School where I took course in Marxism — I might, even today, compromise some of my good American friends. Suffice it to say that my most loyal friend, of whom I was very fond, was a short, bandy-legged Scot from Glasgow whose enthusiasms were divided between Italian opera, Lenin and liberation from the Jewish orthodoxy in which he had been brought up.

New Jersey: 1935

In the landlady's garden
we walked entwined in moonlight
Luella and I
tree and shadow of tree
linked white and black.
It was a time
before this present darkness
before flashes of violence
tore clouds with lightning crack—
but in the moonlight
we were visible
walking the landlady's garden
we were seen entering her house
climbing upstairs for supper.
And when Luella had left
(at least she waited till I closed the door)
the landlady shoved her shoulder
into mine
    and her frog eyes
into my face:

131

"Was that a coloured girl you dared to bring
into my home?"
"Why, yes, a social worker;
we have jobs together in the Settlement House."
"For that I could whack
the liver out of anyone. Don't ever
let a nigger enter my door again."
"Why no! — I never will—
nor a white girl, either."
And I went upstairs
to pack.
They say it's the same thing, now
even in the North, the same
animal fear, frog eyes—
and in response
the same dark guttural laugh:
"You jest don' understand things, honey."

And I guess I don't understand
for I haven't been back.

"The Times Were Different"?

a radio play by Dorothy Livesay

SOUND: (Music: theme of the nursery song, "Boys and Girls come out to play," fades into the sound of a skipping rope and a small girl's voice)

CHILD: Blue bells, cockle shells, evy ivy over.

SOUND: (A boy's wagon rumbling over wooden planks).

BOY: Toot' Toot' Out of my way!

CHILD: Blue bells, cockle — hey, stop that, Roger!

SOUND: (Children's voices in excited play, montage effect): You will! I will not. That's not fair. I won't play. Aw, don't be a meanie. I will so. EEnie meanie minie mo, catch a nigger by the toe. . . . Rah rah rah. Red white and blue. Your father is an Irishman, your mother is a Jew.

(Music up and out. Dead silence.)

MARGARET (as an adult): When I was a child, I thought as a child. It was a small and sheltered world. A short street — white pavement — with a boulevard running down each side. And wooden sidewalks, along which I used to skip.

SOUND: (Skipping rope turning, child skipping)

CHILD: Blue bells, cockle shells, evy ivy over.

MARGARET: It was fun, sometimes when you had nothing to do and there was no one to play with, to watch the ants busily hauling away their loads — and sometimes to squash them with your feet.

CHILD: (Skipping) Step on a crack, break your mother's back.

MARGARET: It was a good feeling, on a cool summer morning, with the dew still on the grass, to wet your black patent leather slippers or, all by yourself, to take a rubber ball.

SOUND: (Ball Bouncing)

CHILD: One two three alairy, four five six alairy

SOUND: (Theme of "Boys and Girls" soft in B.G.)

CHILD: seven eight nine alairy; ten alairy, catch me!

MARGARET: When the boys and girls came out to play, everything got faster and faster. We played tag, hide-and-seek, cheese it. . . .

SOUND: (Child counting, very fast: "one two three four five six seven eight nine ten — CHEESE-IT" Repeats, fading)

MARGARET: Sometimes it would get wilder and wilder and there'd be a fight between our gang and the gang up the street. . . .

SOUND: (Children's voices, montage effect: "You can't play here!" "We can so!" "Aw, get on your own side of the boulevard." "I can stay here if I want to." "Sure he can." "Jew boy, Jew boy, Davey is a Jew boy." "Well, you're a Catholic, so there!")

BOY: Rah rah rah, red white and blue, your father is an Irishman your mother is a Jew.

CHILD: Never mind, Davey. You know what to say to them.

BOY: Sticks and stones will break my bones, but names will never hurt me!

CHILD: Come on Davey, come into my yard, and play.

VOICES: Sissy, sissy, plays with the girls.

BOY: I can fight too. Just come over here and see.

GIRL: Aw, let's not have fights any more.

ANOTHER: Let's play Hide-and-Seek . . . Not IT!

VOICES: Not IT! Not IT! . . . Margaret's IT.

CHILD: (Counts fast to ten) Ready or not, you must be caught, hiding around the goal or not! O-U-T spells OUT!

MARGARET: (low, as if to herself) Ready or not, you must be caught. . . . But when I was a child, I thought as a child. When I grew older, I put away childish things . . . I began to read books. . . .

SOUND: (Music up. Dreamy theme).

MOTHER: Margaret? Margaret! Where are you, child? In a book again, I suppose . . . Margaret, it's time now.

MARGARET: (as a child of 13) Yes, mummy.

MOTHER: It's supper-time. Close the book; and come and set the table.

MARGARET: Okay, mum. Just let me finish this one chapter . . . see' it's only two more pages.

MOTHER: Very well, then. . . . What is the book you are reading?

MARGARET: Er? . . . Oh, it's one out of Daddy's bookcase.

MOTHER: But *what* is it? One of Thomas Hardy's?

MARGARET: Uh huh.

MOTHER: Let me see it. Not . . . not *Tess*?

MARGARET: Why not? Daddy said I could choose whatever I liked.

MOTHER: He just wasn't thinking. . . . I think you'd better stop reading.

MARGARET: But that's not fair, Mum. I'm just in the middle.

MOTHER: Never mind, just now. I'll discuss it with your father.

MARGARET: Aw, gee. Spoil sport.

MOTHER: That'll do, Margaret. . . . Anyway, it's time to come in. Supper's nearly ready.

MARGARET: (adult) Ready . . . Ready. . . . Ready or not, you must be caught — But I wasn't caught that time Daddy won out! I was allowed to read all of Thomas Hardy — and even the moderns, like Hemingway and Lawrence. But it was different with one book, one written by a woman!

SOUND: (Music, soft in B.G.)

MARGARET: I was lying in the hammock one summer afternoon, half-asleep, a book in my hand. The gate clicked, and I heard mother coming up the walk with a friend. . . .

MOTHER: Shall we sit in the garden to get cooled off, and then have tea?

FRIEND: That sounds just right to me.

MOTHER: There, take this chair, with the foot-rest.

FRIEND: This *is* a peaceful spot. . . . Does Jack do all the gardening?

MOTHER: Every bit of it. As well as the antique-collecting and the book-buying!

FRIEND: What was it you started to tell me about that book?

MOTHER: Oh . . . *that* one! (laughing) The one I gardened with?

FRIEND: Gardened with?

MOTHER: I simply could not finish the book . . . it left the worst taste in my mouth.

FRIEND: Who wrote it?

MOTHER: A woman, if you please! This Virginia Woolf who's supposed to be so wonderful. *Jacob's Room* it's called. And it's all about his room and what goes on there — creaking bed and so on — the innuendo, my dear! You've no idea.

FRIEND: Well, it does sound intriguing. Better not let your daughter get hold of it.

MOTHER: But I've told you — she can't! Not now. I've seen to that.

FRIEND: You mean you burned the book?

MOTHER: (laughing). Better than that. I hated it so, wanted to do something about it, with my own hands. So I got Jack's trowel and went out into the garden. I dug a hole, under the oak tree — and there I buried it!

FRIEND: Lillian! You didn't!

MOTHER: I certainly did. I'll show you the spot, over there beyond the hammock. . . . O-h-h! Margaret! I didn't know you were there.

MARGARET: (15)(yawning) I didn't either! I've been asleep, I guess.

MOTHER: Well, run along into the house, will you dear? And put the kettle on . . . Mrs Fenwick's with me.

FRIEND: How do you do, Margaret?

MARGARET: How do you do, Mrs Fenwick. Okay, mother, I'll get the tea.

SOUND: (Music up: "Polly Put the Kettle On")

MARGARET: (adult) But as I passed the oak tree, I noticed that there was a pile of fresh earth, upturned. . . . Would the tree be poisoned, I wondered? Would the tree die?

SOUND: (Music up and out . . . then fast into a Charleston).

135

MARGARET: At university, in the late twenties, it was all so different. Freedom to read. Freedom to think. Freedom to talk and act. There was a boom in the air, a kind of feverish excitement. Individuals were all that mattered. We talked far into the night, drinking Italian wine, gesticulating in the candlelight. Or we danced, skated, went sleigh-riding by moonlight. . . .

SOUND: (Sleigh-bells, horses' hooves muffled on snow).

MARGARET: Oh, I wish this could last for ever and ever.

DAVEY: Well, it won't.

MARGARET: Cold comfort Davey.

DAVEY: Look, Margaret, it's our last year. Gather ye snowflakes while ye may. . . . Here, I'll put some down your neck.

MARGARET: (squeals) No you won't. Oh Davey, *don't!*

DAVEY: Just to remember me by. Cold comfort!

SALLY: I wonder where you'll be this time next year, Davey.

MARK: In Russia, he'll be — probably. The workers' paradise! Ya!

DAVEY: A lot you know about it, you silk-pajam'd capitalist.

MARGARET: Now don't let's argue . . . not on a sleigh-ride! . . . Will you really go to Russia, Davey?

DAVEY: No, I don't suppose so. Paris will be good enough for me.

MARGARET: Paris! Oh . . . if only. . . .

DAVEY: Do you think you might get there, Margaret?

MARGARET: I'm afraid to think of it, I want it so badly. But it all depends. . . .

DAVEY: On that scholarship?

MARGARET: Yes, And, of course, it depends on my mother.

DAVEY: What has she got to do with it? You have to stand on your own pins, my girl.

MARGARET: I know. But that's hard, when she keeps sticking her pins into me!

SALLY: Shame on you, Margaret! Such disrespect.

MARGARET: Well, Sally — what about *your* mother?

DAVEY: (humming) What are little girls made of, made of? What are little girls made of? Sugar and spice and—

136

SALLY: Come on everybody, let's sing! (She begins) "There's a long long trail a-winding"

SOUND: (Half a dozen mixed voices singing, gradually fading into the distance, accompanied by sleighbells.

MARGARET: I did have my year in Paris, . . a last fling at swotting in libraries, browsing among prints along the quais, sitting in the Tuileries gardens on a windy Sunday; a last fling at running the cafes along the Boul. Mich., watching the French berets mingle with black heads from Africa, a Turkish fez, a Hindu turban. There was no race hatred in Paris. But there was something else. . . .

SOUND: (Horses galloping: A shot fired. Screams of "Les flics, les flics! Courez, les flics sont ici.")

DAVEY: Margaret, we'd better get out of here!

MARGARET: I can't. I can't move.

DAVEY: You'll have to . . . I'll go ahead of you, and push.

MARGARET: But Davey, wait a minute! What's all the trouble? What has happened?

DAVEY: The police have shot somebody. See, one of the demonstrators. Look over there . . . they're trying to make a space around him. . . .

SOUND: (Sirens. . . . Roar of a crowd, in French. Slogans etc.)

DAVEY: There's the Black Maria. Come on girl, for God's sake. Look — this way. Hurry, or we'll be caught.

CHILD'S VOICE: Ready or not, you must be caught, hiding around the goal or not. . . .

MARGARET: We were not caught, exactly. But outcast. Then out of France. Out of Europe. . . .

DAVEY: But not out of the depression!

MARGARET: The strange thing was, it was just the same in Canada as in Europe — men surging in the streets, parades, demonstrations. The Mounties called in at Estevan. In Montreal, men on horseback lashing out with whips . . . I saw it on St Catherine Street. And the Black Maria. . . .

SOUND: (sirens)

MOTHER: But Margaret, you can't read that stuff.

MARGARET: I will.

MOTHER: But Margaret, you can't talk like that.

MARGARET: I will.

MOTHER: But Margaret, you don't understand!

MARGARET: Then I will understand! I'm going back to college. I'm going to study to be a social worker. I'm going to live like these people live — then I will understand!

SOUND: (Repeat earlier montage effect of children playing on street. A fight. Name calling.)

CHILD: (Crescendo) Eeenie meanie minie moe, catch a nigger by the toe, when he hollers let him go — eenie meanie minie moe.

MARGARET: Here, what's all the row about?

CHILD: (sobs)

BOY: Shut up, you. . . . Here comes the Welfare Lady.

MARGARET: Why, Mamie! You're crying. . . . What's the matter?

MAMIE: She — she called me names.

CHILD: I did not.

MAMIE: You did so.

MARGARET: Well, you know, Mamie: "Sticks and stones. . . ."

MAMIE: I don't care. I still love Georgie, see?

MARGARET: Which one is Georgie?

CHILD: That kid over there. See him, he's runnin' home to his ma. Scaredy cat.

MARGARET: Oh, the little coloured boy.

MAMIE: He's not little, he's sixteen. I don't care what they say, he's my boy friend.

CHILD: Eenie, meanie, minie moe. . . .

MARGARET: Never mind, Mamie. Come along with me. . . . I was just going to your house. Is your mother home?

MAMIE: She's home all right. But she's drunk.

MARGARET: Oh well, I've brought her a cheque she might need, for groceries . . . maybe we could go to the store, and stock up? Won't you come along, Mamie?

MAMIE: Okay.

SOUND: (Footsteps up and out. A clamor of children playing again, a voice counting; "96, 97, 98, 100! Ready or not, you must be caught. . . . (fading) hiding around the goal or not")

MARGARET: Well, Mamie was caught. I had thought there was something I could do for Mamie. In social work, you can't do anything for adults, they have to do it themselves . . . but for children, I thought! If Mamie had been put into a foster home when she was little, away from that street . . . away from that mother . . . if anyone had loved her. Oh, George, the coloured boy, loved her, after his fashion — yes. But too well . . . I heard afterwards that Mamie had been put into a Juvenile Correction Home, where her baby would be born. In Mamie's case, in Catholic Montreal, it wasn't because of intimate race relations that Mamie went through the courts, it was because she was labeled as a Juvenile Delinquent. My own feelings were pity, even perhaps identification with those young lovers, but on my next job I found out that I was supposed to have quite different feelings. It was across the border, in New York City.

SOUND: (Train bell ringing. Cries of "Boa-oa-r-rd.")

DAVEY: Well, I guess this really is goodbye?

MARGARET: I guess so, Davey.

DAVEY: Sure you won't change your mind?

MARGARET: No . . . but please understand!

DAVEY: I'm trying to.

MARGARET: I just have to go.

DAVEY: Well, gather ye rosebuds. . . .

MARGARET: Davey, you're so cruel.

DAVEY: You're not, of course.

SOUND: (All aboar-r-rd)

MARGARET: Davey, don't you remember?

DAVEY: Remember what?

MARGARET: The sleigh-ride! . . the snowflakes? And you said — it was you who said it!

DAVEY: Said what?

MARGARET: 'You have to stand on your own pins.'

DAVEY: (laughing in spite of himself) Okay, girl. And when you've stood long enough, you can come and lean on mine — and be a teacher's wife!

MARGARET: Oh, thank you, Davey. Thank you, darling.

SOUND: (Boar-rd!)

DAVEY: G'bye.

MARGARET: 'Bye then.

SOUND: (Train begins to shunt off. Margaret's voice, very low, keeps time with the train wheels: "Ready or not, ready or not."... a long whistle, and fade).

MARGARET: Well, I was here! In New York, with only fifty dollars in my pocket. I took a cheap room, with only space enough to turn around in, in a cell-like, dark-smelling, rooming house near Washington Square. Autumn, 1934. Then I started looking for a job, climbing up the stairways of shabby buildings where private employment agencies siphoned the few from the many. Sure, there was a job in a bookbindery, or a job in a fish curing plant if I got out there by six in the morning. "But I might's well tell ya flat, Miss, ya look too kiddish for that kinda work." So instead I went to the Social Workers Exchange in a modern office building and got a job within the week. There was a depression in the States, too, so what with NRA, WPA and all the private agencies, social workers were in high demand. I had chosen the right profession! I was sent across the Hudson to a small Settlement House in a New Jersey town. I rather liked the look of my new boss, a plain, grey-haired, New England woman. I liked her for talking out plainly. . . .

MISS JAMES: I think you'll fit in here, Miss Morell. You have a kind face. But there's one thing, one more thing we should perhaps talk about, before you decide. Half our community, you know, is Negro...have you thought about your attitudes to that? What is your point of view on the Negro problem?

MARGARET: Problem? Well, I don't think it is a problem, at home in Canada — not yet, anyway.

MISS JAMES: I mean, how much prejudice have you run into, up there?

MARGARET: For myself, none, Miss James.

MISS JAMES: But coloured people are not accepted socially, are they?

MARGARET: Well, I hardly know. I haven't come across it. Of course, there was Mamie.

MISS JAMES: Mamie?

MARGARET: A case of mine. She was a white girl, in love with a Negro bell-hop. She had a baby.

MISS JAMES: That kind of thing would never happen here! The boy would be lynched.

MARGARET: At home it was the girl who went to jail.

MISS JAMES: Well, I see you have a rather different set-up.

MARGARET: Have you ever heard of the "Freedom Train"? During the Civil War Negroes escaped to Canada, and became free. . . .

MISS JAMES: Well, they are free here now, of course. But you must understand, for the social happiness of all, white and coloured work side by side, but after work they go their own ways, amongst their own people. On our staff, for instance, we have three coloured social workers — very fine people, you will see, when you meet them. Sometimes we have get togethers, staff parties. But even then, there can be no dancing between white and coloured.

MARGARET: No *dancing*!

MISS JAMES: I see you have a lot to learn, my dear. Let me put it this way; if you are ever in a jam, and don't know what to do in this matter, come to me, will you? Feel free to come to me.

MARGARET: Why yes of course, Miss James.

MISS JAMES: It's agreed, then? You'll stay?

MARGARET: I'd like to try it.

MISS JAMES: Good Well, as you know, our last case worker left a week ago — for family reasons. She's married, gone to Australia! So we are in immediate need. How soon could you come?

MARGARET: Oh, anytime you say, Miss James. Tomorrow!

SOUND: (Music up. Negro spiritual music. Young voices singing).

MARGARET: Oh, I beg your pardon. Is this a rehearsal?

SOUND: (Laughter)

PAUL: Well, if that don't take the cake. The lil' girl from way up north never done hear any singin'.

DONNA: Come on in, chile, and shut that door. Here's where we all take our lunch, and do some singin' besides . . . Did you pack a lunch?

MARGARET: No. Miss James said I might boil an egg, in here.

DONNA: And so you can, honey. Right over here on this hotplate.

MARGARET: Oh, thank you.

DONNA: You've been made acquainted with everybody, have you Miss Morell?

MARGARET: Yes, I think so. Mr Alden was in the office this morning.

PAUL: Paul is the name.

DONNA: I'm afraid we don' stand much on ceremony round here, Miss

Morell. Especially Paul doesn't!

PAUL: First thing we'll have to do, we'll have to teach her to sing. Honest now, don't they sing where you come from?

MARGARET: Not very freely. Unless you are a French-Canadian.

PAUL: That's *your* minority problem? If you sing, you're a minority!

MARGARET: Maybe you're right! It's more of a split personality problem: French versus English. . . . In Montreal, though, there is a Jewish problem.

PAUL: So if I'm Jewish I'm out in the cold — and if I'm coloured, what?

MARGARET: Given the money, you'd go to school and college like all of us.

PAUL: Huh, just try that here . . . a coloured boy getting into Yale or Harvard.

DONNA: What are you talkin' about, honey chile? You is the one that went and done it.

PAUL: But only by bluff. By not sending them my photograph. And me hailing from a nice genteel town like this one: and a nice New England name tagged onto me.

MARGARET: Is that the way you got to College?

PAUL: Uh huh. To college in the North. And a fine time I had. Taken into the finest homes — spoiled, I was.

MARGARET: So it can be done!

PAUL: It can be done, if you get the gift for bluffin'. But you know what, Miss. . . ?

MARGARET: Call me Margaret.

PAUL: Margaret? Margaret's too big a mouthful for the likes of me, with my limited education! . . . I'll call you Meg.

MARGARET: Meg! All right then. That's what my Dad used to call me when I was little.

DONNA: Go way then, Paul. Mind you be a good Daddy to her.

PAUL: Why can't you never take me seriously, Donna? Meg, you'll take me seriously, now won't you? Because I'm dead serious about this thing. Honest now. I want to get it straight! Miss James, she told me she couldn't find an ounce of prejudice in you. So — (He is laughing)

MARGARET: So what?

PAUL: Every day, sister. Every day I'll be watchin' you.

SOUND: (Donna starts picking up the words and making them into a spiritual: "Every day da Lawd is watchin', every day da Lawd is watchin', every day da Lawd is watchin' — YOU!" General singing and laughter).

MARGARET: But the strange thing was, I discovered it was Paul, really who was prejudiced. There were four of us who went around together: Donna and Paul, the coloured social workers; Red, a Scottish character who was working for WPA but who had an old car; and myself. We went to meetings, lectures on socialism — always egged on by Red, who was a "Red"; and sometimes we went dancing in Harlem. Miss James' supervision did not extend across the Hudson to Harlem.

SOUND: (Hot dance music a la Ellington. Hand clapping. Laughter. Margaret is laughing freely.)

PAUL: Laugh again, Meg. Laugh again.

MARGARET: Why, Paul?

PAUL: Because you almost caught the laugh o the deep south.

MARGARET: Can't white people laugh the same as Negroes?

PAUL: No. No they can't.

MARGARET: Just "almost", eh? I can be almost like you but I can never quite make it.

PAUL: Aw, don't let's argue, honey. Come on, let's dance.

SOUND: (Music up, then change to slow blues tempo, and FADE).

MARGARET: But even when he danced, he was separate. He was so careful to hold me at a distance. Only once, by accident, as we were walking along a street, my hand brushed against his. I could feel his body go cold, as if into stone. Or he would set himself mentally apart, somehow: and say the cruelest things. One night, after a meeting, we were sitting in a cafe, the four of us.

SOUND: (Juke box music, up. Rhythm of "Every day da Lawd is Watchin'" which Donna starts to hum, low).

MARGARET: Well, Paul, *have* you been watching me? How will I do?

PAUL: You do pretty all right, Meg. You've worked with a coloured boy, been on a public platform with one, eaten with one — even danced with one. I wonder now, how much further would you go?

MARGARET: Does it have to stop there?

PAUL: That's what I want to know. Would you kiss a black man?

MARGARET: Of course I would — in private. I don't kiss any man in public!

PAUL: I'll let that one pass. How about this one? Would you marry a Negro?

MARGARET: Why not? If I loved him, that is; and if he loved me.

PAUL: You see! There's an 'if' to it.

MARGARET: There's an 'if' to any marriage.

PAUL: All right then. Let's get down to cases. Meg, would you marry *me?*

MARGARET: No, I wouldn't.

PAUL: I thought so. I understand.

MARGARET: (vehemently) No, you don't understand at all, Paul! That's the whole trouble with you. For you, everything has to be tested out, like in a laboratory. You . . . you just don't understand about love — at all.

DONNA: Hear, hear. Now you're gettin' it, boy.

MARGARET: Red, come on. Shall we go? (chairs scraping) I just don't want to talk anymore. . . . Will you see me home?

SOUND: (Minor notes, saxaphone)

MARGARET: I guess Red, and Donna, and just about everybody else knew the way I felt about Paul. But he didn't feel that way, so he didn't know. Or else, perhaps — if he did, he hid it very well. He was used to hiding things. . . . I didn't see him, socially, for quite a while. Then one night I was serving coffee and sandwiches at my place for some of us who had been arranging a concert . . . and Donna persuaded Paul to come along. Upstairs in my tiny flat he helped me cut sandwiches in the kitchenette.

PAUL: It's a right neat little place you've got, Meg girl.

MARGARET: Yes, I do like it. Sorry you didn't come before.

PAUL: Just scared, ain't I?

MARGARET: Maybe . . . but what of, Paul? What is there to be so scared about.

PAUL: What about? Huh. Listen girl. Was your grandfather shot, running across a field? Was you uncle hung on a tree and lynched?

MARGARET: No.

PAUL: Well, mine was. In the south. Can I forget that?

MARGARET: Does it help, to remember?

PAUL: I have to remember.

144

MARGARET: The more you remember, the worse it is for you. The harder it is to fight it.

PAUL: Then you recognize the fact that I do have to fight?

MARGARET: Yes, but I think you are fighting in the wrong way.

PAUL: How would *you* go about it?

MARGARET: It's not such a lone battle, as you make it out to be.

PAUL: You know Meg, that just happens to remind me of the fable of the blind bird.

MARGARET: What was that?

PAUL: Well, this ol' Mr Bird, he nearly got shot one day. So, for a while his eyes were blinded. He just couldn't see where he was flyin' to. Pretty soon he came up to a wall; and there he clung, feelin' himself along it. Then he came to a window sill and beat his wings against it. If he could only get through that there window, he thought, then he'd be free. Then he'd fly free in the wide wide world. So he started makin' little runs against the window and WHAM, banging himself full force against it, wings outspread. After a long spell of this when he was nearly done in, he made one big special effort and smashed through the glass—

MARGARET: And that killed him, I suppose?

PAUL: No sir. He was still alive. But he wasn't free. He was in an attic room, more closed in than he'd ever been before.

MARGARET: I never heard that story before.

PAUL: No more did I. I just made it up, this minute.

MARGARET: Oh, Paul. . . .

PAUL: For you to think about. . . . But maybe you'll find out, by yourself, just how it is with us. . . .

DONNA: (calling) Hi, you two! Is the coffee ready?

RED: I'm fair starvin', Meg. Are ye ready or not?

MARGARET: (low) Ready or not, ready or not, ready or not you must be caught. . . . (UP) Coming!

SOUND: (Music bridge. Brisk change of voice and tempo)

MARGARET: It was the next morning that Miss James called me into her office.

SOUND: (Knock on door)

MISS JAMES: Come in.

MARGARET: Good morning, Miss James. Did you want to see me?

MISS JAMES: Yes, Margaret. Sit down, won't you?

MARGARET: Thank you.

MISS JAMES: Margaret, do you remember when you first talked to me, six months ago, you agreed to come to me with any problems you might have?

MARGARET: Why yes, Miss James.

MISS JAMES: I was wondering if there was anything on your mind, just now.

MARGARET: I don't think anything has happened, specially. Everyone here has been awfully nice to me.

MISS JAMES: And you have been nice to everyone else. Perhaps that is the trouble?

MARGARET: But is there trouble? What do you mean? I've been good friends with Donna and Paul, gone out with them, that's permissible, isn't it?

MISS JAMES: Well, my dear, I'll stop beating about the bush. Whatever has occurred, I am sure you meant well. This morning, Margaret, your landlady phoned me.

MARGARET: Mrs O'Hara?

MISS JAMES: Yes. She's very upset. Some of the neighbours noticed last night that there were coloured people going into her house, a man, particularly.

MARGARET: But that was only Paul!

MISS JAMES: But that's it. In the area where you live, Margaret, coloured people don't visit.

MARGARET: You mean I can't have my friends at my place?

MISS JAMES: Not if the landlady objects.

MARGARET: Then I'll change the area where I live. I won't live there another day.

MISS JAMES: Where will you go?

MARGARET: To the east side of course, where everybody lives, all mixed up.

MISS JAMES: But that is where most of our clients live.

MARGARET: And does that matter?

MISS JAMES: I'm afraid it would matter, to the Board. You see, staff members have always lived on the *west* side of town.

MARGARET: Unless they were coloured!

MISS JAMES: Yes, that is true. Unless they were coloured. My dear, I know this is hard for you to take. I foresaw this sort of thing coming up and I tried to warn you. But I don't want you to make a hot-headed decision now. Think it over for a day or two. We like your work on the staff. We like *you*. We want you to stay with us. But there are limits outside which a staff member may not go. . . .

MARGARET: (low) Beating against a window-pane. . . .

MISS JAMES: What was that?

MARGARET: Nothing, Miss James, do you mean this: do you mean that I have to go on living in that house with that woman who won't allow Negroes to visit?

MISS JAMES: Not necessarily. You could find another apartment. Or a boarding house.

MARGARET: But even there — even there I could not have my friends to visit?

MISS JAMES: No.

MARGARET: Then it's impossible. I can't stay here!

MISS JAMES: Margaret, I ask you not to decide right away. You are more involved than I had supposed — personally involved.

MARGARET: Personally? You mean. . . .

MISS JAMES: I mean, in regard to Paul?

MARGARET: I know nothing about Paul's feelings and I don't tell him mine!

MISS JAMES: No, of course not. All the same, it's not the happiest of situations, is it?

MARGARET: It's not the happiest — not for Paul. It's Paul who is unhappy. It's Paul who is afraid.

MISS JAMES: Well, my dear, I've known that for a long time — ever since the days when he had no job at all, though he was a qualified lawyer. At least here, he's treated as a professional person. But he has to work out his problem his own way. And he's so proud, Margaret — he will let no one else help him. Least of all, a white woman.

MARGARET: I know that.

147

MISS JAMES: Well, if you know it, think hard. Think what is the best way out for all concerned. Now you can run along, my dear. There's a client waiting for you.

MARGARET: Thank you, Miss James.

SOUND: (Door closing. Bridge to Paul's voice singing: "Nobody knows the trouble I've seen.")

MARGARET: Paul?

PAUL: Oh, good mornin', Meg.

MARGARET: I'm sorry to disturb you, Paul.

PAUL: You couldn't disturb me . . . any more'n you have done!

MARGARET: That's just it. Paul, I have to speak to you.

PAUL: Are things that bad? Then maybe you better not, honey. You might get your wings scratched up.

MARGARET: Please Paul! For just this once, you have to listen to me.

PAUL: I can listen, gal, I can listen. But you can't make me talk.

MARGARET: I know that. But I have to tell you, the first, Paul, I'm going to leave here.

PAUL: Back to Canada?

MARGARET: Yes.

PAUL: That's no news. I saw that coming. But so soon? Does it have to be this soon?

MARGARET: I don't want you to think I'm running away! If anyone would keep me, I'd stay.

PAUL: Listen here, Meg girl. Look at me!

MARGARET: I'm looking.

PAUL: Do you see what's in me? I can't ask anybody to step into my cage. I can't do it. I'm not that kind of guy, I guess. Not much use for nobody but myself.

MARGARET: And you hate yourself.

PAUL: Maybe I do. But I wouldn't want anyone else learning to hate me too.

MARGARET: All right, Paul. You've said it. That's it.

PAUL: You be a good girl, and fly away home. . . .

MARGARET: (in a whisper) There's a kiss then . . . on your forehead.

PAUL: Goodbye, Meg girl. . . .

SOUND: (Door closing. Child's voice: "Lady bug, lady bug, fly away home. Your house is on fire, your children are gone.)

MARGARET: So I had to go home then, defeated. I hadn't been able to make race relations work, any more than anyone else. . . . Up in Canada the houses were the same. The people were the same. The street was the same. . . .

SOUND: (Child skipping. Child's voice: Blue bells, cockle shells, evy ivy over)

MARGARET: But I was different! One summer evening, walking against all the traffic sounds, the robins singing goodnight in the elms, the children's playing hide-and-seek. . . .

SOUND: (Child cries and counting in B.G.)

MARGARET: One evening I tried to explain it all to Davey. You see, Davey, I've always fought against things that seemed wrong — but this thing, I don't know how to fight it. I feel beaten. I can't solve anything!

DAVEY: *You* can't solve it! Who do you think you are, Jehovah? Heavens, woman, things as big as the race question have to be solved by the people themselves. It's the blacks will have to fight it out.

MARGARET: But shouldn't the whites be responsible too? There must be something even one person can do — there must be something?

DAVEY: There is. But it's just not on the grand scale you planned for, Margaret.

MARGARET: What, then?

DAVEY: Just keep on, living and acting the way you believe.

MARGARET: Surely there's more?

DAVEY: Sure there's more! Show you're not prejudiced, by marrying a kike, for instance.

MARGARET: Davey!

DAVEY: I mean it. I've always meant it.

MARGARET: But we're just old friends, Davey. I'm not in love with you.

DAVEY: But you will be! Give me a year, Margaret — just a year of marriage . . . and you will be in love with me!

MARGARET: I don't know if I'm ready or not. . . .

DAVEY: But you're caught, Margaret, you're caught! And it's my turn to count — like this (He begins kissing and counting. She laughs.)

SOUND: (Child counting, to the same beat. Margaret joins in)

CHILD: Ninety eight, 99, 100 — Ready or not you must be caught, hiding around the goal or not. O-U-T spells OUT!

SOUND: (Music up and climax to finish.)

Herbie

At headquarters the game was easy, leaning back in a swivel chair with a good cigar, waiting for a poker crowd to get started, listening to Andy tell that one about the Prince of Wales. Even the grunt McNeil gave when he slithered through the ice like lightning, charging along on light feet, even that appraising grunt gave you a comfortable friendly kind of itch down your spine. Then little Pinky coming, Jesus the guy was funny, like a sausage or you know, what's in a name, anyhow he always pretended to be breaking out of his skin when he saw one of them cartoons in the bastard paper, supposed to be sarcastic about the Chief, or leering at Wesselwein because the poor stiff got shot one night and they demoted him.

Well, 'fore no time McNeil said Wesselwein would go up again like a rocket, he had the brains that guy, he had it down to a science. And that didn't hinder the boys from pulling out Pinky's bottle from the lavatory lockers whenever there was damn well anything in it. You hadn't used to drink in the mornings but now it made all the difference, jacked you up for a big day ahead. "After all it's a responsibility," Pinky said in his squeaky voice, "it's not everybody has a job behind the scenes."

When Pinky said it that way, you just knew he was right, somehow. But you couldn't do much about it except sit round. Different when the Chief said the same thing. That was some pep talk, all about brain and brawn swinging along together, and keep your finger on the pulse, and keep at it boys, don't falter and we'll have the buggers in the small of our hand. You felt big then, and the next hour or so when McNeil came slithering through, you tossed the cigar away and jammed on your hat. "Well, I guess I'll be doing the rounds."

Outside the wind hit you. Along Fort Street and up Palisade it tried to whinny round your legs, setting you thinking of that horse Minny that used to wheedle for carrots over the pasture gate. That was a dead life if you like, rotting in the ground like potato seed in a wet season. Now you could push along like a machine, bigger than most, not caring for the wind or the blue faces milling around, sucking up to a cafe window as if they could get a free cup of coffee. The lazy bums wouldn't use their legs and arms, couldn't move a muscle of their brains to help themselves. It takes guts to go out and land yourself a good job.

Well, now, where were you steering yourself. About time you headed for the bookstore, it would be about time for a batch of that Rooshian stuff, and anyhow on account of being so busy the last two days you hadn't gone in to get your *Worker* and the girl might get wise.

Maybe it would only be the old woman in there like it was the last time. Jesus, if it would only be the girl again, the nigger bitch, and you could just catch her two wrists till the blood ran, pay her back for that day last week when your fingers got near her thigh and her wrist flicked and there you stood like a fool with knuckles stinging. The way they used to sting when Ma rapped them with a pencil and you felt worse than if she'd taken down your pants and lit into you with a brush.

It should be easy to make her though, all the boys said them coloured flashes were rearing to go, they asked you after each trip, "Did you make a date?" And you kind of winked and stuck your front out. But the bitch, she wouldn't even give you any back talk, just asked you how you liked the paper, standing there unsmiling with breasts pointing at you, ready to lie cool in your hand like fruit. Yet you couldn't get near her — the light was between you and her as it falls around a statue of Mary, keeping you off.

Christ, you must be going crazy, as if a black bitch had anything to do with religion. It was like calling the confessional a speak-easy, the way Pinky did. Now, there wasn't any reverence about her, she was just stuck up, a branchy tree in need of some pruning. Wait'll he seized her arm this time (easy but firm) and asked her to go to the show!

This was the right block now, leery with second-hand clothing stores and cheap hardware. These Reds were always in the dirtiest sections of the city, attracting all the rats. Now here was her window, flashing bright with filthy print. Across the door as you waited a second to take everything in, a blaring poster showed a big prize fighter stooping to pick up a skimpy coon. "United We Rise" were the words printed on it. Funny kind of wrestling match that must be.

You push open the door and saunter in. There she is.

"G' morning comrade."

"Good morning." Her hands, dark leaves, flutter among the books.

"How've you bin, sister?"

"Business is brisk. You haven't been in for your *Worker* lately."

"No I — I bought it somewheres else."

"Oh? At the newsstand on Sherbrook street?"

"Yeah, that's right. . . . Don't you get kind o' tired hanging around here, sister?"

"No. Did you read the article on war in yesterday's issue?"

"Yeah. That was great. Simply great. I passed it on to a couple of other fellows. Say, you know. . . ."

"I guess you want your copy of *Soviet Russia Today*. It's just out."

"Yes. That's right. That's what I come for. And there was another one — something about 'Red Plays'."

" 'Red Plays'? Possibly you mean, 'New Theatre'?"

"Yes. Of course. That's right. And I'm told there's something else — written by a fella named 'Comin . . . Comin. . . .'"

"Of course. I thought you would be wanting the Comintern Resolutions. I am sorry, we are all sold out."

"Oh. When'll they be in?"

"Possibly next week."

"I see. O.K. I'll be in — Say, what do you do with your evenings, sis — Comrade?"

"Well, tonight there's a meeting on 'Sanctions'. . . . Are you for or against sanctions?"

"Gee, that's easy. I'm against it, of course."

"That's the wrong answer."

You look at her, expecting to find her eyes lowered, searching the books on the counter. She is staring right at you, her eyes sly and mocking. "That's the wrong answer."

Jesus, you'd like to smash her eyes out, twist her arms behind her till she screamed, set those limbs flashing and quivering. But your tongue is stuck between your teeth.

"Here, how much do I owe you?" The dollar bill flutters to the counter.

"Twenty three cents. Thank you very much." Her voice flowing soft and her head bent to show the part down the middle. You'd like to crush her in your hands, but she would be stiff like steel, snapping down to throttle you like steel. . . .

The change stuffed in your pocket, towards the door.

"Wait. You've forgotten what you came for." Your turn and she hands you the parcel and she will not let her hands touch yours.

You slouch out of the door into the blank street.

Toronto 1936

Day and night
Night and day
Till life is turned
The other way!

All these three social work years I had abandoned writing any poetry which was personal. But in New Jersey, so near New York, in trips to Greenwich bookshops I delved about — perhaps seeking some relief from the orthodox Marxian literature I had been consuming for so long — Masses, The Daily Worker, and countless pamphlets and political tracts along with some heavier economics and Engels, Lenin and Stalin. What was my astonishment and unbelief to find some slim volumes of English poetry — revolutionary poetry but full of lyricism and personal passion! C. Day Lewis first, then Spender, then Auden and MacNeice. There was nothing like it in America or Canada, but it was a movement that followed exactly where I had left off with my Paris thesis — it threw Eliot aside and proclaimed a brave new world. I think I must have wept over this discovery, but there was no one of my friends and comrades who would have taken any interest in it. All I could do was write a poem myself, celebrating the new horizon.

It was soon after that I went home, supposedly with an ulcer but actually, I think with a slight nervous breakdown. I had a month's holiday in which to recuperate which I spent in our country home at Clarkson — with one week alone on an Ontario farm north of Galt. It was there that I wrote "The Outrider."

Although I returned to my job in Englewood I was not well enough to carry on and the doctor sent me home for the winter. I spent it slowly getting well — probably psychoanalysis would have been the cure at that stage and writing. Besides the new poems eventually included in the volume Day and Night. *I did quite a number of short stories, some of them published under a pseudonym in the new united front monthly,* New Frontier. *This was the literary magazine launched by my old university friends, Ross Parmenter, Jocelyn Moore, Stanley Ryerson, Margaret Fairley, "Jim" Watts now married to editor Lon Lawson.*

Dec. 5, 1935

My dear Dee:

"Day and Night" is a splendid bit of work. I will publish it in the opening issue. [*Canadian Poetry Magazine*]. This is one of the best things I have ever seen you do.

Dee, I think a little punctuation in the short-lined verses might clarify poetic intention. I am aware of some of the changes going on in that direction, but I am afraid the public might put the newer styles down to oversight in proof-reading. I do not like to do much punctuation myself, but I think the verses are a trifle scant in any case.

Would you send me a final copy so I might send it direct to the publisher. I have to save my time in every possible way.

Thanks again Dee, I am more than delighted to have you in this start-up.

Yours
Ned Pratt

Day and Night

Dawn, red and angry, whistles loud and sends
A geysered shaft of steam searching the air.
Scream after scream announces that the churn
Of life must move, the giant arm command.
Men in a stream, a moving human belt
Move into sockets, every one a bolt.
The fun begins, a humming, whirring drum—
Men do a dance in time to the machines.

2

One step forward
Two steps back
Shove the lever,
Push it back

While Arnot whirls
A roundabout
And Geoghan shuffles
Bolts about.

One step forward
Hear it crack
Smashing rhythm—
Two steps back

Your heart-beat pounds
Against your throat
The roaring voices
Drown your shout

Across the way
A writhing whack
Sets you spinning
Two steps back—

One step forward
Two steps back.

3

Day and night are rising and falling
Night and day shift gears and slip rattling
Down the runway, shot into storerooms
Where only arms and a note-book remember
The record of evil, the sum of commitments.
We move as through sleep's revolving memories
Piling up hatred, stealing the remnants,
Doors forever folding before us—
And where is the recompense, on what agenda
Will you set love down? Who knows of peace?

Day and night
Night and day
Light rips into ribbons
What we say.

Welder (United Ship Yards, Montreal, 1943), Louis Muhlstock. Collection of the artist.

I called to love
Deep in dream:
Be with me in the daylight
As in gloom.

Be with me in the pounding
In the knives against my back
Set your voice resounding
Above the steel's whip crack.

High and sweet
Sweet and high
Hold, hold up the sunlight
In the sky!

Day and night
Night and day
Tear up all the silence
Find the words I could not say. . .

4

We were stoking coal in the furnaces; red hot
They gleamed, burning our skins away, his and mine.
We were working together, night and day, and knew
Each other's stroke; and without words, exchanged
An understanding about kids at home,
The landlord's jaw, wage-cuts and overtime.
We were like buddies, see? Until they said
That nigger is too smart the way he smiles
And sauces back the foreman; he might say
Too much one day, to others changing shifts.
Therefore they cut him down, who flowered at night
And raised me up, day hanging over night—
So furnaces could still consume our withered skin.

Shadrach, Meshach and Abednego
Turn in the furnace, whirling slow.
    Lord, I'm burnin' in the fire
    Lord, I'm steppin' on the coals
    Lord, I'm blacker than my brother
    Blow your breath down here.

    Boss, I'm smothered in the darkness
    Boss, I'm shrivellin' in the flames
    Boss, I'm blacker than my brother
    Blow your breath down here.
Shadrach, Meshach and Abednego
Burn in the furnace, whirling slow.

157

5

Up in the roller room, men swing steel
Swing it, zoom; and cut it, crash.
Up in the dark the welder's torch
Makes sparks fly like lightning reel.

Now I remember storm on a field
The trees bow tense before the blow
Even the jittering sparrows' talk
Ripples into the still tree shield.

We are in storm that has no cease
No lull before, no after time
When green with rain the grasses grow
And air is sweet with fresh increase.

We bear the burden home to bed
The furnace glows within our hearts:
Our bodies hammered through the night
Are welded into bitter bread.

Bitter, yes:
But listen, friend:
We are mightier
In the end.

We have ears
Alert to seize
A weakness
In the foreman's ease

We have eyes
To look across
The bosses' profit
At our loss.

Are you waiting?
Wait with us
After evening
There's a hush—

Use it not
For love's slow count:
Add up hate
And let it mount

Until the lifeline
Of your hand
Is calloused with
A fiery brand!

Add up hunger,
Labour's ache
These are figures
That will make

The page grow crazy
Wheels go still,
Silence sprawling
On the till—

Add your hunger,
Brawn and bones,
Take your earnings:
Bread, not stones!

6

Into thy maw I commend my body
But the soul shines without
A child's hands as a leaf are tender
And draw the poison out.

Green of new leaf shall deck my spirit
Laughter's roots will spread:
Though I am overalled and silent
Boss, I'm far from dead!

One step forward
Two steps back
Will soon be over:
Hear it crack!

The wheels may whirr
A roundabout
And neighbour's shuffle
Drown your shout

The wheel must limp
Till it hangs still
And crumpled men
Pour down the hill.

Day and night
Night and day
Till life is turned
The other way!

The Outrider

Swift outrider of lumbering earth.

—C. Day Lewis

in memory of Raymond Knister

PROLOGUE

He who was alien has retraced the road
Unleashed, returns to this familiar earth.
The gate falls open at his touch, the house
Receives him without wonder, as an elm
Accepts her brood of birds. Along his road
Crows charivari chattering announce
His coming to each thronging sentry-post.

The old man standing with his hayfork high
Can let it rest, mid-air, and burden fails
And falls within the sun-dipped gloom of barn.
The young boy bowed behind the clicking mow
Feels his spine stiffen as if birds had whirred
Behind him, or a storm had clapped its clouds.
A girl, chin pressed upon a broom, will stir
As a warm wave of wonder sweeps her out
Whither her musings never leapt before.
And so it is.

His coming dreamed of long
In the recesses of thinking, in the hard
Hills climbed, his face a resting-place.
In winter warming hands at roaring stove
His doings crackling as autumn wood. . .
And so it is. Now summer's all swept clean
He comes with eyes more piercing than before
And scrapes his boots—swinging wide the door.

160

I

THE GRANDFATHER

The year we came, it was all stone picking:
Sun on your fiery back, and the earth
Grimly hanging on to her own. At the farm's end
A cedar bog to clear. But in the dry season
Not enough drink for the cattle.
The children gathered blueberries, and ate corn meal.
We danced no festivals.

Children stretched lean to manhood. One day
Wind prying round, wrenched free the barn
And lightning had the whole hay crop
Flaming to heaven. Trying to save the horse
Arthur was stifled. His black bones
We buried under the elm.

I stumble around now, trying to see it clearly.
Incessantly driven to feed our own ones, but friendly
    to neighbours:
Not like the crows, hungry for goslings,
But sober, sitting down Sunday for rest-time
Contented with laughter.

I stumble around now, lame old farm dog:
When I'm gone, one less hunger
And the hay still to be mown.

* * * *

THE FATHER

The buggy on that whirling autumn day
Swayed in a rain rut, nearly overturned.
And you stood by the roadside, brown and gay,
Black hair drawn tight in pigtails and your eyes
Searching the sky. Brave was your body then
And I brought you home to discover the answer to
    hunger,
The peace of loving, the stay of restlessness.

Trembling as a birch tree to a boy's swinging
You were again and again my own small love.
But love was never enough, though children sprang
Year after year from your loins—never enough
For my yearning though your eyes burned strangely—
And earth has kept you far more fierce and safe.

* * * *

THE SON

My mother caught me in her skirts and tossed me high
    high into hay I bounced.
The straw tickled and a swallow, frightened, flew
    before my heart could cry.

I remember this, the startling day of early fear,
    bird beating me back
And somehow no way—hard to know why or where
    she was no longer near.

Brothers would later tease me with a feather tail
    or loose a crow they caught
And I must swallow the fear with my hunger, to learn
    how the yearned for will fail

How the expected sunlight will shrivel your pounding heart,
    the seed you plant be killed
The apple be bitter with worm, but your honesty firm
    seeking another start.

           *   *   *   *

I grew up one evening, much alone—
Resolved to plunge. The thing I feared, the crow,
Was hoarse with calling, whirling, diving down
And suddenly his urgent social bent
Was answer to my inwardness. His cry
Throbbed and echoed in my head, his wings
Caught all reflections in my mirrored mind.
I would then follow where his footless tread
Led on; I would no longer be the beast
Who ploughed a straight line to the barrier
And swung back on his steps—my father's son.
It would take long. But from that summer on
My heart was set. I raced through swinging air,
Rumpled my head with laughter in the clouds.

2

It was different, different
From the thoughts I had.
Asphalt and factory walls are not
Soft ending to a road.

It was different, different
Standing tight in line
Forgetting buffeting clouds above
Trying to look a man.

It was different, different
To lift the lever arm
And see farm beasts revolving by
Their dripping blood still warm.

On lazier afternoons
Deep in clover scent
Neither beast nor I could dream
What the speed-up meant.

A thousand men go home
And I a thousandth part
Wedged in a work more sinister
Than hitching horse and cart.

Dark because you're beaten
By a boss's mind:
A single move uneven turned
Will set you in the wind.

His mercy is a calculation
Worse than a hurricane—
Weather you can grumble at
But men can make you groan.

   * * * *

    (Down in the washroom
     leaflets are passed.
    "Say, Joe, you sure
     got those out fast."

    "Yes. Now's the time
     to give them the gate:
    Speed-up right here
     is legitimate!"

    An old worker stares:
     his wizened face
    Sceptical still—
     Years in the trace.

    But young, lean face
     opposite me
    Reads, and alert
     watches to see

Who will respond
who's first to talk—
Our eyes meet, and greet
as a key fits a lock.)

Early morning
stirs the street
men go by
on urgent feet.

Early morning
litter still
in the gutters
on the sill.

Early morning
sky shows blue
men are marching
two and two.

Men are surging
past the gate
where last week no one
dared be late:

Surging—though
a siren's shrieks
warn that someone
called the dicks. . .

＊ ＊ ＊ ＊

It was different, different
Because I learned: for this
You plough the fields and scatter
The toil of days and years.

You die in harness and are proud
Of earthen servitude
While others that live in chains have sought
To shake the rotting wood

Upheave the very earth, if need
Insist, banish the fence
Between a neighbour's grudging hate
Rise in your own defence

Against the smooth-tongued salesman
"The cottage built for two"
The haggling on market days
Desperate to know

How winter's service shall be slaved—
Will this hay last the year—
Where are the taxes coming from—
Must we sell the mare?

Cities that sell their toil, must put
Possessiveness to shame
And draw you to them in the fight:
The battle is the same.

The blowing silver barley grain
And skyline wide, serene—
These shall be your gift to those
Who wield the world's machine!

3

This is your signpost: follow your hands, and dig.
After, the many will have parachutes
For air delight. Not veering with the crow
But throbbing, conscious, knowing where to go.
There's time for flying. Dig up crumbling roots,
Eradicate the underbrush and twig—
Pull snapping thistle out and stubborn sloe—
Those backward ramblers who insist they know.

Employ your summertime, at union rate:
Conveying energy on this green belt
Of earth assembled, swiftly known and felt.
Faster! Speed-up is here legitimate:
Employ your summertime, before the thrust
Of winter wind would harden down the dust.

EPILOGUE

We prayed for miracles: the prairie dry,
Our bread became a blister in the sun;
We watched the serene untouchable vault of sky
—In vain our bitter labour had been done.

We prayed to see the racing clouds at bay
Rumpled like sheets after a night of joy,
To stand quite still and let the deluged day
Of rain's releasing, surge up and destroy.

We prayed for miracles, and had no wands
Nor wits about us; strained in a pointed prayer
We were so many windmills without hands
To whirl and drag the water up to air.

A runner sent ahead, returned with news:
"There is no milk nor honey flowing there.
Others allay the thirst with their own blood
Cool with their sweat, and fertilize despair."

O new found land! Sudden release of lungs,
Our own breath blows the world! Our veins, unbound
Set free the fighting heart. We speak with tongues—
This struggle is our miracle new found.

Six Years

Mrs. Dakin lived in the third house from ours. Maybe I remembered it best because it was the only house on the street where I hadn't set foot inside the doorstep: though I reckon I knew the outside by heart, with its neat box hedge planted gay-like with geraniums and salvia, its windows trim with polka dotted curtains, and the bungalow roof nestling down comfortably over the clapboard. It was one of the nicest cottages on our straggly street, the look of it made you wish the town council would hurry up and pave out our way. And Mr. Dakin they said made good money where he clerked, somewhere in the city, shot up flight after flight each morning by the elevators.

Those were good days, and most of our men were working at the starch works, taking their dinner pails with them as they left home at six thirty in the morning. We women were up betimes too, washing and scrubbing and tending to the children. It wasn't till along about ten o'clock that Mrs. Bennett, Mrs. Dakin's neighbour, could take note of the fact that Mrs. Dakin's blinds were pulled up, and she out on the back porch in her wrapper, taking in the milk. Mrs. Bennett may be something of a gossip, but she is kind-hearted all the same — and certainly Mrs. Dakin never gave her curiosity the least bit of satisfaction. She would never even call out good morning sociably like any decent body would. If she had to answer you, her speech would be short and quick like that of city people. They do say she came from the city, and maybe that says as much as the first robin.

166

Mrs. Dakin had only one baby, that she wheeled out every afternoon in his carriage. And when he grew older she let him play about in her back yard all by himself. Sometimes he would talk away to Mrs. Bennett's children through the fence, and Mrs. Dakin would be at the kitchen window, watching every move he made. It was as if she thought her child was something precious and different from all the other children. Almost as if our kids had a disease he might catch.

When the big lay-off came Mrs. Dakin was the only woman on the street who didn't seem to know about it. Maybe nobody troubled to tell her, but she wouldn't have cared anyway. Her man wasn't working at the factory. It's strange to think about in a way, her living so close to us, and yet so far. I used to wonder sometimes, hurrying past her house to the store, how she could live like that, so far away from everything that was happening. Goodness knows, I had enough troubles of my own not to want to drag anybody else into the same net. I did not want her to suffer, no. I just wanted to understand her. She was on my conscience like a frightening dream you have had in the night, and can't quite remember.

One night a group of our men folk were having a meeting in our front room, to talk about getting cash relief instead of vouchers. Bill Sanders was there, Alec Thomspon, Joe Mantoni, Sam Bennett and my Joe. I called out to them to keep the wick burning low, because there wasn't much oil left in the lamp. We would have no more until our two weeks budget time was up. The electricity had been cut off months before. Maybe they didn't hear me, but anyway they got to figuring with pencil and paper, and talking louder and louder. Suddenly their talk was cut off short, like birds voices when a storm is coming. Then Joe said, "Well, I'll be jiggered." I peered through the kitchen door into the front room and there they were, sitting in the dark like I had predicted. I went to fetch some candles and when I came back Sam Bennett was standing at the window with the curtains pushed back. "Well" he drawled slowly, as if talking to himself, "I reckon the only welcome light in this street, that we fought so hard to get wired and brought up to date, is the Dakin's electric light burning up the midnight on their porch."

"And they only came here after we got the electricity installed," Alec said.

Nobody could forget the Dakins.

It couldn't have been long after that when we were sitting home one evening all to ourselves. Joe wasn't going out to any meetings that night so he was feeling comfortable with his shoes off, leaning back in his chair by the stove and reading the paper. I finished giving the baby her bath, put her to bed, and sat down by the table to help Jonny with his spelling. Joe was puffing away hard at his pipe, sometimes reading out some news items, or else just muttering to himself between paragraphs. To tell the truth I wasn't paying much attention to him, just sitting there drowsily and saying yes and no, and telling Jonny not to look in the book when he spelt out loud.

Joe said something about there being a letter in the paper from an unemployed fellow on our street. Then all of a sudden he was jumping to his feet, excited, waving the paper.

"Why, Mary, would you believe it! After all we've been saying and thinking — it says here that the Reliable Insurance Company has dismissed most of its male workers, because they have to be paid more than the girls!"

I just looked at him, not knowing what he was driving at. Sooner or later he would explain when he saw the dumb look on my face.

"But don't you see what this means, Mary! That is where Dakin is working — that is what will happen to Dakin!"

Mind you, I don't think he was gloating. It just hit him like a thunderbolt would, and he didn't know what to think. In a flash I could see Mrs. Dakin taking in those words, wide-eyed and innocent, not understanding, and the fear like a bad dream swept over me.

If the truth must be said, most of us were somewhere near the front window for the next few mornings, along about the time that Mr. Dakin went up the street to catch his trolley. There he was, same as usual, his slight, bony figure walking along at a quick pace. It was only after two weeks that Mrs. Bennet said definitely, "He couldn't have been laid off. He goes back and forth regular as clockwork."

I was glad. Yet there was a kind of ache too. The Dakins seemed so far off.

That winter was the worst winter we had had. Instead of stretching further the relief we got seemed to shrink. Joe said prices were going up and they didn't make vouchers out of elastic. Then there was always new things needing to be bought, shoes and medicine for the children, kitchen necessities, cleaning materials that weren't on the relief list. For a while we skimped. And then we began to get mad. It was when Alec Thompson's little girl was so sick with pleurisy, run down from lack of vitamins, and they wouldn't take her into the hospital. That was when the Unemployment Association got going strong. Most of us women were on the women's auxiliary and grievance committee combined. We investigated families that had been given a rough deal, we went on delegations down to the relief office.

One week when the struggle was at its pitch we decided to hold a euchre and social at the Association hall, so as to raise money for delegations to the county council and for emergency aid to blacklisted families. We women were discussing it beforehand over at my place. Mrs. Thompson came plump out with what was on our minds: "If we want to raise money we can't take the pennies out of our own tin boxes that we keep on the mantle. That's no way out. We've got to invite people who are working."

"Such as?" said Mrs. Mantoni. Then she named a few people who are skimping along on wage-cuts.

"What about the doctor's wife? And the minister's wife?" someone else pointed out.

"And what about the Dakins?" said Mrs. Bennett. Everyone just laughed, as if that was a good joke.

"Mrs. Dakin is still wearing the winter coat she had three years ago," Mrs. Thompson said. "But she passes you with her head in the air. The other day I said good morning to her on Main Street, but she was staring in at a windowful of flowers, and made as if she didn't hear me."

"If she can buy flowers, she can buy a ticket to a euchre," Mrs. Mantoni said. That gave me the courage to say that I would drop in at her place, and ask her.

The very next morning I was unlatching the little green gate, and ringing the front doorbell. I would have felt more natural going round to the back, but I didn't somehow like to. It took a long time before she came to the door. She opened it about a foot and stood on guard between me and the house, her black hair wrapped up in a dust cap, her hazel eyes sort of defiant.

"I'm Mrs. Morrison. I was asked to call on various people on behalf of the Unemployed Association."

"We don't belong to that," she said, very quick.

"I know. It's just that we're having a social and get together. We thought maybe your husband and yourself would like to come."

She hesitated. It was a bright cold morning, and easy to see she was shivering. But she did not ask me to come in. "I would have to ask my husband," she said.

"Maybe if I left you a couple of tickets," I said, "You could decide later." I held them out to her. "They are fifteen cents each."

She drew back, almost closing the door. "I really don't think he would want to go," she told me. "You see, the baby is sick and I would have to stay with him."

"I'm sorry." That's all there was to say. She had got quite definite all of a sudden, when at first I thought there was a sort of yearning in her, to come and meet us all.

We held the euchre without her. Mr. Conroy dressed up in his clown suit and had us all laughing instead of worrying about the relief. Somebody had a fiddle and Sandy McPherson, who was supposed to be at death's door with his weak heart, went tearing through the hall like a stick of dynamite, leading the square dances.

That night Joe and I walked home tired but happy-like, he carrying the baby and I dragging Jonny and Isabel, who were almost walking in their sleep. The sharp, starry night quickened our breath, so we threw our heads back. Finally we saw ahead our own street, and rounded the fenced-in corner that is Dakin's corner.

The Rummage Sale (1940), Miller Brittain. Collection of the National Gallery of Canada, Ottawa.

"Joe," I whispered, "there isn't any light on."

"Well, they're in bed, I guess. Or gone to a movie."

We moved on, almost past Mrs. Bennett's house. But she tapped at the window and I stepped in alone to see if she wanted anything. Mrs. Bennett had not come to the social because she was expecting a new addition to the family.

Inside she seized my arm breathlessly. "Mary, it's happened!"

"And you didn't get to the hospital?" I was horror struck to see her standing there.

"Not me. I mean the Dakins. Their electricity has been turned off!"

"But — but that's impossible. He's working."

"All the same, the electrician went by there this afternoon."

"But he's working."

"Who knows?" I turned to the door.

"Then they need our help."

"They don't want our help, Mary."

"Never mind." I didn't feel excited any more, or happy like at the social. It was with a funny kind of quietness I went out of Mrs. Bennett's yard and turned in at the Dakin's gate as if I was going there for the first time in my life. The front doorway was dark and bolted so I made my way round to the back, knocking on the kitchen door. Everything was quiet.

I knocked again. Someone stirred. The door opened by a tiny crack and the faint glimmer of one candle lighted the room. Almost hidden behind the door Mrs. Dakin said uncertainly: "Everett?"

"It's I. Your neighbour. Mrs. Morrison."

She opened the door without a word. Once inside the dim, muffled light of the kitchen I did not know what to say. Mrs. Dakin seemed to be alone, and from what I could see of her face it was all puffed up with crying.

Finally I said that I had come from an unemployed gathering. We believed we would get better relief to fit the rise in prices.

"I wasn't there," said Mrs. Dakin. "Sit down, won't you?" She was standing up herself. Her body seemed too rigid to sit. I pulled a chair up to the kitchen table and sat looking up at her. "I am on the grievance committee, so I happened to think that if there was any matter we could take up, to help you out—" I was faltering, and she did not seem to comprehend. "Perhaps you would want to talk to your husband first?"

"Oh he's not in, he's gone out for a walk." Her voice was still nasal from crying. "You can talk to me all right."

I told her what the Association had been doing. I told her what the relief officer was like and how it might be difficult to get on relief for the first time, unless you pushed hard. She did not seem to be listening, standing on one foot and making circles on the floor with her other shoe.

"You see" she said, still hard and set, "we don't want to go on relief.... I don't know what right you have to tell me to do it."

I got up, then, in a hurry. "I'm awful sorry. I didn't mean to intrude. I don't know why I thought your husband wasn't working."

"Who told you he wasn't working?"

"Nobody . . . I was mistaken, I guess. It was your lights going off. I thought it would be neighbourly to ask what was wrong. Please excuse me."

"It's true," she said.

"What's true?"

"That he hasn't been working."

"But he goes to work every morning!"

"That's a lie too." Suddenly she was nearly crying. "He was laid off three months ago. He only p-p-pretended to be going to work. There, now you have it. Now you know everything I was trying to hide — everything."

We were facing each other, she young and desperate and I older and trying to understand.

"There wasn't nothing to hide" I said. "We're all the same way."

"But we were saving up to move, and to send Jimmie to school in the city, and to go up north in the summertime. . . . You wouldn't understand. And now there isn't anything left. . . . And I'm having another baby. . . ." She began to sob then, and slouched down into the chair.

She was so young and she thought she could do everything by herself. It didn't matter what we were planning to do to help ourselves, she wouldn't count herself in on that. But I knew there wasn't any other way out.

I figured I'd have to leave her there, crying, and go on home. But when I had got as far as the door she stopped me.

"I've been awful mean to you," she said.

"No. I see how it is."

"I used to watch you going by on the street with your head up as if you were really going some place. And I'd want to run out on to the street and say hello. But I was scared that if we got to know the neighbours it would keep us back somehow. I didn't want Everett's boss to stop by and catch me gossiping on a corner. Everett said we didn't have anything in common and now you're the first person to come."

"I didn't come out of pity," I said. "It isn't kindness."

"Then, what. . . ?" she faltered.

"Just to say you've a right to live decent . . . but it won't come the way you've been thinking."

We looked straight at each other.

"I'll tell Everett," she said.

New Frontier, 1936

A Criticism

The editors of New Frontier asked Morley Callaghan to comment on the stories in our first issue. Mr. Callaghan writes as follows:

These three stories have one good quality in common; they are honest. Unfortunately the three of them are to some extent variations of the same theme — the man out of work.

Mrs. Innis writes very sensitively. She has a nice feeling for words and for people and she is determined that her stories shall come out freshly, but in this particular story the emotion is too diluted, especially in the body of the piece. She has sympathy and she is close enough to her characters but she simply fails to record her good feeling sharply. That may always be her trouble. In her case I don't think it's so much a matter of whittling down but of getting the sharp feeling before she begins. That's what she should try to do anyway!

The Katherine Bligh piece "Six Years" is one of those long, honest pieces, the authenticity of which can not be questioned, and where there is no doubt that the author's heart and even her head maybe is in the right place, but which for all that is singularly devoid of feeling. Right here is the place to state emphatically that class consciousness, or an intention directed toward that end is not enough. Then, too, there is this to be remembered: if you are going to write in the colloquial speech it is assumed that that is being done so you will get added freshness and life in your stuff. If you don't get it, it means that you are picking out the cliches of speech rather than getting the juicy racy flavour you ought to get.

The brightest and most amusing of the three pieces, but probably the least authentic is "Friends, Romans, Hungrymen." A.M. Klein knows how to use words sharply, and in this piece he often gets a sharp and vigorous feeling. Its weakness is that the very great determination to pull off striking effects defeats the authentic quality of the bitterness of the piece and leaves you with a feeling that few men out of work and walking on their heels would be quite so determined to be so amusingly bright.

It is odd that these three pieces should have been on the one theme — the man out of work. The editors tell me that this was not a deliberate selection, but that nearly all the stories they received were about men who were out of work. If this keeps on it will appear that either all the young writers of the country are out of work, or that they all feel a little frustrated, a little cynical, or even defeated, and that living in this country doesn't leave one with a strong feeling. That may well be. But soon we ought to be hearing a lustier crowing, soon someone ought to tell us that there is some passion in the land.

Morley Callaghan.

New Frontier, 1936

They Shall Inherit the Earth by Morley Callaghan Macmillan's $2.50

In an estimate of Canadian books, most critics are so apt to fall into wishful thinking that the value of the book, as compared with contemporary literature, is completely obscured. There is little to be proud of in the record of Canadian novels: and where we do have younger writers who face the problem seriously, they have to flee to the United States for recognition and encouragement. Canadian novels have been so far removed from reality, not only psychologically, but from a social point of view, that when Morley Callaghan writes of Toronto as he sees it, the book is banned from the library.

Our hope for good literature remains not in the blind hands of the middle class as a whole, but in those members who are awakening to the implications around them, and to those forces of the working class which are fighting reaction and searching for a fuller life. The process may be slow, many new writers may be discouraged as was Raymond Knister before his death, but the roots are bound to take hold. There is so much to say about Canada! And so very few have begun to say it.

In the light of this statement, it is interesting to take a closer look at Morley Callaghan's work. Since his first short stories, his honesty has been apparent, his search for style. He was interested in maintaining a scientific objectivity akin to Hemingway's and other members of the post war "lost generation." In reality however, Callaghan is a step ahead of the generation. The years of the depression have been with him as he grew. Instead of becoming cynical, his essential belief in life has challenged him to give a more affirmative statement concerning the world about him. In *They Shall Inherit the Earth* this conflict and affirmation are made quite clear.

At the risk of distorting their importance, I shall first mention certain aspects of the book which show the writer's awareness of the social forces around him. The apparent theme is the separation that has developed between a capitalist father, Andrew Aikenhead, and his son Michael, an unemployed engineer. Contrasts between the former's glittering but empty life, his slow realization of defeat, and Michael's dissatisfied insecurity are vividly brought into play. Michael's surroundings in a poor working-class rooming house are sympathetically done, as are also his petty-bourgeois down-at-heels friends. Even more might have been made of these "background" characters, the woman-hunter, the Jewish student turned Christian, the sectarian communist. They are much more alive than the stiff portraits of Michael's wealthy relatives, which have a two-dimensional unreality.

Michael is slowly brought to life by his contact, friendship and love for Anna, the only "proletarian" in the piece, who is delightful, but sometimes too good to be true. It is here, if we are seeking symbolism, that Callaghan's object would seem to be to show how it is only thought alliance with the honest and life-giving class that salvation comes. "They shall inherit the Earth."

I very much doubt if this is his intention. He steers away from a revolutionary conclusion, and he does it by means of his style. Throughout the book, more noticeably during the first half, there is a curious lack of that reality which makes writers such as Josephine Herbert so outstanding.

In Callaghan's writing however, beneath the simplicity of the style, there is a strong poetic current, an intense sympathy for mood that reminds one consciously of Saroyan. Michael's despair becomes tender and soft, shunning the truth as if he were hiding under a leaf. The poet dominates, hitting the high spots but neglecting the slow collection of detail which is part of a novelist's weapon.

What is the significance of this style? Surely I do not mean that poetic feeling is detrimental to a book? Not at all. But in this case, as in the case of Saroyan, I would say that the poetic feeling springs not from a revolutionary grasp of the situation, but from an idealist orientation. The real theme of the book is Michael's search for security. He is a trained professional, unemployed, with an unemployed girl dependent upon him. One would think that security first of all would mean his bread and butter and his job. Yet in the course of a year, Michael does not have to resort to relief, he does not borrow from his father, he gets a job for two weeks and that is all that is said about it, he sends his wife to a semi-private ward in the hospital. These may be small details, but if you and I were up against them, they would loom large. No, the real theme is Michael's mental and "spiritual" security. His actual day to day existence is considered insignificant.

This is a familiar middle-class point of view, since day to day existence for people comfortably off is not a struggle. Their conflict is an internal one. And it is also true that the thousands of middle-class people today who come face to face with economic insecurity do not find poverty the most appalling aspect of their situation. They are lost souls, bewildered and shaken, longing for peace. In this sense, Michael is truthfully portrayed. He couldn't, the author is arguing, act otherwise. He couldn't be like his excited revolutionary friend, who is typical of the narrow-minded unfriendly communism which seizes new recruits from the middle class, and who says: "You know damn well you'd feel a lot better if you, yourself, had something to live for." Michael answers him:

"I agree absolutely, Bill. Listen, you don't think you hate the way things are any more than I do, do you? Drive along your band-wagon and I'll get on it. I'll go with the parade right up to the big tent. But I've learned something else. I know it will help a lot to clear the land away and so it'll be easier to live, but there's more to it than that. The personal problems will begin all over again then. You seem to think that you just have to have an economic housecleaning and we'll all get justice. None of us will get justice, personal justice, and we start hungering for it all over again."

There is the crux of the matter, the key to Callaghan's thought. Our "communist" makes the unfortunate answer of wit, "You want a little private orgasm with the universe," instead of pointing out that by solving the economic problems in a revolutionary way, so that they are radically changed as well as solved in the old sense, we will have directed an individual freedom to grow, an entirely new security in every sense. Communists, real communists, do not ignore that aspect of things. They believe there will always be struggle, personal struggle, but it will be on a vital, happier basis. Ilya Ehrenburg's novel, *The Second Day of Creation* is an example of this difference.

Callaghan's hero, instead of accepting the full implications of his situation, dives down a blind alley, achieves a psychological peace with his broken-down father. His solution is an individual solution which does not solve the enigma at all for his class, for the millions like him, or even for himself — a year hence. For this reason, the novel, which appears at first to be so well knit, so logical and skilful, has the effect of drawing you up tight when you have been running fast. A hammer is being used to drive in a pin. For Callaghan has the power, he has the understanding, but somewhere he is afraid. Should he overcome that fear, his freedom will be immense. We would like to see him break out of bounds and play hooky.

Reviewed by Dorothy Livesay

The poem Pink Ballad appeared in the magazine Masses *in 1934 and represents the hard line against social democracy and magazines like the* Canadian Forum.

Pink Ballad

Hot stuff, baby! Hot stuff, baby!
A crack and a joke and a smile.
Hot stuff baby, hot stuff, baby:
Sunshine and socialist guile!

Take a look at Woodsworth—
See his nice goatee.
Who's to save the country?
No one else but he!

Agnes too will help him
She's never read Karl Marx
And so she says she's fitted
To drown the bosses' barks.

And then the two together
By "reason", not by force
Will form a little commonwealth
And make each other hoarse.

Shouting about happiness,
The "will to live," free bread,
When Capital and Labour
Will share the self-same bed.

O then we'll all be equal:
Free leisure, work, repose
While Woodsworth is our premier
And Aggie hugs her foes!

Chorus: Hot stuff, worker! Hot stuff
    worker!!
A crack and a joke and a smile.
Hot stuff, worker. Hot stuff, worker
Sunshine and Socialist guile!

Depression Suite

i

If there are prayers, it is the walls
That hear them, lavatory walls
And smart swift taps that spurt.

If there are tears, and cigarettes
It is the walls that hold such
And then erase the hurt.

If there are girls who still have left a song
The midnight scrubber does not heed
But mops it up like dirt.

This is the wall, the enemy
Who keeps our hands from striking free.

ii

I can be a vagabond and still
Be framed within a window sill;

I can nurse a little cloud
And yet not mention it aloud;

I can sing down deep within
And not let anybody in.

But I can't stretch a hand out yet
To someone I have never met

177

And shout the answer, stride the wall
Crying, here is room for all.

I am a coward yet, the task
Is too stupendous that you ask.

iii

I sit and hammer melodies
Upon the keys; the snappy tunes
Go pounding down the room; O quick
My girl! Yessir, and click click click,

She's at it harder still, the fear
Like rigid tentacles, like arms
Gripping her back; a wave of heat
Must be fought down, the lips drawn in

And faster faster, Sir, we have
Your letter of the fifteenth instant
How do you like my harmonies
Better than jazz dear Sir, click click.

Better than jazz and kisses are
The pounding minutes, nickels, dimes
The dancing whirling hours, the fear
The keys, quick, quick, the fear!

iv

You have no heart—
That's what she said:
You haven't a morsel
Of brains in your head.

You hobble along
Like a limping horse;
With face unshaven;
Your jokes are coarse.

You ask for a kiss
When I want a show:
Shall we go to a dance?
You reply, "Aw no."

It isn't any fun
Going with you
So don't come back.
That's all; I'm through.

* * * *

Feeding the destitute families at a "soup kitchen" in a public park.

(Miller Services Limited, Toronto)

Well, I've been hungry
For a decent meal
Till the smell of coffee
Has made me reel.

I've had the soles
Of my shoes worn out
And shuffled in line
Like a turnabout.

The moon and the stars
Have lit the dark
As I slept on the ground
In a city park.

And morning has been
Raw white and chill
With an ache in the bones
And my mind stock still.

Yet there's a hunger
Worse than these:
When a girl goes by
Gay as you please

And a fellow meets her
And they smile deep—
That's a hunger
Won't let me sleep.

Makes me wonder
If I'm just
Like a lump
Of trodden dust

Sets me thinking
Faster yet;
Hurry, Mister
Don't forget

Thousands like us
Lying in bed—
"You have no heart"
The boss once said:

"You've only arms
And legs for me
Time in, time out—
And then you're free."

Free: to stumble
Down a street
With sullen look
And restless feet—

Thousands like us
Lying in bed:
We might be shouldering
Men, instead!

We might be marching
With firm tread—
"You have no heart"
That's what *she* said.

v

The boss was a friend of mine
I was close to his heart
(Snatch the plank from the saw
Heave till your muscles smart)

The boss liked the way I ran
Fast as the mill hum
I, a revolving bee
And wood my honey comb.

Pile up, pile up for him
Sweet steaming logs that wheel
Blasted by logger's hands
Peeled raw by men and steel.

Speed up, speed up, the sweat
Greases our chains, our breath:
Never stumble nor pause
If a man is crushed to death.

The boss was a friend of mine—
I flashed my union card:
He spat and turned away
Slow, in the mill yard.

vi

The man you knew in Galilee
Walked also in the market-place,
Stood at the warrior's monument
With weather-beaten face.

Crying against the shrunken slums
He held the city Council mute—
Down in a Hastings Street cafe
He touched a prostitute.

He came back hungry from the camps,
Rattled a cup on bargain day
And selling flowers was sent to jail
For leading other men astray—

* * * *

You who approve the Mountie's whip,
Tear gas, and the rearing beast:
Mark you the faces underfoot!
His was of these, the least.

vii

Even although the skimpy relief investigator
Pressed by you in the hall, afraid of a hot glance
And you heard her thinking aloud: "Why don't they get jobs?"
    You're alive, still, alive!

Even although the woman you love is the one you can't marry—
You can fornicate and besmirch love, but never make it secure
(That's not allowed by the government)
    You are standing erect and alive

Even although Maisie looks furtively every day
At the bright dashing dress in the store window
And your hands seem pinned to your pockets

Even though fruit is spilled onto the sidewalk
Black thick grapes like a kid's curls, oranges,
Peaches like the sun going down, bananas

Even although you can't taste them
    You're alive, by yourself, alive.

You can smell the essence of sweet fall fruit
Summer itself falling and the sea wind changing
Clouds bluffing the sunlight

You can chase shadows and guffaw at prosperity's cower
You can stretch muscles and shout
You've got it, got what it takes
To be living, alive!

The West 1936

*"We knew we were being watched, for by this time I
had written several articles for the left press about
company towns in B.C."*

In the Thirties we did not know the term "cultural
shock." The phrase reached me long after I had
reached the West Coast. Language must have evolved
like that! And how much clearer is the experience,
in your mind, when you can name it. Is this perhaps the main reason for
becoming a writer?

I had never travelled west of Winnipeg before (except as a small child
during World War I, when the family visited my aunt Helen in B.C. We
paddled in the ocean at English Bay, wearing fulsome navy blue bloom-
ers. I saw sea and sand and sky. All to remember).

But I had never known the mid-west, the foothills, coal country, mountains. To get the feel of the prairie workers and their union struggle I took
the train to Estevan — then Regina — names that had become very
familiar by 1936. In Regina there was a cousin I was supposed to look up,
Helen Gordon, daughter of Judge Percy Gordon. After spending my first
night at Jack King's house, learning about the On to Ottawa Trek and that
fatal Dominion Day, 1935, I telephoned my cousins and was invited to be
their guest. "How was it you got here this morning? There's no train!"
Somehow I lied myself out of that one and was made comfortable in a
spacious, sunny house. Too comfortable, I thought, trying to adjust
myself to talk of boarding-school days from talk of poverty and struggle. I
remembered Helen as a child, a wild red-headed maverick; now she was

the polite young lady, properly performing as hostess to guest. Much as I liked her still I had to keep my real self to myself. The right hand was uppermost! And so I soon headed for Calgary. "Calgary" for me was a name before it became a place (was there a Stampede in those days?). I was to speak there as part of my New Frontier promotion tour. Of course I had no money to spare. I was no longer travelling on my father's purse; but a relative of his had left me a small legacy, which purchased my train ticket to Vancouver. So instead of staying at the YWCA or an hotel I looked for some comrades.whose address I had been given. "The Party" was underground, so I had to avoid telephoning and simply "land" and ask to be put up. The family lived on the welfare side of Calgary in a row of small frame houses, down-at-heel in every respect. They were living on relief but welcomed me with warmth and curiosity. They said I could have space in a double bed. That night there were three of us, girls in the one bed. My second shock was the realization that they had scarcely any food in the house. For supper I think I bought a cake for them; I should have bought meat and vegetables.

That day I had been interviewed in a newsroom by two rival young women reporters: Edith McCook of the Calgary Albertan *and Maudie Ferguson of the* Calgary Herald.* *Then in the evening I gave my lecture in the Public Library on the new developments in English poetry: Auden, Spender and Day-Lewis — reading their poems, I believe, rather than my own — and commenting on the relationship between politics and literature as it applied in Canada. On recent tours across Canada I have met people who attended that meeting. In Victoria I have met Maudie, now Mrs Farquarson, whose journalist husband knew my father. Maudie does not remember that after the occasion in Calgary she drove me home. I say "home" because I had to explain to her that no, I wasn't staying at the Palliser or at the "Y", but with friends. I gave her the address, never realizing that Calgary is a city drearily numbered, western style, and you have to designate an address as being east or west, north or south (right or left!). The young reporter simply assumed that I was staying on the "right" side of town. So my confusion was great when we drove through streets of solid brick middle class houses, in contrast to the poor huddled houses where I had spent the night. "Something's wrong," I stuttered. Good-humoredly, but with obvious surprise, Maudie drove me all the way back across town. I dared not give her the correct house number for fear she would look up the owners and reveal their name in the press, so I concocted a "next-door" number and was duly deposited there. But Maudie was polite, and watched me safely up the porch steps. I fumbled in my purse as for a key; but as she was still waiting I waved her on. Once the car was safely out of sight I walked to my friend's house on the left and*

---

*See *New Frontier*, page 220.

rang the doorbell.

My experiences in the coal-mining towns of Alberta were equally unusual for a middle class girl who had never stayed in a working-class environment, nor witnessed a long drawn-out strike, nor square-danced! The difference between Calgary, and Corbin or Blairmore lay in the fact that here I was welcomed as a reporter for New Frontier *and* The Worker. *It was the mayor of Blairmore (Emlyn Williams, I believe) who made me feel most at home. He lined up for me men and women who would talk about their experiences. I marvelled at what they had gone through and at how they had still retained their humanity, their solidarity, their ability to laugh and to make their own entertainment.* For the barn dance that week-end the women had managed to bake scones and cakes and there was always a brew of tea. Liquor was unthinkable as well as unpurchasable. Although very shy about dancing, I was led out onto the floor and somehow managed the bewildering steps, due no doubt to the fiddler's exhuberance. Then, for the next few days Williams put himself at my disposal with the utmost courtesy, driving me to other mining communities. Our goal was to reach Fernie, across the mountains in British Columbia. In the Fifties Nabokov went to Fernie in search of small blue butterflies; but in the Thirties a Canadian writer searching for the story of men locked out in what was almost a ghost town.*

"I don't know if we'll get through," Williams said.

"Get through what?"

"Why, it's the border. The police will be searching every car."

"For contraband?"

"For contraband people*! Union organizers! You'll have to say you're going to visit relatives. Remember, it's a company town."*

A company town! That sinister phrase was to haunt me in B.C. for the next few years. During the following summer I holidayed in the mountains at Bridge River gold mines. By now Duncan Macnair was my inseparable companion. In search of work, he got a job placer-mining in a small camp some miles from Bridge River. I took a room in the local hotel and every evening he trudged over to meet me. We knew we were being watched, for by this time I had written several articles for the left press about company towns in B.C. Nonetheless it was a shock when the manager of the rickety hotel gave notice that I could only stay one more night. "Why not? You aren't full up." "Them's the rules, Miss." We had a last evening walk and climb into the gaunt ridges of greyish, clay coloured rock: valley after valley of silent uninhabited peaks.

---

*Anne Marriott's poem "The Wind Our Enemy" has beautifully described such scenes.

*"I am being watched in the town," I thought, "but amongst people.
Here there's nobody. Only the mountains are watching." I felt fear. . . .
"Let's go back!"*

Dominion Day at Regina

We, from the prairies' sweep
reared with the wheatfields
who followed the gopher
home to his mating

Kin to the pine tree
tossed with sea foam
in rusty rock's heart
blasting a home

We from a mining town
seared with black dust
suckled on bosses' oath
schooled by our struggles

Give us no uniforms—
warm walls instead;
pierce with no bayonets
we ask for bread!

We offer our hands
our sinew and bone—
Give us the work
and it shall be done!

Demonstrators on the prairies, demanding work, give the communist salute.   (Miller Services Limited, Toronto)

Out West

There were four of them in the cell, a room walled with brick, white-washed, containing four steel beds bare except for a grey blanket neatly folded at the foot. At eleven o'clock precisely, a skimpy shaft of sunlight shone down from the high window, reaching the floor. It was then, if the boys were not in the halls working, that they squatted down, sun on their faces, and played their game.

Will Murphy and Sam Matchluk had worked it out. They told Sean they had practised it first at the relief camp, when lights were out and one fellow wanted to talk to his neighbour in the lower bunk without disturbing anyone. It was simply a code, so many taps meant such and such a letter of the alphabet. Will and Sam could use it with great speed, but Sean caught on to it quickly. As a reward Will said Sean was a bright lad and would probably do well in an intelligence test — whatever that was. They were overjoyed to find Sean so receptive, because before he came they were "stumped." The Czechoslovakian, who always sat in a corner by himself, his face screwed up like a monkey's could not understand English. Accordingly, their code was lost on him.

"We were crazy," Will said, "of course we should have an international code. Now why didn't I learn the deaf and dumb languages — or telegraphy?" He socked himself cheerfully on the jaw.

Sean liked watching Will think out loud. He was an odd little fellow, bony and freckled, full of enthusiasm for things he had learned and always chastising himself for not knowing more. He had never been able to go to school, but was self-taught "from the ABC up." He said he had made a point of learning something from every person he met. That was how he became acquainted with Sam, at the relief camp.

Sam was born in Europe and still remembered it. He told Will how his people dreamed of America, as Pharoah's slaves dreamed of the promised land.

"I thought this country needed men to build it up," he had said. "But the only home I've found here is the road, and the only wages, twenty cents a day in a concentration camp."

Will had flared up at that phrase, "concentration camp." "Why don't you go back where you came from? It's only in Europe they have such places."

From that moment they were fast friends, because Sam had a way of saying things that made Will curious. Before he knew it Will was talking, like Sam, telling the other boys, "We will be castaways all our life unless we fight for our future. It's a swell slogan, that." On that slogan they built the camp union and, for leading a mass refusal to eat sour food, they were "shown the door" and whisked to Edmonton out of harm's way. So Will related the tale to Sean.

The boy listened, quiet as he had always been. Maybe, when he got out of jail, he might head for a relief camp himself. It might be interesting.

188

En route to Ottawa, 1800 unemployed stopped at Regina, Saskatchewan, June 1935.
(Public Archives Canada C-24840)

Meanwhile he was restless. At night, staring into the dark, he couldn't sleep. Not enough exercise, Will suggested. Sam winked and said he needed a girl, which made Sean blush. He thought of Jennie, forced into the streets. That was all he knew about her. And he knew even less about himself. Nothing his father told him had come out right. To make living an adventure you had to pinch yourself. He was so bewildered about it he could not even sit down and write a letter to his mother.

* * *

She had planned his life for him. But it was his father's plan he had been unconsciously following. Sean's father had been a mining prospector, out west. He was a big grizzly man with surprisingly blue eyes, and a hearty way with him. In those days "out west" meant towards the Great Lakes, so Sean had a very definite picture of the country as being of rock and pine, snow-bound and isolated in the winter when the camps broke up and the men had to row to the railway in large "pointers" crudely built but strong enough to carry horses and equipment. His father, at the end of these journeys, would hold Sean on his knee and recount his adventures, telling of the new friends he made among the settlers, strong men who were "fighting the bush" and "taking it."

It's a great country, son," he would say, "and mebbe someday we'll see ourselves settled on the land, building our own log house."

Whereat Sean's mother would sigh, and cross to the window where the small town lay smooth before her eyes. She longed for a settled life. Eventually it came to her, after Sean's father was killed in a brawl, trying to hide away a man who was searched by the Mounties. After that, Sean's mother went to live on her brother's farm, taking Sean with her. Later, as he grew into his teens they moved to the city so that he could go to high school and learn a trade.

His mother planned his life for him. She didn't want him to be a farmer or a miner. Perhaps if he studied to be a mechanic or an electrician he would some day have a business of his own. Then they would have plenty of money and be able to move out of this down-at-heels district and buy an electric range, maybe have a car.

Sean had not bothered to question much what his mother had in store for him. He was a lanky, ungainly boy, with a bumpy sort of face, quiet in his ways. His main interest at school was baseball, riding around on a bicycle, and when the mood took him, devouring history books. At the back of his mind, scarcely expressed, was the image of his father "out west," vigorous and young like the country itself. His philosophy had been, "You've got to take it, son." Sean's dreams did not stretch much beyond that. Prodded by his mother, he concerned himself with graduating from high school.

It was after graduation that Sean woke up. He had to get a job. It was his mother's idea that he get an apprenticeship with a mechanic of some sort. Two years before, Mr. Rigby, an electrician who lived down the block, had promised to take him on. But when Sean went to see him he was told times were bad, Mr. Rigby had had to lay off some of his men and the rules of the union would not let him take an apprentice unless he had a certain number of men working for him.

"Too bad, you know, that unions are like that — maybe next year things will pick up."

It was the same with every place he went. The "boom" was over, he was told, there was nothing doing. He began desperately following up ads in the newspapers, racing all over the city on his bicycle. As the cold weather came on he returned each evening to face his mother's pinched reproachful look.

"But gee's Ma, it's the same all over. All the boys say it. Why, none of my class is working, except Joe Miller, who is in the store with his old man. You shouldn't blame me." But he knew she did.

Finally he got a job delivering groceries for the A and P, for $3.50 a week. That was because he had a bicycle, and the boy who formerly had the job had had his wheel stolen.

When spring came Sean was eighteen years old, and fully grown, almost as tall as his father had been. He used to tear along the street wheeling at top speed, his head pushed down and forward as if he was making a charge. That way he did not have to look at people. That way the sun could not set fire to him, the soft sky held no promise. That way the furry green leaves, so clean and new, could not make his eyes smart. It was only at night there was no escape. The sweet cool night crept into his room like a woman, yet did not stay his tossing.

One evening the boys were standing outside the cigar store, talking casually, staring at every "skirt" that passed, and listening to Louis Tiboldi's "hot stuff." Their harsh, unrestrained laughter had an empty sound. It was during a lull that Red Burroughs said, kicking the step with his toe, "Well I'm good and fed up. I'm going out west."

"How?" The others were curious, sceptical.

"Oh somehow. Hitch-hiking I guess. They say there's work on the farms. Anything's better than this."

Out west. The phrase set Sean tingling. The great gateway. The free land. His father had said it was a great country. . . . Before he knew it Sean heard himself saying to Red, "Well, I'll go with you. Riding the rods or whatever." But underneath he was saying to himself, "What will your mother say?" All the boys were thinking it too, but they said nothing.

Sean fought it out with his mother by passive resistance. Her tears were of no avail. He said he was going, and he went, telling her finally, shortly, that his father would have wished it. Her reign was over.

They started out the new life whistling, thumbing their way. Sean had sold his bicycle for ten dollars, but this money he was keeping for a tight corner. They found they could get lifts easily in the farm country, and sometimes a square meal was given them in return for odd jobs. They

191

slept in a barn or a school shed, their feet getting hardened and their clothes weathered. Even though spring rain might soak them to the skin, they would say to each other, "This is the life, boy."

But they wouldn't have had any idea of how to reach Winnipeg from North Bay if they hadn't met up with Sandy Petersen, who initiated them into the tricks of railroading. He had been all over the continent, from San Fransisco and Vancouver down to Saint John, N.B. He was a brakeman, a longshoreman, anything you wanted. He was going as far as Port Arthur to see his girl and there was nothing he did not know.

"A fine fella" said Sean to Red.

"Uh huh, Swedish, wasn't he?"

"Guess so."

They were inured now, their shins no longer bruised by boxcars, their stomachs accustomed to a feast of water for breakfast.

In Winnipeg Sean thought he ought to write to his mother, but he couldn't somehow. Instead he sent her a postcard, a picture of the Parliament buildings. Winnipeg wasn't a bit like its Parliament buildings, it was a jumbled dump of small frame houses, in need of paint, flat and treeless with wide streets and foreign faces. Still it was on the prairie, and this he had come to see, this was refreshing after weeks of forest, swamp and rock.

They searched out a hostel, on the advice of a fellow traveller, but after a couple of nights of the raw springs and the fleas, Sean decided a park bench was better. They sat all day in Kildonan Park, eating some peanuts. Red said he didn't feel like tramping about just yet. Sean had been out that morning, hanging around and employment bureau. The only men wanted had to be "experienced." "Gees, we'll never get a chance to be experienced," he was thinking.

Towards evening, a soft spring evening, Sean began to feel empty, himself. He hadn't the heart to follow Red over to where two janes were sitting. He just sat there dully, watching Red fooling around. Reluctantly he went over when Red called insistently. Red was very jocular, obviously jacking up his nerve.

"This is Madeline, Sean, and that's Jennie . . . we were wondering, how about a little dinner party?" Sean laughed awkwardly, thinking it a joke. But Red gave a meaningful wink, pointing at Sean's back pocket. Then he knew Red must mean the ten dollars he was saving. For a time he hesitated, thinking he wasn't going to give in as easy as all that. But Jennie, the little soft one who was easier on the eye, began to chirp up to him. He saw that her dress was darned in one place, and that her flimsy shoes were almost worn out. I guess they are hungry as we are, he thought. He gave in.

They had a five-course meal at a brightly lighted restaurant near the park. The girls ordered highballs so Sean and Red had them too. They were hilarious about nothing at all, and Sean felt dizzy with happiness.

He hadn't felt so good for a long while. . . . And here he was, the hero of the evening, giving everybody else a good time.

For a while they danced to the radio music, then Red said, "Aw let's get out of this. Let's get some air in the park." Sean could have gone on dancing all night, and Jennie went somehow limp in his arms when Madeline told her to hurry up. Red and Madeline were game.

Sean stopped talking to Jennie and she didn't have anything to say either. They walked behind the others to the park, and moved towards the woods. A soft twilight had fallen.

When she lay down in the leaves he knew she expected him to be like anybody else. God knows he had wanted this enough at home, long ago. But she wasn't somehow the girl. He sat beside her awkwardly, and said finally, "Do you mind if I don't?" Then he was overwhelmed to find that she was crying, sobbing roughly with her whole body. He spent the night comforting her until they fell asleep, exhausted, an unseen sword between them.

In the morning Sean stood up and stretched, ready to move on. Red did not want to leave, so Sean headed alone for Edmonton. He had sixty-seven cents in his pocket.

It was just as tough in Edmonton. After the second night he was hauled in for "vag" and padlocked, along with some street walkers, perverts, and a couple of boys from the relief camp. He was hardened to it now, he scarcely felt ashamed at all. Back home he would have died rather than go to jail, his father's eyes would have been upon him. But after all the old man had said, "You've got to take it." The old man made friends with everybody and kept his chin up, even though life for him couldn't have been quite like this.

* * *

Now in the cell, lying sleepless, his head burning with a whirl of thoughts, Sean suddenly threw off the blanket and sat up. It was not dawn yet, but he couldn't lie there another minute. His feet, touching the icy floor, recoiled. He fumbled around for his boots, then he stood up and stretched.

Tap tap tap. Will, whose bunk was next to his, was tapping out the code. "It will be over soon. There's a great job ahead. Sleep while you can."

Maybe. But Sean could not sleep. He sat down sheepishly at the foot of Will's bed. "I wish I had had a real job once," he said, in an undertone.

"Why?"

"Then I would feel as if I was worth something."

"I know, kid."

Sean realized he had never said such a thing to anyone before. Perhaps he had never thought it. But Will knew, all right. Will had learned much more than school had ever taught Sean. Sean was only a greenhorn, who

Unemployed in Vancouver demand jobs instead of relief. (Public Archives Canada C-27900)

just went places because of the name — following names as a child would follow a penny held out of his grasp. "Winnipeg", "Edmonton", "Out West." Places where he thought he belonged, because he was young. Now Sam was saying that the young did not belong anywhere. He would have to chew that over.

In the dark room Will and Sean were silent, listening to each other breathing — the snores of Sam and the rough troubled sleep of the Czechoslovakian, who couldn't express himself but who cried out sometimes sharply in the night. Sean did not feel so alone any more.

A grey light was slowly penetrating the cell. Sean stood up again, fumbled in a corner, and pulled out a pencil. He began writing to his mother.

In the morning, before they filed out to breakfast, he read some of the letter to the boys:

"Just now, after those hard experiences, you will be glad to know I have a job. I am living in a boy's school, cleaning brass, washing dishes, etc. The food is very good, three whole meals a day, and they treat you as if you were a human being. There are some nice girls working here and a couple of boys who've had a private school education. So you see I'm in good company. Who knows where I'll fly off to from here? You've no need to worry about me."

Will laughed heartily, and Sam grinned. "That letter won't be censored!" he asserted. Then they all laughed, Sean as gaily as the others. But he felt mean. Not because of the lie to his mother. But because of all the lies. Because of the school kids back home, and because of Jennie. His father, even, had been wrong. For it was not just this letter, but his whole life that had been censored.

"You can't speak! You can't work! You can't live.!" These were the slogans.

And his generation — the crowd around him, Red as well as Will and Sam and the boys back home — would they go on taking it?

He wanted to know.

The Beet Workers

By Dorothy Livesay

He came from Poland six years ago. "I have plenty trouble" he said, his eyes that were lost in a furrow of wrinkles suddenly opening wide and blue. "My brothers come to grow wheat. No good. Rain no come, grasshopper instead, then frost. Winter time I get out to Calgary for t'ree month, work in a barber shop. Only two t'ree days every week I work. No more."

Now that the chinook had sucked up the last snow he was returning to the farm. "Maybe good days sometime . . . if in Europe no war?" He left the question unanswered, his eyes opening wide again as if he stood in a field, watching the sky.

Wheat in Alberta is still a question mark, farmers who bought up huge sections of land watch it withering away under their eyes with soil drift. There is no Five Year Plan to give the wheat a meaning, and so in many parts it is being abandoned. Now there is a new upsurge, a new means found for exploiting the land — and the farmer: the sugar beet.

The Rogers Sugar Company at Raymond, Alberta, has started the ball rolling. By keeping three hundred or so men working during the winter in the factory, when there is plenty of competition for jobs among the idle farm workers, the sugar monopoly is able to keep wages down to forty-five cents an hour and less. They haven't been bothered with union trouble, anyone knows a girl is glad to get a job these days. Then the company hands out an ultimatum to the farmers. You grow so many acres of beets and we will give you a fifty fifty split on net sales of sugar — depending on the fluctuation on price. After which, having caught the farmer nicely in this agreement, the company hands out a separate contract to the farmer, under the terms of which he hires his beet workers, from April to November.

The land is undulating, bare to the sun. The beet workers, or contractors, live in small shacks on the farmers' land, settling there one month before the real work begins. One contractor handles from ten to fifteen acres of beets at twenty dollars per acre. That is, for thinning twenty-two inch rows he gets eight dollars per acre: for hoeing, two dollars; for weeding, one dollar and fifty cents; and for topping and piling, eight dollars and fifty cents per acre on a yield of ten tons per acre. In the actual harvesting season a contractor's own family has often to come out and bring in the beets on time, for "the harvesting of the beets shall commence at the time specified by the Sugar Company in their notice to the grower to dig. . . . If the grower has not commenced digging beets by October 5th, weather permitting, the contract may be declared cancelled and the grower shall pay the hold back to the contractor who is free to seek other employment!" Often in the rush season the contractors have to hire other help, at the rate of one dollar and fifty cents to two dollars per day. If beets are planted which give a greater yield than that needed by the

196

William O'Brien Unemployed (1935), Louis Muhlstock. Collection of the National Gallery of Canada, Ottawa.

company, the contractor loses out.

But the main "catch" to the contract is the fact that it does not apply uniformly. Instead of being an agreement between the Beet Growers Association and the Beet Workers' Union, the reactionary leadership of the farmers association had it read simply as an agreement between one grower and his contractor. As a result, terms of the contract can be changed at will.

It is against this arbitrary character of the contract that the Beet Workers' Union is struggling now, and which caused the strike last spring when the RCMP were brought in by the Company. Labour on the beet farm is skilled labour, and when it is withheld the beets suffer. The most effective method of strike action has been that of occupying the shacks but of refusing to sign the contracts until the terms are generally recognized. Evictions have been attempted but in general, and this is increasingly true, the growers are in sympathy with the beet workers.

This fact is going to make all the difference in future struggle. The Union has pointed out that both growers and contractors are at the mercy of the company, and common action will get best results. Thus unity was actually achieved when the union supported the growers in their demand to the Federal Government for a Sugar Tax rebate, on the understanding that if this was achieved the growers would pass thirty-one per cent of it on to the contractor. In the same way the Union supported the farmers' demand for seven dollars a ton from the Company, instead of the fifty fifty split on net sales. Gradually therefore, the monopoly clutch of the company is being dealt with in a united fashion. This year there will be twelve hundred men in the fields, and fourteen thousand more acres under cultivation than before. The task ahead for both the growers and the contractors is a tremendous one.

But sugar is not the only monopoly in Alberta. While thousands of miners are unemployed, the Canadian Pacific Railway has been quietly linking up smaller mine companies by means of its subsidiaries (like the Consolidated Mining and Smelting Co of Canada, which it controls and which, besides having a hand in International Nickel, has ten "daughter" companies of its own — plus E.W. Beatty, Sir Herbert Holt and four other bank directors.) In this way the CPR has taken over two mines in Coleman and has merged four in Lethbridge. Shortly after this last merger Mine Number Six was closed down, throwing seven hundred men out of work. Then, after the Coalhurst disaster of December 9 last, that mine was abandoned. Coalhurst, a semi-circle of shacks around the tipple, is now a "ghost town." It's inhabitants are in receipt of provincial relief, which is only half the amount given out in the city of Lethbridge. Half the houses are owned by the CPR, with evictions pending: the other half, owned by the miners, must either be lived in as they are, or abandoned completely with no reimbursement (visitors won't be in the habit of wanting to buy or rent houses in Coleman). The CPR also, of

Pioneer Survival (1938), Charles Comfort, O.C., R.C.A. Collection of the National Gallery of Canada, Ottawa.

course, owns the water system, so in order to avoid losing its water supply the town is struggling to have this taken by the government. They are holding out, too, for government ownership of the mine and for a new shaft to be sunk, to keep the town alive.

Shaugnessy was the third mine in the merger. With four hundred working there now, the men figure it will only last for two more years, then it too will be "abandoned" and the human lives involved flung back into a ghost existence. Instead new mines will be sunk, as the new Number 8 mine at Lethbridge, containing so much modern machine equipment that less and less men will be needed to work them. In Number 8 the CPR has taken care not to get involved in any responsibility towards the miners, refusing to let them live on its property and thereby taxing them with the extra burden of bus fare to the mine. Blacklisting of the Mine Workers' Union is of course one of the main aims, plus the possibility of a cut in the agreement which the small "home local" may find it hard to fight alone.

Here is Alberta then, seeing no future in wheat, being clutched at on all sides by the hand of monopoly — by the biggest corporations and the biggest bankers Canada possesses. But Alberta isn't taking it lying down. One of the first steps is unity between all the mine unions, whether local, Canadian, or American — and that is on the agenda at Calgary on May 10. Then there is unity of farmers and farm labourers, just in its beginnings, but promising well for a future where both labour and farmer groups will be together, struggling politically as well as economically for a common future freed from the exploiting hand.

new frontier

A CANADIAN MONTHLY | MAGAZINE OF LITERATURE & SOCIAL CRITICISM

TORONTO
JUNE 1936

Corbin
A Company Town
Fights For Its Life

Dorothy Livesay

A Direction for Canadian Poets . . . . *Leo Kennedy*

United Front in Toronto—1872 . . . . *Betty Ratz*

$150.00 Prize Contest for Canadian Plays

VOL 1, NO 3   25 CENTS A COPY

Corbin—A Company Town Fights For Its Life

By Dorothy Livesay

Pushing its way through the dusty mountain roads of the Crow's Nest Pass, Alberta, the car spurts up an incline, slows to a stop. From an office at the side of the road an officer steps out, red-faced and bull-necked, wearing the uniform of the British Columbia Provincial Police.

"Where you from?"

"Coleman," the driver beside me answers.

"What's your name?" The officer jots down the answers in a note book. Then he searches the driver's face, with a puzzled look. "Coming back tonight?"

"Yes."

"Going far?"

"Corbin."

"Corbin, eh? Who you going to see there?"

"My sister."

The officer gives us the onceover, appraisingly. "O.K. You can try it. But the road's in bad shape."

The car darts forward. We lean back, smiling. Plenty of other cars from the mining towns of Alberta have never got across the boundary. Leaders of the Mine Workers' Union of Canada are on a blacklist. This isn't Germany, but British Columbia, April, 1936.

The Corbin road is a narrow track skirting the edge of mountains, almost washed away in some places by snow slides. For an hour it climbs above desolate valleys, snow slashed, some green with jackpine, others sentinelled with trees like burnt fingers. There is no one else on the road, no settlements. We push ahead under a grey sky.

"Sure, it's romantic country," my driver says. "And a rich country. Over twenty-five years ago the mine was opened, and there's still seventy-five million tons of coal to be mined. But I wouldn't live or work up here — though I've been a miner all my life. For one thing — you have winter, and then July. But that isn't the only reason. You'll see."

Corbin lies in a narrow crescent between mountains. Three rows of identical shacks, unpainted and soot-coloured, are perched on the slope facing the tipple. There are no lanes or streets between them. An empty store and a cafe, a boarding-house, a school and a union hall are the main public buildings, likewise unpainted. Above the village there is only snow and burnt timber. There is no sound or activity anywhere: since the strike fifteen months ago every hand has been idle. The town is living on contributions from other miners.

Today is ration day. Miners of all nationalities — Scotch, Welsh, Belgian, Czechoslovakian — are crowding into the union hall to get the week's rations for some two hundred families. The relief committee, consisting of men and women, is on hand to mark off lists and parcel up the provisions from behind a counter. One of the single men, who "batches" with his mining partner, explains how many supplies each adult is entitled to weekly. All staples are covered, such as flour (five pounds,) sugar (three-quarters of a pound), butter (half a pound), potatoes (six pounds). Jam or peanut butter cannot be had every week, beans and cheese are likewise rare, one pound of meat has to go for ten days, eggs vary from two to eight per person per week.

"But we get along pretty good," the young man grins. "I can make such swell bread now I'm baking everybody's, almost."

"And can I wash floors," another man adds.

"Well, none of you can beat me at puttin' out a snow white washin'," says a third. I begin to wonder if the women have anything left to do, so one of the miners suggests I go up to his home and "meet the Missus."

It is one of the shacks in the middle row, with scarcely any room between houses for children to play, and the front family's back yard with its ashes and garbage almost on this doorstep. The kitchen and front room are neat, but shabby, with the oil cloth worn bare and the walls askew. Mrs. W., a thin, freckled young woman, greets the visitors happily. "Well, imagine you being from the east! I was born down in Ontario. Come in and sit down."

"I see you brought the flour, Ben. Now I can make some biscuits." She laughed then. "We women had a terrible time about the flour. You see, the union had to base the rations on some budget, so they used the army list. I guess the men in the army like lots of hot cakes, so they need lots of flour. But our children don't. We had some time to convince the committee to buy more vegetables and less flour."

The supplies, she explained, were brought up every two weeks from Lethbridge by truck. Union and Corbin defence relief funds are allotted at the rate of sixty-eight cents a week per person, and the diet expands or is restricted according to market prices.

"It's hard sometimes to make a meal seem different, especially if you have no meat. The biggest trouble is not having any fresh fruit and so few green vegetables. We can't always get the dried fruits. That's hard on the children — they aren't really undernourished but they're not getting everything they should have. And if a person is on a diet it is impossible to get it — we couldn't ask the union for that."

Milk comes — about a pint for each family — from a dairyman who gives credit in exchange for having his hay brought for him. "But two of his cows died, and he lost two because he could not pay up for them."

Since Corbin is a company town (Corbin Collieries, Ltd., an American firm), everything in it belongs to the company. The water system was frozen all winter, and nothing done about it; electricity was turned off "so our radios are no use"; sanitation has "gone out of business"; stores are closed; rents are unpaid — "they wouldn't dare evict us because that might draw too much attention to the condition of the houses."

Most irritating of all, Corbin miners are no longer taxpayers, so the school trustees are no longer elected by them, but appointed by the company. "This year there is only one, Walter Almond, who doesn't know anything about schools or teaching. He supplies fuel as well, and acts as janitor — which is against the law for a trustee. But what can we do?"

The only thing the company has been forced to do is to keep open the school and pay the two teachers. Classes only reach the eighth grade, however, and there is no way of getting children to a high school. For two months during the winter the only doctor was fifteen miles away, so the government had to keep the road open. Then finally a doctor came, his salary partly paid by the government and partly by the miners themselves, who are supposed to supply rations, rent and electricity. They are greatly behind on the doctor's rent, so he is leaving at the end of April.

"Corbin is fairly healthy, except for influenza," the doctor told me. He is a military man, used to hard fare. "The diets are all that prairie children would get. The great trouble is weakness of the heart, especially among many of the women. It's due to the high altitude and of course has nothing to do with the present situation.' He meant with the attitude of the company, which refuses to negotiate with the miners.

"I'm glad you want to know the truth about Corbin," another miner's wife told me. "At the beginning I used to send stories about our life up here and why we went on strike to the Nelson News. Then they began sending letters back asking, 'is your story authentic?' They would not print our facts, but lies that came from the other side. After that I quit bothering. But it makes you sore to think that people on the outside don't know what happened."

"Yes," another young woman said, with some bitterness, "some friends of mine in Lethbridge would hardly speak to me because they read I was throwing a fence post at an officer. The newspapers helped the police to frame us."

"Tell me why you went on strike?" I asked a group of miners up in the union hall, men both single and married who had been strike leaders.

"A year before then, our strike should be," a Czechoslovakian burst out.

"Yes, we must have been asleep, though we were all in the union since 1925. It wasn't the wages so much, it was the conditions we had to live under."

"Yes," agreed another, a Nova Scotian. "It got so we saw that life was dearer to us than the mine."

They told the story of those shacks built in 1909 of green lumber, costing only $175 to build and bringing in $5.00 per month rent ever since, besides $3.50 for water and light, 50 cents for radio use, 50 cents for a garbage collection that only came twice a year. The house shrunk, fell apart, and with only an outer wall it was not uncommon that snow drifted across the bed at night. Ice formed on the wall and even stuck to the beds and any effort to get the carpenter to come and do some patching was met with vague promises and a general run-around. It took one man two years to get his door lintel mended. The health officer reported that the houses were "absolutely antiquated," and he condemned 78 out of 80 houses.

Besides these conditions there was the situation in the mine itself. Nearly a mile from the village where the bath-house is the men had to walk to the mine in mid-winter clad only in their work clothes, and were often held up outside the mine to do road work. As a result they might start work soaked to the skin, and return home with the clothes frozen to their backs. In one mine there has been a fire blazing for years, and nothing done to protect the men. Pay checks went through some extraordinary gyrations, sometimes being short and taking months to get adjusted, or else being much too high. In the latter case the correct amount was pencilled in on the envelope and given to the miner, but the mistaken amount remained on the books. "Somebody was getting something."

"The company's excuse was always that they weren't making money. Yet in the B.C. mines report for three years back of 1934 it shows that Corbin was getting 5.4 tons per man, as compared with 1.1 tons on Vancouver Island and 3.0 tons at Michel. The seam is one of the richest, that's why we want a government investigation, to prove to the world the mismanagement of the company."

Mismanagement was shown most clearly in the negotiations that went on between the Mine Workers Union and the Company. In the face of an expiration of the agreement in March, 1935 and the possibility of a wage cut at that time, the union set forth its demands in January of that year. The union secretary, J. Press, had been fired by the company on the pretext that he did not work full time one day (this situation had been "fixed up" by the foreman). Reinstatement of Press was the first demand and equal to it in importance was the demand for repair of miners' houses. Equal distribution of work was requested, to stop abuses in that direction, and also it was held essential that miners taken from the working face should be paid the full rate of $5.60 per shift. The miners were willing to arbitrate these demands before calling a strike.

The company dilly-dallied but for two months after the strike was called no effort to work the mine was made. Then there were open hints that "The Big Show", which is a huge face of coal projecting from the mountainside and requiring no mining operations but only a steam shovel to work it, would be opened shortly by non-union men. Then at the beginning of April, about six provincial police were called for by the company and took up their residence in the town. Against all provocations the miners continued their peaceful picketing.

On Tuesday, April 16, the company met a delegation of the strike committee and appeared to be willing to sign the agreement. Then they stated that they would have to wire the head office in Spokane for a final decision. The delegation reported this to a meeting of the miners and it was agreed that they would deal with Spokane. But on returning with this decision to the company the delegation was told that they were "too late." A telegram had just come from Spokane refusing to deal with the demands.

"After that," as one of the strike leaders put it, "we knew something would happen. The police were getting restless, they had been called in to keep law and order and there wasn't a single instance of any trouble. On the morning of April 17th I walked down the road early and saw that the scabs from out of town were manning the caterpillar tractor, and filling it up with gas and water. We called out every man and woman in the town and had a mass picket line, feeling that we had to stop the tractor from taking those men up to the Big Show. The womenfolk were grouped in the middle and some were up front. Suddenly, as at a signal, the full detachment of police ran out from the hotel and grouped themselves in two squads on either side of the caterpillar, flanking the picket line. . . . Before we could understand anything the caterpillar was moving forward, straight at our women. And the police, instead of clearing the way, suddenly closed in, hemming us in on both sides, beating miners and their wives with pick handles and riding crops. . . ."

Mrs. W. was one of the women at the front, heading the women's auxiliary. "That morning," she said, "we didn't have any fear. We'd been told that the police were there to protect us, and we just imagined they were called out to clear the road for the tractor. Then the tractor advanced with its sharp knife edge right on us, cutting at us women in front and the cops moving forward with it. We turned to run and the police closed in, beating us. . . . That was when our men went wild. They had no weapons at all, for all the lies them witnesses told. They had to go down to the creek and dig up stones out of the snow to throw at the police, so as to protect us.

"There was nobody killed, though the papers made out there was. The police, some of them just youngsters, started all the violence. Before that happened I used to be patriotic. I'd stand up on my little Maple Leaf in front of anyone. But I learned my lesson. We all did. The police were sent down by the government to protect the American company — not the Canadian workers. Yet all we were asking for was a decent existence. We couldn't go on the old way any longer. . . . Well, one thing it done, was to bring all the miners together — solid. We've never been separated since."

Mrs. C. was one of the women who was badly hurt — a young, lithe European woman. "As the tractors moved down on us, Inspector Elmsie leaned over and hit me on the back of my head. I got away somehow, and was walking in the opposite direction toward the Cafe, when I saw a bunch of cops looking kind of queerly at me. But I was alone, and just running away, so I didn't take any notice of Inspector MacDonald coming up alongside me. All of a sudden he struck me a blow from the rear, across my right ear, it must have been from his riding crop.... Anyhow, I was knocked down unconscious.... For days after I kept fainting, and the whole side of my face and neck was swollen.

"I testified at Corbin, but not at Fernie. Maybe the lawyer thought I'd get too violent and spoil things. I felt violent, when I seen the way they lied — swearing they had seen all seventeen of the arrested men during the riot, when those same police were passing them by in the street the next morning, out with a warrant unable to identify them! And going into garbage piles to find steel bed rails which the miners were supposed to have been armed with! No one was showing the bloody pick handles the police were swinging, but we found them afterwards hidden under a mattress!

"I sure learned something about governments during those days, something I never would have believed before. My husband used to get *The Worker* and I just couldn't believe the stories I read in it. After the riot, 'You see, I was right,' he says to me.... Before, I never would have believed they would attack defenceless people. I guess the moral is, go armed....

"Sure, right now I feel pretty bitter, I don't go to no meetings because it makes me feel too sore. Here the government is doing absolutely nothing for us and we're just living on the sweat of other miners. Maybe I shouldn't say it, but we in Corbin are just sapping the life-blood of Crow's Nest Pass miners. I figure we ought to be getting relief instead."

Getting relief is the big question in Corbin. It is not so simple as it sounds: many workers think it would be a mistake. In the first place, the doctor definitely told me he had it from the Government Inspector that Corbin could not receive provincial relief unless the families agreed to leave the town and go to a place where work might be possible. The miners feel that this would just be a move to help the company: as soon as the town is cleared of union men the company can move in scabs to work the Big Show — a very profitable operation not requiring skilled miners. Wages would go down to about three dollars per shift and this would mark the beginning of a move to rush the union in other towns. Again, going on relief would have a bad effect on the single men, many of them union leaders, by forcing them out of the town into relief camps. For in spite of the Federal Government's promises, these camps remain open in Alberta and B.C. Lastly, relief would not be granted to all miners, as a goodly number of them have property in the shape of automobiles bought during boom days — the only means of communication with "the outside."

Possibly the greatest argument against relief is the fact that in this way the company can no longer be negotiated with, and full government inquiry into the management of the mine, the riot, and the keeping of five men in Nelson jail (even after one of those committed, David Lockhart, died there on March 6), would be ignored. The report of the committee on evangelism and social service of the United Church declared that "nothing less than a judicial inquiry would satisfy justice." Dr. Hugh Dobson, one of the United Church secretaries of social service, in a wire to the Provincial Secretary, urged "an impartial inquiry into all circumstances." As well as this a strong fight in Parliament has been led by Mr. T. Uphill, Labour M.L.A. and the C.C.F. members in the B.C. house. Such actions, the strikers feel, justify a further attempt for an investigation.

"Maybe we will have to go on relief, to stop draining Blairmore," one of the miners said. "But if so we will all go on relief together, and stay in our homes, and bring the real question to the fore: that of getting the mine reopened. It is still being kept in condition, though fire has burned out one mine entirely. But the equipment is still here, the upkeep continues. What are they waiting for? Spokane will give *us* no answer. But what if the Mackenzie King government should live up to its pre-election promises, and threaten confiscation of the mine if the industrial magnates refuse to co-operate? It looks as if the Canadian government and the American company are sleeping in the same bed.

"Well, the miners are together too. Not only Corbin is holding fast, but all the miners of Alberta are behind us, each man in the union from Blairmore giving two dollars a month to keep our children alive and our union strong."

This is why Corbin is waiting. Corbin is not through fighting.

Blairmore

By Dorothy Livesay

It is pay day in Blairmore. Pocketed lengthwise between mountains, some silver-headed, some grey-green with fir trees, the main thoroughfare, Tim Buck Boulevard, is alive with people. Bareheaded, in cotton dresses, the women dart in and out of stores, the men saunter or stand earnestly talking at street corners. It is a spring day, but the sun pours down warm as midsummer.

In the union headquarters on Eighth Avenue, the secretary, Joseph Krkosky, is sitting behind a table. He is young, friendly, scratching away at his pen as one after another workers come in and toss him a two dollar bill. A Finnish woman, tall and vigorous, opens her purse laughingly and shows there is nothing left.

"Wait a minute. You get fifty cents back" he reminds her.

"I didn't forget. That has to last me two weeks." She said it quite undaunted. An English miner, leaning beside her across the desk, waved his bill. "Don't forget about me now." He smiles understandingly at the woman.

"O.K." The secretary marks it down. "That's seventy-five cents for the union and fifty cents for Corbin." He marks book after book. Some pay the month's quote in full — $1.50 for the union and $2.00 for Corbin. After they have gone out he explains a little.

"The miners in Blairmore have only been working about three days every two weeks — that's at five dollars a shift. Every month, nearly a whole day's pay is given to organization — to the Union, to different drives and assessments, to the striking miners of Corbin. If a man has a large family, it hardly leaves enough to live on."

"But the strike in Corbin is fourteen months old, at least. Has Blairmore helped all that time?"

He nods his head, smiling.

"And they don't kick against it?"

"Hardly a soul but doesn't do it willingly. Even those that are earning about eight dollars every two weeks bring their money in regularly. Sometimes it's hard to take it. But Corbin helped Blairmore during the 1932 strike. It's turn and turn about."

That made me want to know more about Blairmore. It isn't every town that has a union and a philosophy like that. Blairmore's stand must rest on something much firmer than that of a having a Tim Buck Boulevard.

I asked an old Finnish miner about it. He has lived here twenty-five years, spending most of them in the Green Hill mine, Blairmore's mine owned by the West Canadian Collieries, a French firm. In those days, they worked five and six days a week fairly steadily; the town hummed with Europeans, Italians, French Canadians, building their own frame bungalows or renting them from the company. It was easy to live, and the mountain air was good. The miners settled down and married, watched the town grow.

Now, for six years everything has been different. The same men are working, but so infrequently that what was once a week's pay is now a month's. A speed-up has been introduced, yet miners who were vigorous twenty years ago are now aging. Instead of their boys getting jobs, it is the old men who are still working, some of them walking two miles to the mine and then doing a day's work. They have to work or the family will starve.

Then old age pensions in Alberta are no solution to the problem: they are only obtainable at seventy years. "I will get a good pension in my grave" the miner said, with his wise, laughing air. He pointed up to his "future home", the graveyard on the hillside, flanking the mine.

But Blairmore people are so vigorous, so generous, I was thinking. There's a friendliness in the air . . . what made it? The answer came from a miner's wife, an old-timer and a fighter. "We haven't got much" she said, "but we have had the strike."

That was in 1932. A seven-month strike against the threat of a wage-cut and for recognition of the Mine Workers Union of Canada, the right to join any organization of the miners' choice.

"It was in that struggle we forgot we were Italians and Slavs; we forgot we were men and women. On the picket-line we were all workers together. That's what we have in Blairmore."

Out of that strike came the first labour council slate elected in Canada, something that rode into power on the upsurge of feeling, something that has had to be fought for hard since, so that it might be maintained as a vital force. For that labour council was not a Soviet. It had power over municipal services, water and light, roads, education, taxes: but it could not control the life-blood of the town: the mine. It could not take over the food services, the transportation. It could not control the provincial police, nor the magistrates. IT COULD NOT SEIZE POWER! Nor smash the power of the state. Lastly, being raw and somewhat unsure of itself, it could not protect itself against reactionaries and opportunists in its own ranks. As a result, it has had to face the failure of a police chief who was sent to jail for two years on an extortion charge!

Side by side with these things, the Council has made definite achievements. Besides street improvement, schools have been renovated, showers installed, free text books and cod liver oil are given to the children and free medical and dental care is arranged for. The town has hired a full-time visiting nurse, so that general health care is improving and the particular difficulties women underwent in childbirth (being unable even to pay for a midwife) have been eliminated. Teachers are more highly paid than in similar towns elsewhere, and they hold joint meetings with the Council to discuss educational problems. Unemployed families have been recognised as a relief problem and recently all single men have been registered with a view to getting relief for them.

Just now, the Council is taking a new lease on life. In January last, it met and conquered its biggest threat, an election slate drawn up by the company. Previous to this, the Blairmore Council consisted only of miners from the Mine Workers Union, the strongest union in the town. Realizing that this situation was driving away other miners and small professional and business people, straight into the arms of the company, the Council slate for January was composed of only three miners from the MWU, one from the "home local" (which has about thirty members) and two businessmen, besides the mayor, a mine carpenter. This slate for the first time united all the exploited groups in the town against the mine company, and it is this slate which is now in office.

What is it doing? For one thing, it has found that working men and business men have many things in common. For instance, where the town had allowed a fifteen per cent discount on prompt payment of taxes, it was realized that this meant an insignificant saving to the small business man, but a saving of some four thousand dollars to the mine

210

company. Accordingly, the discount has been abolished. Similarly, a tax on business frontage has been removed, and two and a half mills has been added to the mill rate to help get the town out of debt. In general, the policy is to tax the monopolies, not the small man.

Many problems still remain for Blairmore — some solvable, others not so under capitalism. Taxation is high, water and electricity rates are one dollar and three dollars respectively, per month. Few homes, although well built, have complete sanitary plumbing, and the cost of living is abnormal as compared with larger cities. The question of relief, one third of which has to come from the town under the present Ottawa arrangement, will become more pressing, especially if the mine remains so inactive, and partial relief to those "employed" becomes a necessity.

In this sense, Blairmore is in exactly the same dependent position as many other municipalities in Canada. Higher taxation (locally) is a boomerang, since if it is in the form of a mill rate, it drains the miners. However, certain things like evictions can be avoided: the town does not believe in taking over its own houses!

Again, like other municipalities, Blairmore has to solve the question of its youth, some three hundred of them without work and no prospect of it, spending their time on street corners and in pool rooms. There is no technical or vocational school anywhere near, no recreation halls or swimming pools. Blairmore wants these things, and young people are talking about getting them, perhaps by uniting all shades of opinion in a Youth Council. As one of the young fellows put it: "we have a lot of fight in us yet. During the Corbin strike last April it was the young fellows of Blairmore who insisted on heading the miners march to aid Corbin after the riot, in the face of provincial police and their guns."

What lies ahead for Blairmore? The answer can be found in any miners' meeting. A committee is reporting on an interview with the boss to discuss a new agreement. For the first time the Mine Workers Union is not alone, but in joint delegation with the Bellevue "home local", men who were previously regarded as "scabs" and given the name "fascists" by children in the street. "Now we come up to the boss smiling" a delegate reports. "He's not used to seeing us miners smiling but we've got a reason now." He goes on to describe how the company agrees to everything except the check-off, whereby the company would have to take the union dues off each pay check. This helps the union in an unorganized place like Bellevue, so the company refuses.

To Blairmore this is a small item; to Bellevue it means a lot. Will Blairmore hold out on the agreement till Bellevue wins its point? There's hardly any discussion, the men don't hesitate: every hand goes up like one man's. That's unity, and Blairmore is forging it. With Corbin, then with the "home locals," lastly with the United Mine Workers of America.

"Once we have that, we'll be strong enough to force the federal government to take over some of our problems: relief, a works program, the opening up of closed mines." That is the feeling. And with it is the feeling that you don't get anywhere else except in Blairmore: 'We've a long way to go yet, but this is *our* town!"

This was the time that Vancouver was famous all across the country for its production of Waiting for Lefty. *Garfield King, a lawyer, recruited a cast of about fifteen — just from the unemployed. They used the Stanislavsky method. Their production was so good that, with the contributions of individuals, they went to the Dominion Day Drama Festival in Ottawa and won a prize.*

The Workers' Theatre on tour; (back row) "Jim" Watts, Percy Matthews, J.P. Smith, Toby Gordon (front) unidentified actor and Avrom Yanovsky.

212

Mail and Empire, 1936

Radical Drama
Is Well Directed

Theatre of Action Presents
Good One-act Play at
Margaret Eaton.

By Pearl McCarthy

"Waiting for Lefty," by Clifford Odets, that American playwright who drew the attention of most conservative people to the left wing theatre, was given the first of three performances in the Margaret Eaton Hall last night. This one-act drama lived up to the highest praise that has been written of it. But the Theatre of Action and the Student League which presented the piece, put their good taste in question by presenting, as a complementary piece, as trashy a bit of circumstance as we have ever seen labelled drama. This unsavory curtain-raiser was "Private Hicks," a play which won a prize from the American League against War and Fascism.

The Odets play is so good, so genuine in craft and spirit, that not even its propaganda flavor can mar the enjoyment. With reason, sincerity and the most acute use of dramatic possibilities, it shows how exasperation with an existing economic system may drive men to drastic action. Every step is given motive by true, basic human feelings. It was well directed by Miss Jim Watts and

Jean Watts, director.

Martin Loeb, and consistently well acted by a large cast.

An engaging device of the play is the union of auditorium and stage, the stage scene being a hall platform, and the hecklers of the meeting speaking from the audience.

"Private Hicks," by Albert Maltz, dealt with a young American soldier who refused to shoot strikers. It had no reason beyond a boast of blockheadedness expressed to blasphemy.

Jos. Lavallee With Bowl of Soup (1931), Louis Muhlstock. Collection of the artist.

A Cup of Coffee

He was standing on the corner of Robson and Granville, his hand jingling in the near-empty pocket. What the hell was he going to do now, he wondered, with all his gratuities gone? Sunk into Vet's Fuels, Inc. Might as well have been thrown into a ditch as thrown to that stinker, Eddie. But he might have known it would turn out like this. Everything had turned out black since way back, since before he knew Hilda, even. . . .

Hilda. The name came easily to his mind. His lips opened slightly, as if the name were like taking a breath. What was it the welfare lady had said? Cold, chilly words as he stood there in the hall, hot with sweat.

"I think you would find her changed, Mr. Metka." Maybe she would be. Maybe — He took his hand from his pocket, slowly mopped his brow with it, as if to clear his thinking.

B-r-r-r. A siren blared. A car screeched to a stop as the light changed. A girl, about to cross the street, caught herself back quickly. Then she half turned on her heel, swinging towards him.

"Hilda!"

The girl turned sharply, violently. Seeing him there she made as if to dart across the street. But the traffic was against her. He took a stride towards her and drew back towards the drugstore window.

"So, it's you." That was all she said.

He took her in at a glance. She looked the same, only thinner. Her hair hung long, in yellow ringlets. He did not like it that way.

"Gosh. How locky I been." In the shock of seeing her he lost control over his accent.

"And I suppose you were lucky the first time you saw me. Well, I wasn't. And I'm not now." Yes, she was hard as nails, like the welfare lady had told him. Still, seeing her was a thousand times better than sending messages through the government hook-up. It meant. . . .

"Now looka here, Hilda. We gotta talk, see?" He took her arm and began walking fast up Granville St. "Come and have a cup of coffee."

"Aw, Nick, I haven't got the time. I'm busy."

"Busy? How long you been in town?"

"A coupla days. I lost that job in Kamloops. So I'm looking for one here."

"Well, come and have a cup of coffee on me." He steered her into the cafe, headed for a quiet cubby-hole at the rear.

"Two coffees — and doughnuts, hey Hilda?"

"O.K." Huh. He thought likely she'd be hungry. Probably hadn't had any breakfast. He beamed across at her, intoxicated at his good luck. But before he said anything, he'd wait till after she'd eaten.

"What went wrong on your job?"

"Nothin. Business was bad. They didn't need me."

"Well, you're a good waitress. Shouldn't have no trouble here."

"I had trouble enough before."

"Sure. I know that. I mean, gettin' a job. Seen George yet?"

"Uh huh. He's keepin' me in mind. But it's not any of your damn business, Nick."

He flushed hotly. She was still mad, eh? "Well, maybe you don't think it's my business. But I do. Looka here, Hilda. Chust because I kin hardly keep goin' myself don't mean I don't worry about you. . . ."

"Oh yeah? You been workin'. I know."

"Sure I been workin'. Truckin' sawdust. It looked good, too. I put all my gratuities into the outfit. We was workin' it up, me an Eddie. Gettin' orders for the winter. He had a hookup with a new mill, out East Hastings. It looked O.K."

"Then what?" She didn't sound interested. Just sarcastic.

"I tell you it looked good. Looked like I'd be able to get onto my feet, and make you a real offer. Then the mill folded up — the son of a b---, Eddie he run off with the truck. Just quit cold and left me holdin' the bag. I got nothin'."

"That's an old story — from you. You had enough dough in Nelson last week-end to take a dame to a beer parlor."

"It's a lie." He pounded the table with his fist.

"Well," she countered, "I'd take somebody else's word rather than yours."

"Who told you such a thing?"

"Your own cousin."

"Frank? Oh, so that's it. Is that all? Why, that was *his* girl, Hilda! He had to go out o' town and he ast me to keep an eye on her."

She lit a cigarette, puffing it into his face. She was beginning to get excited. "Huh. Do you expect me to believe that?"

He stared at her, mouth gaping. It had been true. It mightn't uv been but it was, for chris' sake!

"Awright, Hilda. Believe what you want. That don't stop the facts from bein' so. And it don't make my bank account any bigger, either. I tell you. I'm flat. I gotta get a job, fast."

"Why don't you go back to the woods?"

"It's my lame back. Ever since Italy, I can't do the work I use to do, and it ain't easy to find jobs no more — in town, that is. Not like it used to be."

Her mouth tightened again. "And d'ya think it's easy for me? If I'm workin', what do I get. Twenty bucks a week. And rent to come out of that, and clothes, and car fare. And seven dollars for Tommy's keep. . . ."

She broke off quickly, biting her lip, but it was there. She had said it. He leaned forward across the table, breathing fast.

"Heelda! Heelda, why won't you let me see him?"

"I've told you why — too damn often."

"But Heelda! *If* I could pay. Look at me, Heelda. Can't you see it's the trut'?" Even if I was making twenty a week, I would give you give — for him. If I had it. Last Christmas, didn't I. . . ."

"Ten bucks. Ten little measly bucks. To pay a year's board, I suppose?"

It wasn't much. Not much. But he had thought maybe — "You're awful hard, Hilda."

"And why shouldn't I be? Who made me that way? I got fooled once and now I'm not taking any chances. I've got to look out for myself — and for Tommy. Nobody else will."

"But what harm would it be chust for me to see him? Chust once't? Can't a man see what his own kid looks like?"

"Oh. So you *still* want to be sure he's yours? And then, maybe, you'll pay up? Well, for your information, he's the image of you — brown hair, brown eyes — dark skin — poor kid."

"I know that. The welfare lady told me. That's why. . . ."

"Oh! She did? And what else did she tell you?"

"Nothin'. She wouldn't give me the address. Not till you'd o.k.'d my goin' to see him. Aw, Hilda. . . ."

"Well, I give them that much credit. You can trust their word."

"Listen, Hilda. Ever since I left the old country, kissing goodbye to my little mother, ever since, I wanted to have a home of my own, and a little kid, Hilda. What's gone wrong? Why can't we have it?"

She was putting on her gloves. "Do we have to go over all that again? I'd be keeping you too, as well as Tommy. I got more sense."

He sighed, leaned back in the hard seat. She had changed so he hardly knew her. It would be like cat and dog between them now. He had enough sense to see that. But she mustn't go yet. He had one more card to play. His heavy hand reached for the small gloved one.

"Well, I won't ast you that. I won't even ast to see him. But I got a plan, Hilda. It ain't easy for you to keep Tommy, I can see that. And it ain't easy — it ain't possible for me to keep him. But I want to help, and you gotta believe that. . . ." He paused a minute, wondering how to say it. . . . She fidgeted, pulled out her make-up box. He put his hand over that too.

"Chust a minute, Hilda. O.K. Please listen to me, this once't. You know Jan — my brother, Jan?"

She nodded, her eyes narrowing.

"Jan and Emma they been married six years. They got a good farm, good fruit country. They got a nice, snug house, and a dog, and chickens. But there's somethin' they ain't got, Hilda. Somethin' that you and me's got, see? They ain't got a kid, Hilda!"

"You mean. . . ?"

"Sure I mean. Jan could keep Tommy. He wants Tommy. He'd even adopt him if we liked. You wouldn't have to pay no board. You could see him whenever you wanted. He'd have all the fresh air, and the milk, and the strawberries he needed. And he wouldn't be with strangers no more."

He paused, waited. Her face looked empty. She wasn't saying anything.

"Hilda!" He leaned over, his two hands seizing her wrists.

"Don't. Don't touch me!" She yanked herself away. Her coffee cup rolled over and spilled its dregs on the oilcloth. She turned sidewise, pulled herself out of the seat.

"Hilda. You ain't going like that?" He sprang up to face her in the aisle.

"Leave me alone. Let me out of here!"

"No," he said. "No. You gotta answer me, Hilda."

"Answer what?"

"About Tommy — goin' to Jan."

She stood still opposite him. "Give him to Jan? After two years that I've kept him myself? Give him away to *your* folks and probably never see him again? Say, you must be crazy."

"Hilda." He shook her roughly. "It's sense. It's the only sense there is. It'll give the kid a chance't."

"A lot you've cared about his chance — or mine either." A gulp came into her voice. Amazed, he saw that she was crying.

"Hilda. Hilda." Roughly he patted her arm. "Sit down. Sit down a minute."

She crumpled into the seat again, burying her head on her arm. He just sat there beside her, at a loss what to do. Gradually the shaking body quieted. She found a handkerchief and blew her nose. He just sat there.

"I didn't mean to cry" she said, in a stifled voice.

"Sure you didn't. You're strong, Hilda. Strong."

"But I couldn't have you take my baby away from me. I couldn't."

"Sure you couldn't."

"He's mine. He's all I have. I don't see him often, but he's mine."

"Sure, he's yours."

"I'm sorry to make a scene on you like this."

"It's awright. He was folding a paper napkin and squeezing it into a small ball.

Gathering together her bag and gloves, she stood up quickly.

"Well, goodbye, Nick. I'll have to go fix my face. Get cleaned up. Make the rounds."

"Sure. Goodbye, Hilda."

They shook hands, then she ran out of the cafe.

The waiter brought him his bill. Two bits. That left him thirty-seven cents for the rest of the day.

New Frontier 1936-1937

"It is my thesis that the function of poetry is to interpret the contemporary scene faithfully; to interpret especially the progressive forces in modern life which alone stand for cultural survival."

*There is definitely a whole movement and trend, of which I am a part, of poets writing politically oriented social criticism. It began in the thirties, when A.M. Klein published his radical poems in the Ca-*nadian Forum. *Then Leo Kennedy, a young Montreal poet of the McGill group, turned "left" and repudiated his "bourgeois" poetry. As soon as the Toronto magazine* New Frontier *was started (with dissidents from the pale pink* Forum), *in 1936, Kennedy, Klein and myself appeared in its pages, chiefly with poems about the Spanish struggle.*

New Frontier *was a "united front" magazine set up in contradistinction to another, more radically communist magazine* Masses. *It was to rally the middle class intellectuals and artists to the cause of the international working class against war and fascism. Lon Lawson was editor in chief, with his wife, now Jean Watts Lawson, providing the funds from her capitalist grandfather's estate. Thus, NF was not a strictly Communist Party organ; but it was adamantly, to begin with, against the* Canadian Forum's *pallor. J.F. White had been an editor of the* Forum *but now joined the editorial committee of NF, along with Margaret Gould (a social worker) Jocelyn Moore (a librarian), Ross Parmenter (a newspaper man who had been part of the* Varsity *crowd), Leo Kennedy and myself. Other assistance came from the Progressive Arts Clubs. The biggest impact made by me on behalf of the magazine and the new writing took place in Vancouver. A convention of the Canadian Author's Association was taking place ... I was asked to speak; and Guy Glover of the Progressive Arts Club theatre of action also made his views known.*

Calgary Herald, April 17, 1936

Literature of Today
Comes Nearer People,
Miss Livesay States

Canadian Poets Slowly Finding Way of Expressing Life About Them

A deeper understanding of life and an awareness of the spirit of the day is characterizing the newest poetry and literature in general not only in England and America, but in France and through Europe as well. While no one Canadian may yet be said to have wholly exemplified the new progressive outlook, the general trend of the younger poets in particular is in that direction. Such was the message brought by Miss Dorothy Livesay of Toronto who spoke on "A New Hope for Canadian Literature" in the public library Thursday evening. Miss Livesay is herself a poet and writer of the younger school.

Common Man Untouched

In the early part of the twentieth century, poets, by their very withdrawal from the world, ceased to express the spirit of their day. Theirs was an 'escaped' poetry, as exemplified in the work of T.S. Eliot. These poets ran away from the world about them, and this flight from reality was characteristic of poetry until the time of the War. Literature thus was a preserve for intellectuals only and left the common man wholly untouched, Miss Livesay pointed out.

War Awakens Poets

But the impact of the war brought a realization of the world about them and they awakened to question the need of such horror. War's effect on literature has however been depressing. But depression has done even more to bring the world's state to the quick of the poets' mind. So today the poet finds every subject is a fit subject for their pens. Out of it all is coming a keener realization by today's progressive writers of human brotherhood, of kinship, and of the dignity of love. This is not propaganda, the speaker warned her hearers. The very fact that an artist is bound to be highly sensitive to what is going on around him makes him today a social realist.

September 29th, 1936.

Dear "J.F.B. Livesay":

You may be interested in the enclosed clippings which I have saved for you and which gives me the impetus to write you a long intended note.

We are all delighted in having "Dee" at the coast and those groups working in causes in which she is interested consider her a great asset. Personally I am becoming fonder and fonder of her.

You have a very fine daughter and I am a bit cross at you that you gave me the idea that she is a bit hard-boiled (whether you intended to do this, of course, I'm not so sure). But you did it.

Then when I met her and looked at her fine sensitive face, heard her speak, with that rising inflection in her voice, and that look towards heights, on which she glimpses things the rest of us don't vision, intuitively I feel that here is a very unusual personality. She certainly stands out as a leader of youth today.

I think she's shy too — and yet has the courage of a lion when fighting for a cause. Of course she's unconventional, but often it takes more courage — and there's more generosity and a sense of giving and service than with the Rotarians and the Babbits and the rest of them.

You have given me many pleasurable experiences — your lovely home and garden, the thrills of working for the C.P. (I like telegraph reporting best of all) but nothing connected with you equals this fine frail daughter of yours. Whatever I can do for her, I certainly stand ready and am looking forward to meeting her fairly frequently in Vancouver.

Of course too I think she is wasted in the Mother's Pensions business — the same as in the newspaper reporting. She should be writing all the time because that's her rare and precious gift.

Perhaps you'll get out here to visit her and, as usual I'll be glad to see you. How are the inhibitions. Sublimated I hope.

Sincerely yours

Elizabeth B. Price

Calgary Albertan, April 17, 1936

WRITING TOO OBSCURE FOR COMMON MAN

But New Hope for Canadian Literature Held By Dorothy Livesay

"The reason Canadian literature has been so long locked in the cupboard is because of its isolation from the public viewpoint," said Miss Dorothy Livesay, outstanding young Canadian writer in an address in the public library last evening. Miss Livesay held that the correction of this discrepancy was a new hope for the national literature and culture of Canada, though at the present time she felt that such qualities were sadly lacking except in a few cases.

The speaker, who has herself published two small volumes of verse, and is a member of the editorial staff of "New Frontier," the magazine which has most recently made its appearance on the Canadian scene, pointed out that the writers of the nineteenth century were vitally interested in their times. Shelley, for instance, devoted much of his writing to a challenge for freedom.

Zola and other writers of his time realized that to create living characters, they had to understand the world in which they lived. The great writer proved over and over again that first he must be a great scientist. So today, the speaker maintained, writers must seek to know all, even the horrors, brutality and misery.

This seeking after knowledge on the part of writers had a natural revulsion, and the school which followed turned its face deliberately from realities to see only beauty. T.S. Eliot and his followers were of this thought, Miss Livesay said, and as a result literature became a preserve for the intellectual, going into obscurity. Poetry was miles away from the common man.

Return to Realism

But this swing backward could not go on forever either. There was a mood of sudden realization after the war that such horrors need not have been, and the pendulum of poetic expression turned back toward realism again.

Yet the general effect of war on literature was rather a depressing one, the speaker continued. It remained for the aftermath of war, the depression to finally arouse the writer. For the first time he was not secure himself, and there were thousands round about him who were not. He began to realize that every subject was a fit subject for a writer. Writers in Germany and Italy who wished to be free to express their views on conditions had to leave their homelands to get their works published. Those who remained were forced to conform to the dictatorship, and there ended the poetry.

In Canada itself there were conditions which made the writer stop to think. Articles published in the States had not been allowed to cross the border, and others published in one province had been confined within its boundaries. Such things should not be, and writers must express themselves against this provincialism, Miss Livesay said.

Today progressive writers were choosing a belief in human kinship, in the dignity of brotherly love. There was a positive reaction rather than a negative one.

Social Realists

But it was a mistake to think that all art must be propaganda. The artist was more or less bound to be more sensitive, to see farther ahead than the average man and to be a social realist. But there was no outstanding example

222

in modern writing to show that Canada was reacting to these influences.

There was a good deal to be said, she felt, for the point of view that the depression had made Canada a nation, and that provincial barriers were at last yielding with the realization of the need for a national program. So the national entity was emerging out of the crisis and a national culture would also emerge, the speaker felt assured.

As a concrete example of the growth of many young writers along progressive ideas, Miss Livesay spoke of her own case. Mere poetic expression of a new world of nature no longer satisfied her, she said. Poetry would never be popular until it was close to the people and for the most part Canadian poetry was sadly lacking in this quality.

At the conclusion of her address Miss Livesay read several of her war poems.

Calgary Herald, April 17, 1936

"The New Frontier" Plans To Encourage Canadian Literature

Miss Dorothy Livesay of Editorial Board is Calgary Visitor

"The New Frontier" is the latest magazine to make its appearance on the Canadian Literary scene, and one of its most able writers and a member of its editorial board is Miss Dorothy Livesay, a Toronto visitor in Calgary for a few days.

The magazine which is to appear the fifteenth of each month has already published one number. The second number comes out this week and will be in Calgary within the next few days.

While it is meant primarily as a literary magazine, "The New Frontier" plans to be an open forum for progressive opinion all across Canada. Already associate editors have been appointed in Halifax, London, Ont., Winnipeg and Regina. Miss Livesay said. William Lawson of Toronto is managing editor, with the editorial board made up of J.F. White, formerly editor of The Canadian Forum, Felix Walter, professor of French

at Trinity College, University of Toronto, Leo Kennedy, Montreal poet; Dorothy Livesay, and Margaret Gould, social worker of Toronto.

To Aid Young Writers

While the magazine's aim is to encourage a Canadian literature, it hopes at the same time to be a medium for young Canadian writers who now are almost forced to write for publications in the United States, Miss Livesay pointed out.

Short stories, criticisms, departments for poetry, art, movies, music and book reviews, as well as three or four articles will make up each issue.

Miss Livesay, herself one of the younger Canadian writers who is establishing a name for herself particularly in the realm of poetry, will speak this evening in the Public Library on "A New Hope for Canadian Literature." She is the daughter of Mr. J.F.B. Livesay, general manager of the Canadian Press, Toronto, and Florence Randall Livesay who is particularly well known in the literary world for her translations of works of New Canadians, most of which she has put into poetry.

Vancouver Daily Province, Sept. 1936

Dorothy Livesay And Guy Glover Address League

Miss Dorothy Livesay

"Rise Up, Comrade, It Is Death to Rest" — the concluding words of a poem written by Miss Dorothy Livesay who addressed the Women's International League Sunday in the Hotel Georgia more than expressed the speaker's sentiments of "The New Trends in Literature" which formed the subject of her address.

The program, a symposium, was given to aid Guy Glover who will leave shortly to resume his histronic studies in the East. Mrs. Rex Eaton, president of the League, introduced the participants who were enthusiastically received. Mr. Richmond Hyslop gave a group of violin selections including a number of his own composition while Mr. J.D.A. Tripp played piano numbers. Dr. A.F.B. Clark read the original translation of a play by the Russian dramatist, Pushkin and in conclusion was the talk on the "Progressive Elements in the Drama" by Guy Glover. Mrs. W.S. Planta convened the program.

Canadian writers have been too dependent economically and politically on English and American influences and an increase of national spirit in Canada is necessary if tradition is to be shaken off, said Miss Livesay. Canadian authors must turn to home subjects and awareness of the changes wrought within the past few years particularly since the World War so that a better understanding of the process of society may be gleaned, she declared.

The speaker declared that this may be brought about if our authors imitate the modern works of the American writers who have taken as inspiration immediate experiences expressed in realism and in the evils exposed through social realism.

I had arrived in Vancouver in April, 1936. Every day was sunny, all that spring and summer; and I was in love. I had met Duncan through A.M. Stephen, the West coast poet who was the brother of Gordon Stephen, Western representative of J.M. Dent. Gordon, all through the depression remained very "square" and establishment, but

"A.M." as he was fondly called had become radicalized. He was the President in Vancouver of the League Against war and Fascism, so it was natural that I looked him up at the very first in order to promote New Frontier. *Besides a request for a list of possible subscribers in the area I asked him if he knew anyone who would push magazine sales in the bookstores. "Why yes," he said, "there's a Scot, a veteran friend of mine from the Twenties who has just returned to B.C. after a long stint around the world and in the nickel mines of Noranda. He's an accountant . . . knows Charles G.D. very well, is a member of the Vancouver Poetry Society. His name? Duncan Macnair — 'Mac', we call him."*

It was arranged that I should meet Mac at the Honey Dew, a Granville St. coffee shop where they served a fresh orange drink. It seemed that Macnair had not ever heard of me, but seeing the name Livesay he thought I must be my mother, Florence Randal Livesay. He was certainly surprised to find me in my mid-twenties, and a left-winger. A tall fine-featured angular Scot who spoke a musical and modified Glaswegian, Duncan attracted me immediately as an enthusiast for poetry. Thirteen years older then me, he had enlisted with the Black Watch at sixteen (pretending to be eighteen) and had managed to come out unscathed from the battle of the Somme. By 1920 he had emigrated to Canada and had met up with members of the Vancouver Theosophical Society, some of whom were poets: A.M. Stephen, Annie Charlotte Dalton, Dr Ernest Fewster. The latter, I believe, had started the Vancouver Poetry Society, a group which appeared to be irrevocably dedicated to Victorian Verse. It would be my task to free Duncan from this yoke! On his part, as more of a theosophist than a marxist, he sought to temper my political rigidities. But those theosophical beliefs in world brotherhood led a number of that persuasion to become active in politics, particularly as supporters of the C.C.F. This was quite a new scene for me! By the autumn I got to know some delightful women in the C.C.F. and in the International Women's League for Peace and Freedom. They invited me to join their monthly luncheon club — acutally a book club — and I enjoyed the stimulus of older women who had been in the suffragette and pacifist movements since their youth: Laura Jamieson, who became an alderman and a juvenile court judge; Dorothy Steeves, who became a C.C.F. M.L.A.: Mrs Planta, a theosophist; Mildred Fahrni, a very active pacifist and C.C.F.'er. She had visited Ghandi in India. We often met in Burnaby at the home of Mary Wood, a keen literary critic.

But my main concern of course was for what I had come out to do: to be the editorial representative for New Frontier. *Until I got a job I was staying in Burnaby with my aunt (Helen Randal, Registrar of Nurses) but I managed to take the tedious interurban street car trip into the*

Hastings St. station where Duncan would meet me. We had a list of names to pursue, amongst them Dr G.G. Sedgewick (the English professor whose brilliance left a deep mark on his students, Roy Daniells and Earle Birney, both of whom I came to know quite well); and professor Hunter Lewis (who became a great ally in the civil liberties struggle in B.C.

I hiked the many miles from Granville St. to UBC, stopping to call on our contacts. By the end of the afternoon I was exhausted, but Duncan could walk and hike and climb for hours so I tried to keep up with him. What I particularly remember about that long sunny trek was Duncan's confession that of all the nineteenth-century writers, he most admired George Meredith for his "Love in the Valley" and "Diana of the Crossways." I had read both, since these works were a part of my father's library. Along with Tennyson and J.S. Mills, I suppose Meredith was one of those Victorian men who supported the cause of women's liberation — within limits of course. Nonetheless, to find a man really enthusiastic about woman's creative independence cheered my heart.

Soon after this I got a temporary job in social work with the Family Welfare; and by fall I had applied for a position with the Welfare Field Service of B.C. which had been re-organized by my former professor, Dr Harry Cassidy. I took an apartment in Vancouver's West End near English Bay and this led to contacts in the area with young unemployed people who were interested in the CCF, the League Against War and Fascism and the Progressive Arts Club. Soon Duncan and I had a writer's group going whose aim was to contribute articles, stories and book reviews to New Frontier. *Members included, at varying times: William McConnell, Barry Mather, B.S. "Pete" Ward, Alice Parsons, Beth Varley, C. Bjarnason, Harold Griffin, Roger Prentice, Vernon Van Sickle, Duncan and myself. Other creative groups started up with the aid of Harold and Mabel Parker, Elizabeth Keeling, a nursery school enthusiast, and Margaret Carter, an unemployed graduate of the Art School. Soon we got support from Laura Jamieson and Mrs Edward Mahon, "esteemed citizens", in order to apply to the Vancouver Parks Board for use of an abandoned bathhouse on the beach at English Bay. We had a building bee, tearing down the cubicles; merchants of the West End donated materials and in no time the West End Community Centre was born.*

In the morning there was a children's play co-op with mothers helping. From that a children's dance group developed. A drama group was putting together left-wing plays. Some of the writer's groups were asked to write for them. There was a speaker's group with a volunteer who taught the essence of Roberts Rules of Order so that people would be able to speak up at unemployed meetings. For three years we flourished.

Unemployed No. 5, Litho by Ernst Neumann　　　　　(from *New Frontier*)

New Frontier, 1936

Direction for Canadian Poets
LEO KENNEDY

Even though they have been frequently lionized by the leisured and philanthropic, English speaking Canadian poets have never been seriously accepted as interpreters of Canadian *life*. Perhaps that is because they have been content to function as interpreters of Canadian landscape. This easy preference sets its own penalty in the mediocre level which official Canadian poetry has reached at best.

Today, in this sixth year of crisis and accelerated repression of civil liberties, the isolation of the Canadian poet from contemporary life is still taken for granted and accepted as an ideal, especially by the poet himself. In this time of impending war and incipient fascism, when the mode and standards of living of great numbers of middle class persons (from whose ranks Canadian poets hail) are being violently disrupted, our poets blithely comb their wooly wits for stanzas to clarify intimate, subjective reactions to Love, Beauty, the First Crocus, Snow in April and similar graceful but immediately irrelevent bubbles. In this they are abetted by what finds currency as Canadian "criticism." Here our professors of English Letters, commentators in the learned journals, and facile newspaper book reviewers are at fault. They have made no effort to locate Canadian poetry in its social place, and to see in its state of health or ill-health a register of the health or ill-health of Canadian society. Regrettably, our poetry is still regarded as an "art" which is to be attained for its own sake by a special cultivation of the senses.

It is the writer's contention that the time is now past for this kind of aesthetic flag-pole sitting. It is the purpose of this article to present the situation of our poets outlined above, out of the mouths of the poets themselves and to suggest a direction to which their energies can be turned, with benefit to their own statures, and to a larger audience than they have ever before enjoyed. It is my thesis that the function of poetry is to interpret the contemporary scene faithfully; *to interpret especially the progressive forces in modern life which alone stand for cultural survival.* And it is my private recommendation that, setting theory aside, middle class poets had better hustle down from the twenty-fifth floor of their steam-heated, janitor-serviced Ivory Tower, and stand on the pavement and find out and take part in what is happening today, before the whole chaste edifice is blasted about their ears and laid waste! . . .

Now consider the published work of some Canadians who do not regularly appear in local chapbooks. You quickly observe that neo-metaphysical verse, so widely popularized by T.S. Eliot, is still being ardently re-written. Though classicist Eliot has retired into Anglo-Catholicism, and his leadership has been generally renounced, the apostolic hand lies heavily on the verse of A.J.M. Smith and others. Edith Sitwell, delicate, graceful as a glass crocus, and just about as useful for the task now confronting Canadian poets is reflected in the work of Robert Finch, A.M. Klein, doughty Zionist, is most praised for those poems in which he displays his considerable Biblical knowledge, and which re-create the ghetto history of European Jewry. Bruce of Halifax writes convincingly of the sea and ships, but his poetry carries the personal, insular emotion of one still unaware of immediates. E.J. Pratt is latterly aware in shorter poems of the deepening social crisis. Reclusive Audrey Alexander Brown, whose curious personal history has gone far to popularize her with Canadian readers employs her undoubted talent in the manner and matter of Keats and Swinburne. And the others are of an ilk. Only Dorothy Livesay and F.R. Scott to date have quite shaken themselves free of the superseded traditions, the former by her study of marxist philosophy; the latter with pungent satires on the more revered of our national institutions. . . .

What phases of the living scene shall Canadian poets write about? *Any — so long as they are genuinely experienced and understood by the poet.* Because I have called attention to poems of factory life by Klein and Livesay, it may be felt that this article invites everyone to write them. Nothing of the kind! Industrial poems cannot be written by middle class poets who have no contact with the subject. The poet whose livelihood is still intact may have trouble conjuring a communicable emotion and indignation out of fifty shabby, unshaven men in a breadline . . . until he has thought the whole thing through and realized that breadlines in a wheat country are illogical and criminal, and that he and his kind may be only some steps removed from a like condition. He must touch life at a thousand points . . . grasp the heroism, joy and terror, the courage under privation and repression, the teeming life-stuff all round him that is also the stuff of great poetry! Poetry that is real, Canadian and contemporary can be written tomorrow by poets who worried about "dreams" and their precious egos yesterday. It will be welcomed by millions of Canadians who want their children to grow up straight-limbed to enjoy a heritage of prosperity and peace, and who want the kind of writing that will help bring this about.

We need poetry that reflects the lives of our people, working, loving, fighting, groping for clarity. We need satire, — fierce, scorching, aimed at the abuses which are destroying our culture and which threaten life itself. Our poets have lacked direction for their talents and energies in the past — I suggest that today it lies right before them.

Proletarianitis in Canada

By Dorothy Livesay

It is not a new sort of writer's cramp we are speaking about. The word 'proletarianitis' expresses precisely what most people are thinking when they hear 'proletarian literature' discussed. It is regarded as one of those strange new diseases which science prides itself on being able to name as soon as it is discovered. Who ever heard of appendicitis one hundred years ago? We have today a genius (or a mania) for putting names to things. And so new movements in Literature also have their christenings.

Proletarian literature, as such, first found its name with the Russian revolutionary writers; although (like appendicitis) it existed in Zola's day also, and might be traced much further back if our critics only dared. Since the depression, there has arisen, in the United States, a definite school of proletarian writing. In spite of the taunts of the classicists and the "harangue outangs" it has made a place for itself commanding of respect. At the present time, England also is seeing a marked development in the direction of industrial novels which express the point of view of the labouring masses, mainly in the depressed areas. Even so reserved a journal as the London Mercury is obliged to take note of the exuberance in this new writing.

Looking homeward, curiosity compels us to examine the literary scene in Canada for any sign of a similar trend. Our entire cultural history is one of derivation, either from England or the United States, and therefore it is surprising to find that instead of following glibly this new direction, our apron strings are at last being nervously yanked. Our critics (and by these we mean the older critics, for there are no young ones) are uniting in a chorus of warnings against the infiltration of ideas alien to the Canadian spirit. One rubs one's eyes. What, are we becoming a nation at long last? Are we standing on our own feet? Are we preparing to create something original, fresh, with the sting of prairie dust in it and the salt spray of our coasts? Then there is room for rejoicing.

But halt. Look through the publishers' lists of the last three years; search the pages of the poetry chapbooks; scan the drama festivals. What is there in them we have not heard before? What shadows of bloodroot and echoes of maples come to us on a Keatsian wave of melody? What second-hand salute is this, O Orpheus?

No. There is no proletarian literature in Canada; but there is no Canadian literature either. It is my theory (and as one of the thousands of Canadians writing verse I am entitled to have my theory) that until we look to the people, and the industries, and the economics of our social set-up, we will have no original contribution to make. Until our writers are social realists (proletarian writers if you will) we will have no Canadian literature.

Supposing, for the argument's sake, everyone agrees with me. What then? That is where the hardest part of the tale begins.

When it has once been realized what vast possibilities in subject matter the writer could have, only a general perspective has been thereby gained. The subjective factor, the writer himself, is also of tremendous importance. All of our writers today come from an educated, middle-class group. Their experience is almost wholly confined to one aspect of life, the consumer's. Well and good; that should not prevent good writing. When however the writer, "the scientist of society" as Zola called him, can only see one half of the stage: when he has no understanding of the life of the producing groups; then surely his picture of what he does know will be lop-sided and untrue?

It was with this problem in mind that Russian and American writers, following the example of the greatest novelists, a Balzac, a Dostoievsky, sought to broaden and deepen their own experience. Today, an American novelist like Dahlberg or Fielding Burke, goes to the scene of action, lives and if possible works with the type of people and community he wishes to portray. In the same way in Russia, writers are given every entry into industrial or farming communities, talk freely with the workers and absorb their point of view. The artist's task is to make his own synthesis from this, to set down his individual and creative reaction to the life around him.

It sounds a simple and happy process, necessary until such time as our education will have given us that broader basis of understanding and until those in the producing categories will speak out for themselves. But in Canada again the problem is not so simple.

Supposing I am a teacher in a city school and I decide to spend the summer months preparing this 'writing' background. I would like to know something about Canada's main industries, mining, logging, fishing, not because I believe I ought to write about the workers engaged in those activities, but for the increase in understanding it will bring when I turn again to my city-bred adolescents for creative subject matter.

The first difficulty presented is that of accessibility. Mining and logging camps are almost invariably off the railroad at the end of hard mosquito-ridden roads. Brush that aside and it leaves a bigger question: where to stay? Who would have remembered, in planning this sojourn, that most of our industries are owned by large companies who create the townsites around their plant. They own the store, the post office, the hospital, the community hall: and saddest of all, particularly in British Columbia, they own the hotels. Any one going into a mining or milling centre goes in because he has some business there. He is allowed to remain on that basis. But do I look like a commercial traveller?. A government official? A circus manager? A varieties dancer? No. Then what is my business? "Writing." *Writing!* Stupefaction becomes distrust; distrust, fear: and after two or three nights in the local hotel your writer, (like this one), is asked to leave.

Such experiences can be repeated over and over; until the problem takes on more than literary significance and gets one involved with ideas on democracy. "Liberty of the individual" — is that what our critics are urging us to hold on to?

Returning then, to our premise that a dive into proletarianitis would be good for Canadian writing. Who is going to do the diving, and how? Will laughable attempts be made and a false note struck? Or will there be none to do it until those who have worked in the mills and mines find voice? Must we go on making ink puddles where crocuses were?

PARAMOUNT PRODUCTIONS, INC.
PRODUCER OF
Paramount Pictures
5451 MARATHON ST. HOLLYWOOD, CALIF.
TELEPHONE
HOLLYWOOD 2411
CABLE ADDRESS
"FAMFILM"

April 8, 1936

Mr. William Lawson
The New Frontier
Toronto, Canada

Dear Mr. Lawson:
   Just a note to let you know that you are entirely welcome to reprint "THUNDER OVER ALMA MATER."
   I'm sorry I didn't get your previous letter, but I have been out here the last few months and most of my mail has gone astray with this new Pony Express system. I understand the Sioux have been intercepting riders and raping the mail between Fort Dodge and Laramie. Lucky mail!

Sincerely,

S.J. Perelman

S.J. Perelman
Paramount Studios, Inc.
Los Angeles, California

24 West Chaldon. Dorchester. Dorset. England.

1. viii. 1937.

Dear Mr Lawson.

Thank you very much for your letter. I shall be very glad to become a contributor to New Frontier. I think that your paper will fill quite as useful a place as Left Review or New Masses, may be, even more useful. For I know from Canadian friends how much Canada has to depend for 'literary' reading matter on the very dowdiest stuff that comes from this country. And with this contribution, which I hope you will like, I send you my best wishes. The copies of the magazine have not reached me yet (papers always arrive later than letters); but as the contents of this article are more or less topical I think it best to send it to you as quickly as possible.

Yours sincerely,
Sylvia Townsend Warner

via Lerwick
The Shetland Islands

10 - 5 - 37

Wm Lawson, Esq.
Managing Editor
"New Frontier"

Dear Mr. Lawson.

I am sorry to have been so long in writing you and accepting your kind invitation to send in a few short articles and poems for favour of your kind consideration. I was delighted to encounter "New Frontier." I had not seen a copy of it before, and liked it immensely. I hope it is soundly established and making the regular headway it deserves.

I now enclose for your consideration two short poems; and will do my best to get off a few short articles to you in the course of next week.

Every kind regard,
Yours sincerely
"Hugh MacDiarmid"
(C.M. Grieve)

October 14, 1936

William Lawson, Esq.,
New Frontier,
989 Bay Street,
Toronto, Ont.

Dear Mr. Lawson:
I am much impressed by the two copies of the "New Frontier" that you have sent me. In respect to art it is decidedly better than the "New Masses". I wish that I could contribute something to the magazine at this time, but it happens that I am just now clearing up the odds and ends of work on hand in order to get away for two months of painting.

I should like very much to lecture in Toronto, but I have put myself in the hands of a lecture manager who has all arrangements under his control. I am sending your letter to him and he will write to you. In January I am starting off for a three months tour.

I sincerely hope that arrangements will be made to bring me to Toronto. Meanwhile, congratulations on the "New Frontier".

Sincerely yours,
Rockwell Kent

In Vancouver, after forming our writer's group to supply New Frontier *with material, we found that our problems out there were different from those in Toronto. The correspondence between Macnair and Lawson reveals the increasing hassles that developed. We were considered to be too individualistic and anarchistic. Eventually Lawson had to come west himself to settle the differences.*

New Frontier Club,
Apt. 15, 1070 Haro St.
Vancouver, B.C.
January, 1937

Room 18,
989 Bay St.,
Toronto.

Dear Mr. Lawson,

We have received and discussed your counter broadside; we are happy to limit our reply, for the greater part, to concrete proposals resulting from a concrete discussion of your concrete questions.

You have asked:

1. What can the Vancouver group do to keep us supplied with stories, humourous material and verse.

We have reached the sound conclusion that the only thing the Vancouver Group can do to supply you with this material, is to write it. But this, you may well see, precludes another change in the policy of New Frontier. Explicitly, this change would be of such a nature as to make possible the acceptance, by New Frontier, of material submitted by this club. If you wish this group to supply New Frontier with certain material, you would do well to wheedle the supply by an occasional publication.

2. How can you assist us in doing away with our sectarianism and in raising the intellectual level of articles and editorials.

Your problem of "sectarianism", as you name it, is automatically solved in the solution of the first question. How you can raise the intellectual level of articles and editorials is beyond us; we are inclined to regard it as an impossibility since it depends entirely on the intelligence of the editors.

3. What can you do to increase the sale of the New Frontier and secure subscriptions from those people who still like the magazine.

This, we find logical to suppose, depends almost entirely on the solution of your first two questions. But we have small doubt that the sale of New Frontier can be increased somewhat by a very aggressive policy of salesmanship on our part.

One more word before closing. We have, so far as New Frontier is concerned, no personal axes to grind, but, since you brought up the issue yourself, you have, you know, answered the specific questions you put to us yourself. Print without prejudice, without preconceived ideas about ideas, and your magazine will not only be a good magazine, but it will also sell; and rest assured, dear sir, we will make even greater efforts to sell it.

Bonaventure,
New Frontier Group
(D.C. Macnair)

February 26, 1937

Dear Macnair,

Trotsky article and review just received — thanks. We cannot print an article under initials. Will you supply either real or if necessary assumed name of author and something about him to put in contributor's column. Also the title must indicate what the article is about — may we change present title, Consider the Evidence (which means nothing in a table of contents) to something relating to Trotskyism in B.C.? Make suggestions, if you wish. I seems to be swell stuff, I just glanced over it hurriedly before getting this off to you. Please reply airmail.

Sincerely,
Jocelyn Moore

April 6, 1937

Mr. Don Smith
Editor, The Federationist
539 West Pender Street
Vancouver, B.C.

Dear Mr. Smith,

I am in receipt of your letter regarding Mr. Ward's article on Trotskyism in British Columbia. I have also read with interest the April First issue of the Federationist, in which you comment on the same article.

I wish to make it clear to you that our motives in printing Mr. Ward's article derived from our general policy of supporting all progressive movements, including the CCF. You are mistaken in believing that we have an interest in attempting to "embarrass" any socialist movement; and a more careful reading of the article in question will show that it is in no sense an "attack" upon the CCF. It is an expression of the opinion of a member of your own organization regarding the activities of a group professing a political philosophy totally alien to that of the CCF; a group which has been carrying on factional work within the Federation in an attempt to foist its own political program upon your membership.

From my personal observation, from conversation I have had with CCF members and sympathizers, from a perusal of the files of the Federationist, and particularly from my first hand knowledge of the inactivity of the CCF in the present Spanish crisis, I am myself convinced of the general correctness of the analysis made by Mr. Ward. If the article contains minor errors of fact, I am sure that Mr. Ward would be just as eager as ourselves to have them corrected, and our columns are open to you for that purpose.

The recent history of the British Columbia section of the CCF has been one of internal struggles, factionalism and expulsions. We believe, together with many CCF members, that this unhappy state of affairs has been the direct result of the infiltration of Trotskyites into your organization. If by publishing, Mr. Ward's article we have helped in the work of driving them out of the CCF, then our magazine has rendered a valuable service to the movement. And these people must be driven out if the CCF is to grow into a really popular people's movement for socialism.

I trust you will give this letter the same publicity which you gave to the article criticizing our magazine.

Yours sincerely,
William Lawson

May 6, 1937

Dear Dee

I like your article all right. It is a little "naif" as you say, and you *do* use the word "ideational" which I think is a barbarism, but outside of that it will do fine. Thanks.

This question of unity with the Forum is a serious one. I am all for it, and would like to start operations right away. But there are a number of catches:

1.   They are still hob-nobbing with Trotskyites, and Birney is still their literary editor.

2.   We are not in a position to make overtures, and we have no way of determining how they would accept them.

3.   If negotiations are opened prematurely, they might put us on the spot.

Therefore we are just sitting around biting our nails and wondering what to do about it. Could you make any suggestions? Would it be possible to use people like Cassidy to put the thing across? The basis of unity would be the exclusion of Trotskyites and putting two or three of our people on the Forum board. We couldn't as I see it do anything about the united front policies for the time being, but that should be no reason for delaying the merger if it can be effected.

Let's hear from you (personally) on this vital subject. I will let you know later about assignments, etc. The only one we have in mind is the editorial on political developments out there. And for pete's sake try to do *something* about subs, or there won't be any magazine to worry about.

Love and kisses
Lon

June 29, 1937

Dear Dorothy

I am leaving on Saturday of this week, to arrive in Paris on July 10. Plans after that date are indefinite, as a new situation has arisen about the possibility of getting into Spain. At any rate I am taking all the introductions I can lay my hands on, and hoping for the best.

Leo Kennedy is in Toronto for the summer, and he will be working on the magazine. Jocelyn will write you in full about our plans for the future, which are still being discussed in various places. We intend to make a lot of drastic changes.

Perhaps when you get back from your holiday you will be able to devote some more time to the magazine, particularly to the circulation end. God knows it needs it.

Love
Lon

August 13, 1937

Dear Macnair,

Thank you for the material you sent, it came too late to be considered for this issue, which will be out in a few days; we were able to get most of the stuff set up much earlier than usual but have been having a hell of a time getting editorials written, so it will not be out much earlier than usual.

I think you westerners especially will approve of the issue, if it is too lively for you let us know. We have enough stuff on hand for October too, unless you can send us something topical, but we would like it if you could get people working on local stuff — the articles on the canneries and forestry camps which were mentioned in the Spring.

As I don't know if Dee is home yet I will send the copies to you and hope you will see they are looked after.

Regards,
Jocelyn

September 24, 1937

URGENT!
SPECIAL!

Dear Dee,

Lon says two months ago he sent you some poems by Donald C. Stewart of Toronto to look at, and has asked you about them since. This man wants his poems back BADLY so please send airmail even if you haven't had a chance to read them. He is making things kind of unpleasant for us and he is a useful man we don't want to make a permanent enemy. Lon says he is absolutely sure you have them. Pour moi, I am well and made mental note about colour of tablecloth, come pay day (Joe's!) Regards, to both

Jocelyn

Spain 1936-1939

Though darkness fall again,
A tattered flag, the men will stand upright,
Spirit sustained, the floor of Spain
A ground not tilled in vain with blood

(From the National Film Board of Canada production *Los Canadiennes*)

241

DECEMBER, 1936

Special Issue On

SPAIN

Why Catholics Should Support
The Spanish Government
FATHER LUIS SARASOLA

Vol. 1, No. 8.

15¢

CANADIAN LITERATURE & SOCIAL CRITICISM

242

New Frontier, 1936

Letter From Dr. Bethune

To The Committee in Aid of Spanish Democracy

"Madrid's the centre of gravity of the world and I wouldn't be anywhere else"
Madrid, Jan. 11, 1937

We have had a very hectic ten days as you may know and I haven't really had the time to sit down and write you a letter but as an Englishman is leaving to-day for Paris I felt I should take advantage of this and let you know the news.

Frank Pitcairn — author of "A Reporter in Spain" promised to write an article on our unit for the "Daily Worker" of London whose correspondent he is. But as he hasn't turned up to-day — he stays with us — I expect he has left for another front. Professor J.B.S. Haldane who stayed with us for two weeks, has returned to London and has promised to send "The Clarion" articles on us. I think these would be better than one I might write myself.

As you know, we have withstood the heaviest attack and the most serious effort of the Fascists to take the city since the first and second weeks of November. Their losses have been terrific — at least 5,000. Our papers say 10,000 Germans have been killed and Franco has taken the Moors away from Madrid and replaced them with fresh German troops. They thought they had a walk-over and advanced in exactly the same massed formation as they did in 1914-1915 in France. Our machine guns simply mowed them down. Our losses were one to five of theirs.

The International Brigade has suffered badly of course as they are shock troops, but large re-inforcements of French, German, English, Polish, Austrian and Italians with some Americans and Canadians, are arriving.

We have been having two and four raids a day for two weeks now and many thousands of non-combatants, women and children, have been killed. I was in the Telephone Building the other day when it was shelled. However, it is very modern and strongly built. No great damage was done — a handful of people were killed only. You simply can't get these people to take shelter during shelling and bombing!

Our night work is very eerie! We get a phone call for blood. Snatch up our packed bag, take two bottles (each 500 c.c.) — one of group IV and one of group II — out of the refrigerator and with our armed guard off we go through the absolutely pitch dark streets and the guns and machine guns and rifle shots sound as if they were in the next block, although they are really a half mile away. Without lights we drive. Stop at the hospital and with a searchlight in our hands find our way into the cellar principally. All the operating rooms in the hospitals have been moved into the basement to avoid falling shrapnel, bricks and stones coming through the operating room ceiling.

Our bag contains a completely sterilized box of instruments, towels, etc. so we can start work at once. The man is lying most frequently on a stretcher so we kneel down beside him, prick the finger and on a slide put one drop each of Serum type II and type III. If his red blood cells are agglutenated by II and not by III — he is type III. If agglutenated by III he is a II, if by both he is a type I, if neither, he is group IV. So now we know what blood he can take safely. If I, III or IV he gets our bottle of blood group IV (the universal blood). If he is a II, he gets blood group II. He could also take IV but as these "universal donors" are about only 45% of the people, we must use II's when we can.

Then the proper blood is warmed in a pan of water and we are ready to start. The man is usually as white as paper, mostly shocked, with an imperceptible pulse. He may be exsanguinated also and not so much shocked, but usually is both shocked and exsanguinated. We now inject novo-caine over the vein in the bend of the elbow, cut down and find the vein and insert a small glass Cannula then run the blood in. The change in most cases is spectacular. We give him always 500 c.c. of preserved blood and sometimes more and follow it up with Saline or 5% Glucose solution. The pulse can now be felt and his pale lips have some colour.

Yesterday, we did three transfusions — this is about the average daily, besides the blood we leave at hospitals for them to use themselves. We collect ½ to ¾ gallon daily, mix it with Sodium Citrate (3.8%) and keep it just above freezing in the refrigerator in sterile milk and wine bottles. This blood will keep for about a week. We are working on the use of LOCKES' SOLUTION to preserve the red blood cells longer and are making up Bayliss *Gum Solution.* (Gum Arabic in Saline.) Bayliss was (or is!) an English Physiologist who brought out this gum solution for shock during the war of 1914-18.

There is a Barcelona Unit who are putting up blood in sterile ampules. I will go there and see the method. It looks O.K.

The International Brigade Hospital needs male and female French and German speaking nurses — not English speaking at present although these may be needed later. Brain surgeons also.

Well, this is a grand country, and great people. The wounded are wonderful.

After I had given a transfusion to a French soldier who had lost his arm, he raised the other to me as I left the room in the Casualty Clearing Station, and with his raised clenched fist exclaimed "Viva la Revolution." The next boy to him was a Spaniard — a medical student shot through the liver and stomach. When I had given him a transfusion and asked him how he felt, he said "It is nothing — Nada." He recovered — so did the Frenchman. . . .

Norman Bethune

P.S. — I nearly forgot to mention the reason you received so little news of me in December was I gave letters to the Foreign Propaganda Chief who was arrested a week ago as a suspected spy. None were sent. Except one I gave to an English woman going out to Paris. There are too many fascist spies here. Please send us periodicals and papers. We have seen no papers or journals since our arrival. Was Roosevelt elected? Please send Montreal Gazette, Montreal Star, Toronto Star, New Masses, New Frontier. We really know nothing of the other world!

An Interview With Ernest Hemingway

TED ALLAN

There were many pictures on the table of the Italian dead at Guadalajara, taken by Johnny the Dutch photographer. "Take a look at this one," Ernest Hemingway said. He placed a picture into my hand. The part of the Italian's face where the forehead should have been overlapped like the edge of a kitchen sink. "We'll take them to the States. Show these pictures of what dead soldiers look like. Let them know what a war is like," Hemingway said.

All dead soldiers seem to look alike. Some still have their faces. Some even smile. There was one picture in which the man winked at you as if trying to tell you that he wasn't really sleeping. Hemingway said after a long silent look at one of the pictures, "We took them at Guadalajara. That was one of the most decisive battles of the world. But I still get a funny feeling looking at the Italian dead. They were my buddies once."

We were sitting in his hotel room. Sidney Franklin, the American bull-fighter, was lounging in a chair. Johnny the photographer was sitting on the bed beside Hemingway. It was the day after the hotel had been hit by three shells, one coming right under Hemingway's rooms. There was no shelling for a change, and so we could concentrate on what we were saying. . . .

When I interviewed him for *New Frontier* I asked what he thought of the military situation. "Sure they'll win," he said with confidence. "They've beaten Franco's Moors, they've beaten the Italians, what can Franco do now?" He emphasized the point that the soldiers on the government side knew what they were fighting for. "That's the real difference in this war from the military angle. During the Great War they didn't know what they were fighting for. Here they do. This people's army in Spain is going to be a military factor after this war is over. They've got a kind of discipline no army in the Great War ever had. Their political commissars are there every minute with the soldiers to put them straight on things, to show them and teach them what they have to know.". . .

The war in Spain will have a very great effect on the world, he said, and believed that it was absolutely necessary for any writer today to see Spain. To Hemingway the war in Spain in relation to the people who come here for various reasons, is like an X-ray. It shows up people for what they really are, and brings out the best and worst in them. He felt that any writer who missed the Spanish war was missing something he would not be able to get again, even though there would be more wars.

When I suggested that he would probably write a novel on Spain when he returned to America he laughed and said "How has anyone got the time these days to write a novel, when we'll probably have fifty years of undeclared wars?"

"What will you do? I asked.

"If there are fifty years of war a man hasn't much time for writing. Perhaps I'll give it up."

(From the National Film Board of Canada production *Los Canadiennes*)

Spain's Democracy

Talks

To Canada

Representatives of the Democratic Government of Spain

Interviewed by

A. A. MacLEOD   HARRY F. WARD

Chairman, Canadian League Against War and Fascism   *Chairman, American League Against War and Fascism*

and other

Facts About the Spanish Situation

5c

CANADIAN LEAGUE AGAINST WAR AND FASCISM
73 Adelaide Street West, Toronto, Ont.

---

16   *SPAIN TALKS TO CANADA*

Pamphlets

WAR IS NOT INEVITABLE—Address by General Poudroux. Toronto, May 22nd, 1936, and a Message to Canada from Lord Cecil of Chelwood 10c

SPAIN'S DEMOCRACY TALKS TO CANADA 05c

FASCISM MEANS WAR—John Strachey 05c

WILL CANADA ESCAPE FASCISM? 10c

PEOPLE versus WAR & FASCISM—Report of 2nd National Congress of League 15c

POISON GAS 15c

WOMEN, WAR AND FASCISM 05c

(Special Rates on Bundle Orders)

Send all orders and inquiries to

CANADIAN LEAGUE AGAINST WAR AND FASCISM
Room 440, 73 Adelaide Street West - Toronto, Ont.

CANADIAN LEAGUE AGAINST WAR AND FASCISM
A NATIONAL MOVEMENT FOR PEACE AND FREEDOM

I believe that War and Fascism menace alike the life and liberty of the common people of the whole world. I therefore desire to support the work of the Canadian League Against War and Fascism.

Name ....

Address ....

Occupation .... Phone ....

Organization (*if any*) ....

Is the government of Spain a "red" government or a "people's" government?
What is the attitude towards it of Liberal Republicans? Of Anarcho-Syndicalists? Of workers and farmers? Of high intellectuals? Of the clergy?
What is its program and what has it done for the people?
Has it persecuted the church or religion?
Who organized the revolt against it and why?
What part are foreign governments playing in fomenting revolt?
What is the significance of the Spanish conflict for the democracies of the world?
What can Americans and Canadians do to help the forces of democracy?

To answer these burning questions Dr. Harry F. Ward and A.A. MacLeod, chairmen of the American and Canadian Leagues Against War and Fascism, on their recent trip to the World Peace Congress in Brussels, arranged a special interview with representatives of the Spanish government.

The conference was held in Paris with the following present:

MARCELINO DOMINGO	DOLORES IBARRURI
ANTONIO LARA	*(La Passionaria)*
LUIS RECOSENS SICHES	MIGUEL GONZALEZ
JOSE SALMERON	FIDORO HERNANDEZ
LUIS SARASOLA	ANTONIO MORENO

This comprehensive delegation gave three hours to answering questions of Mr. MacLeod and Dr. Ward on behalf of the American and Canadian democracies. Sometimes the questions were posed to particular individuals; most often they were discussed by the entire group and then answered collectively. Yet each individual contributed his share to the collective answer.

The questioners will long remember the clear, urbane mind of Marcelino Domingo, with his understanding both of Spanish and of world politics; the comprehensive grasp of legal questions showed by Antonio Lara, the sad, firm nods with which the priest Luis Sarasola affirmed that the "church" should not be confused with "priests who shoot from belfries" and "make God to be a belligerent," and the modest clear accounts given by the three members of the workers' militia.

Most of all they will remember the warm, deep tones of La Passionaria, for whom every question was a matter of passionate conviction too firm to admit of doubt.

The interviewers wish to express thanks to Anna Louise Strong, American writer and lecturer, who took the notes and compiled the material of this interview. . . .

DOMINGO: In declaring itself neutral, Europe renounces what has hitherto been its most noble ideal: the defense of civil power, the spirit of law. This isn't a civil war between two sides of equal right; it is an insurrection against the legitimate government. To supply arms to rebels is an unfriendly act against the legitimate government; it is so in all international law. To blockade a legitimate government is also unfriendly. But Europe has not seen it thus; so she speaks of neutrality. . . . There is no neutrality between assassin and the police, between the thief and the judge, between the aggressor and the victim. Neutrality in this case is equivalent to insensibility, irresponsibility, even complicity. Europe neutral in the presence of a monstrous political crime like this insurrection is no longer Europe.

Spain and World Democracy

DR. WARD: What do you consider the significance of your struggle for the democracies of the world?

DOMINGO: Spain is the first trench of a battlefield which extends across national frontiers into all the democratic lands. If by misfortune the Spanish democracy should be conquered, it is not Spain that will be conquered. Universal democracy would suffer a reverse and the democratic countries would have to prepare for war in which already they would have lost the first battle.

LA PASSIONARIA: Today is our turn. Tomorrow it will be yours. We are defending the cause of freedom everywhere.

What Can We Do To Help?

MR. MacLEOD: What kind of help can the United States and Canada give? Do you need most money or materials?

SEVERAL VOICES: Materials.

DR. WARD: What materials?

LA PASSIONARIA: Surgical equipment and appliances, warm clothing and shoes for the militia, anti-tetanus and anti-gangrene serums, knapsacks, canteens. Food supplies such as condensed milk, sugar, canned fish, potatoes.

DR. WARD: Do you agree with the statement made by Senator Branting of Sweden that it would be possible and good to send machinery, raw materials and experienced workers, with which to make the means for self-defense. He says that in the fight between Socialism and Fascism, the living forces of creative labour are all on one side, and that we should rely on this and send material and machines with which labour can produce.

LA PASSIONARIA (with an indescribable gesture of long-suffering yet restless patience): Yes, send machines and machine-tools. We will ourselves make the rest.

In 1976, long after the fight in Spain had been lost to the rebels, I presented a paper at Bethune College, York University, for the conference on "The Social and Cultural Aftermath of the Spanish Civil War." It was later published in Contemporary Verse.

Canadian poetry and the spanish civil war

And this same pallid moon tonight
Which rides so quiet — clear and high—
The mirror of our pale and troubled gaze,
Raised to a cool, Canadian sky,
Above the shattered Spanish mountain tops
Last night rose low and wild and red,
Reflecting back from her illumined shield
The blood-bespattered faces of the dead.
To that pale moon I raise my angry fist,
And to those nameless dead my vows renew:
Comrades who fall in angry loneliness,
Who die for us — I will remember you.

"Red Moon" by Norman Bethune

That decision of Norman Bethune's — to go to Spain, to throw in his lot with the Republican loyalist forces — had a more profound impact on the Canadian people than merely the rallying of 1200 volunteers for the Mac-Kenzie-Papineau Battalion. It had a profound effect on our culture and our arts. But to understand why the struggle in Spain meant so much to us it is necessary to remind ourselves of what had happened to this country in the preceding depression years, 1930-1935. Added to the prairie drought which brought the price of wheat to nineteenth century levels and reduced prairie farmers to a welfare existence, industry in the cities almost ground to a halt. The average national unemployment figure for these years was 22% (according to the Royal Commission on Dominion-Provincial Relations). The Prime Minister's solution to this was to set up labour camps for the single unemployed at a pay of 20 cents a day. But in the cities and towns tens of thousands of families were on relief rations. At the sight of the social fabric of the nation falling apart the victims were neither passive nor inarticulate. They began to organize. A social worker, Margaret Gould, summed up the resulting situa-

250

When the poor in Canada try to help themselves by organizing into unions and striking for better conditions and pay, the militia is called out to crush them, as in Stratford. When they organize for a decent standard of relief, tear bombs are thrown at them, as in Vancouver. Or they are ejected from the City Hall, as in Toronto. Or they are routed out of their homes and thrown into prison, as in York County, Ontario.

The disgrace of this situation was depressing not only for those involved, but for the onlookers — some of whom were writers. One reaction was ironic despair. Anne Marriott's documentary poem "The Wind Our Enemy" is the classic example, one that aroused great concern when it was published as a chapbook by Lorne Pierce of The Ryerson Press. Another reaction among writers and artists was much more positive: a determination to fight for change, a desire to build a new world where there would be justice and a good living for all. The marxist magazine *Masses* (available now only on microfilm) printed many examples of poetry, fiction and Agitational Propaganda ("agit-prop") playlets which illustrate this trend. Across the country the Workers' Theatre and the Progressive Arts Clubs flourished. In union halls and at unemployed rallies the well-known IWW ballads were sung, and those of Joe Hill, and those of the Canadian Joe Wallace. More often songs were improvised to suit the occasion.

For Canadians conscious of this situation the moment of decision came dramatically when in July, 1936, Spain's democratically elected government was attacked in military onslaught by the mutinous General Franco, in collusion with invading German and Italian planes (based in Morocco) and ships bringing arms. The rest of Europe, meantime, lifted not a finger to intervene. Canadians reacted to these events with varying degrees of understanding. Amongst the deprived, the effect on the single unemployed men was electric. They read of the international brigades that were forming, rallying volunteers to save the Spanish republic from fascism. Although it was illegal for a Canadian to serve in a foreign cause, 1200 young men and some young women managed to get visas to France and from there joined a freedom trek across the Alps. But in Quebec the reverse happened: the Catholic church called for volunteers to aid Franco, and got them.

Reflection of these events was soon to appear in the cultural organs of the period, particularly in *The Canadian Forum* which was the first to publish poetry that reflected frustration and anger. Poets of stature like E.J. Pratt, F.R. Scott and Lorne Mackay turned to satire to express their feelings. Of these poems Mackay's were the most terse and stringent:

THREE SNARLS

of a Disgusted Colonial

I

Freedom, in Spain, exhaled a groan.
Her champion, England, scribbling notes.
Refused as yet to throw a stone,
And only held the stoners' coats.

II

O Ananias! what a waste!
Iscariot too! such gifts misplaced!
For, living now, you'd both be set
To shine in Britain's cabinet.

III

Let Britain's leaders, if they choose,
Be cushions for Benito's hips,
And lick the heels of Adolf's shoes:
But damn them! must they smack their lips!

That poem expresses one of the three themes most current in the artist's immediate response to the Spanish civil war: that of disgust with non-intervention by the western powers, by Britain and France particularly, who established a policy of "neutralism" and embargo against the Loyalists. Another theme is that of the betrayal of Christianity. It was voiced in no uncertain terms by the Catholic novelist, Morely Callaghan:

It seems to me that those who have tried to make the rebel cause the Christian cause have no shame. All those who are heart and soul with the rebels have made a clear cut choice between the things that are Caesar's and the things that are God's. They are on the side of property rights against human rights. I have yet to hear any of these passionate advocates of the high Christian qualities of the rebels say openly that they believe that irrespective of who wins the great estates should be broken up and distributed among the people who work them or that they are opposed to General Franco's plan to destroy the labour unions.

Men often find it necessary to wear strange masks to support unholy causes.

The spectacle of devout foreign legion thugs and pious, infidel Moors, ancient enemies of the Christian Spanish people marching to the tune of Onward Christian Soldiers leaves me very cold indeed.

As if it was a direct paraphrase of Callaghan's prose, here is Mackay's poem. Battle Hymn for the Spanish Rebels:

BATTLE HYMN FOR THE SPANISH REBELS

The Church's one foundation
  Is now the Moslem sword,
In meek collaboration
  With flame and axe and cord;
Deep-winged with holy love
The battle-planes of Wotan,
The bombing-planes of Jove.

With the same message, but in his own rhetorical style, A.M. Klein wrote three poems, "Of Castles in Spain", of which two are satirical. Here is "Sonnet Without Music."

SONNET WITHOUT MUSIC

Upon the piazza, haemophilic dons
delicately lift their sherry in the sun.

Having recovered confiscated land,
and his expropriated smile redeemed,
the magnate too, has doff'd his socialized face.
He beams a jocund aftermath to bombs.

Also, the priest — alas for so much bloodshed!—
cups plumpish hand to catch uncatechized belch.

The iron heel grows rusty in the nape
of peasant feeding with the earthworm — but
beware aristocrat. Don Pelph, beware!
The peon soon will stir, will rise, will stand,
breathe Hunger's foetid breath, lift arm, clench fist,
and heil you to the fascist realm of death!

The revered poet E.J. Pratt was equally forthright. Towards the end of the struggle when asked to make a statement about the Spanish situation he wrote that his sympathies were "Wholly with the Popular Front . . . determined by the following reasons:

1. The government was placed in power by approximately seventy per cent of the population.
2. The rebellion, now unfortunately successful, was instigated and maintained by reactionary agencies seeking to preserve the remnants of a grandee feudalism with all its caste and privilege and priestcraft.
3. The loyalist regime was attacked and broken by militarists, who, failing to get command of the national army, employed foreign mercenaries for that purpose.
4. A genuine and heroic effort to establish a democracy has been smashed by a minority used as the spearhead of a Fascist invasion.
5. A hundred other unprintable reasons."

Pratt's poem called "Dictator" in which he compares a Hitler, a Mussolini or a Franco to a "Baritone" is typical of the way he organized these feelings.

He ascended the rostrum after the fashion of the Caesars:

His arm, a baton raised, oblique,
Answering the salute of the thunder,
Imposed a silence on the Square.
For three hours
A wind-theme swept his laryngeal reeds,
Pounded on the diaphragm of the microphone,

253

Entered, veered, ran round a coil,
Emerged, to storm the passes of the ether,

Until, impinging on a hundred million ear-drums,
It grew into the fugue of Europe.

The third theme which runs through Canadian poetry at this time is that expressed in prose by the artist Charles Comfort, who was also a poet! The War in Spain is seen to be a struggle for all the finest achievements of man, now threatened to destruction not only in Spain, but throughout Europe as well as here at home.

> For anyone trained in the practise and appreciation of the pore pacific activities of democratic existence; for anyone who believes that sociology, art and science can only make ultimate progress in a world adjusted and peaceful; for anyone who abhors war as a barbarism civilization should long have outgrown, the appalling spectacle of the Spanish civil war is like a horrible nightmare from which there is no sudden release or awakening. . .
>
> . . . If the gangster methods being employed to subjugate the Spanish people are successful, does it not follow that the successful technique will be applied elsewhere? . . .

In its July/August issue *New Frontier* published a most unusual long dramatic poem by Kenneth Leslie, a poet from the Maritimes who is only now receiving his due — now that he is dead. His narrative, "The Censored Editor," is the most ambitious of any poems written in Canada about Spain. Ironically, it is not included in his *Collected Poems* (1971, Ladysmith Press), but neither are others of his unusual and original revolutionary poems — as Milton Acorn notes in his poem in this issue.

"The Censored Editor" is a dramatic poem for voices. Interspersed between the long, supple lines spoken by Inez, a Spanish Republican fighter, and her son, the journalist and editor Guido, a traitor to the government, the drama unfolds interspersed with short questioning songs like this one:

Who can say
Our sons must die?
Who can say why?

Some say for bread
We gave these dead
Dust is their bread

You ask me why
Our sons must die
This then, is why:

and the answer comes at the climax of the tale.

To stand up straight
In the narrow gate,
Once to stand straight.

Is that all, then,
Once to be men?
That is all, then!

The stark simplicity of these lines, interwoven with much more complicated rhymes and images suggest that the poet Kenneth Leslie had been deeply moved by Lorca's passionate lyricism; and that he, more than any other Canadian poet had assimilated the lessons of politics and made them one with his art. Lorca's influence of course has continued to be felt by Canadian poets. During those days following his death I wrote a poem for him, and so have other poets more recently: Dudek, Woodcock, and others. Young activists today are putting on his plays and singing his songs. It is true that in the narrow sense Lorca was not a political poet: I believe his association, as friends, with men of both sides led to his betrayal and execution. However, it was because of his deep roots in his own country, Granada, that he was a people's poet. As he has declared:

If by the grace of God I become famous
half of that fame will belong to Granada,
which formed me and made me what I am:
a poet from birth and unable to help it.

How many Canadian poets, I wonder, have had the maturity to say words like those about their own country? We celebrate Lorca, write poems about Lorca; but it is time now to see how the experience of the Spanish Civil War has had reverberations which have stirred Canadians to think of their own human condition. The Thirties poets stated the case, but the Forties poets carried the message further through the Second World War. I think of Waddington, Page, Souster; and join with them, Birney, Layton, Dudek, Mandel. They in turn have directed younger poets of today towards social concern, commitment to change, search for roots. And one has only to mention the names of Purdy, Acorn, Nowlan to realize how they have stirred the imagination of Lane, Lowther, Wayman and Lee. Norman Bethune himself — doctor, painter, poet and fighter — is already a mythic figure for poets like Peter Stevens, as well as for our young Maoists. It is this pattern, I believe, that the harrowing experiences of the Thirties, culminating as they did in the hope and despair of the Spanish people's struggle, have burned into the Canadian consciousness. Thus we can assert that Spanish singers and poets have left their mark not only on countries where Spanish is spoken, but also on this northern place, Canada.

Catalonia

I

The flag of darkness lowers at half mast
Blotting the blood-stained hieroglyphs with eyes
Strained from the smoke, the flares, the rat-tat-tat
Of guns' incessant speech. A sudden lull
Fans wind on brow, betokens from far hills
The ones who rest — oh unbelievably
A girl who rests tired head on easy arm
And sleeps encircled by her own heart-beat.

But we, grey snakes who twist and squirm our way
From hump to sodden hump, roll in a hole
Of slime, scarring our knees to keep awake—
For us horizons reel, groping for a centre,
Stars burn in whirling sockets overhead—
We wrench ourselves over the last trench, down
Down, down in scurrying scramble tossed
Towards lost lines, lost outposts, lost defence. . .

2

The Captain of the Third Brigade
Sprang from a hillock where he peered
Into the flare-lit dark. He crouched
And doubled up, ran to the gunner's nest.

"They've quit" he hissed. "They've left the ridge—
Swarming to cover in the wood.
The tanks? They've left the bloody tanks
Defenceless. Wounded men will be inside."

Sorenson came up. He'd seen
The gashed retreat from our right flank.
Tall and lean as a stripped tree
He hung above the captain, panting words.

"What's that?" The Captain thrust a fist
In the man's face. "You mean it, Sorenson?"
"I'll go" the lean one said. And down
He slithered on his knees, towards the tanks.

3

Within a tank the smoky darkness stretched itself
And stupidly the air clutched at his face,
Acrid with oil. It shoved his nostrils in
Clung to his palate with a gritty clasp,
Burned in his lungs. He choked and coughed

(From the National Film Board of Canada production *Los Canadiennes*)

Tried to restrict his chest from heaving rasps,
Crouched in his corner hard against the steel.
His ribs vibrated with each hammer stroke
Released in jerks from a machine-gun's maw.
Then he was hit. Fire stung his shoulder-blade
His arm, still bleeding, hung beside him limp—
A stranger's arm. He looked at it
And saw himself the same, inertly cut
From human contact, blood of brotherhood.
Then sweat broke on his brow, the blood closed down
Against all sound of guns. He swayed, and fell.

4

The boy he fell upon stirred in his dream
Moaned, and felt out the knife wound in his side.
The soggy bandages were now a wad of blood
Clotted but unavailing. Pain
Throbbed like a heartbeat pounding through the room
—His room at home he thought, all sheltered in
With slanting shafts of light, the chinks of day
Touching this rosy plastered wall, with chairs

Hunch-backed, the cool tile floors with candle grease
Spattered like silver coins beside the bed. . .

But oh, the voice — what voice sang out to him
Screaming in siren tones, arise, awake
Stand up and strike, strike, fight and shoot
Shoot till the last strip fumbles in your hand
And silence yawns about you in the tank.

The tank! He rose up on one arm
Then crawled away from his companion's side.
The fumes, the oily fumes spluttered within his brain.
He dragged himself upright and at the hole
Peered out upon the heaving earth, where still
The blasted flowers of fire bloomed high.

The boy was yet alive, upright, awake
When Sorenson burst open the tank door
And hauled him out. "Here's bandages and here
This rifle you can lean upon and walk"—
The other one was dead. They took his gun
And letters spilling from his pockets, these
The two remembered; then ploughed on to find
The next tank, and the next, where other men
Lay trapped and helpless, ammunition gone.

Now we retreat in better order, confident
Of gun on shoulder, captain in command
The wounded swing in swift-made hammocks, safe
From a long guttering death within a tank.

People are marching down the roads of Spain
Bundled with babies, chattels, straggling tots
A donkey-load of warmth, a basket, light
With bits of bread, dried beans, remains
Of other hasty meals swallowed between
The zoom of air raids over village streets.
People are marching with all song
Gone out, all sunlight flattened grey
Upon their faces. Now in steady haste
Marching to valleys where the mountain shade
Leans kindly down, where snow
Looks fair to sleep upon. No winds can blow
More fiercely than a bomb, the winter's cold
Will be steel needles, lighter far to bear
Than thrust of shrapnel splitting through the skin.
People are marching, marching, and they meet
The tattered tunics of the soldiers, some of whom
Walk bareback in the cold. The people stop
And give a shawl, a skirt for covering

And men march on ahead. March on to make
A further stand.

        Though darkness fall again,
A tattered flag, the men will stand upright,
Spirit sustained, the floor of Spain
A ground not tilled in vain with blood
With bones of young men scattered far;
Not fertilized in vain, O grey-green gloss
Of olives, wind-bent on a hill, of earth
Supported by the vineyards' yield, and wheat
Crisp in the sun. No more sterility
Or drouth or barrenness is yours
O rolling plains: who make a covering now
For breath and bone; for growing hands
Whose fingers work between the roots, to burst
Out of the earth again, another spring!

Lorca

for Federico Garcia Lorca,
Spanish poet, shot, it was said, by Franco's men

When veins congeal
And gesture is confounded
When pucker frowns no more
And voice's door
Is shut forever

On such a night
My bed will shrink
To single size
Sheets go cold
The heart hammer
With life-loud clamour
While someone covers up the eyes.

Ears are given
To hear the silence driven in
Nailed down.
And we descend now down from heaven
Into earth's mould, down.

    While you—
    You hold the light
    Unbroken.

New Frontier

When you lived
Day shone from your face:
Now the sun rays search
And find no answering torch.

If you were living now
This cliffside tree
And its embracing bough
Would speak to me.

If you were speaking now
The waves below
Would be the organ stops
For breath to blow.

And if your rigid head
Flung back its hair
Gulls in a sickle flight
Would circle there.

> *You make the flight*
> *Unshaken.*

You are alive!
O grass flash emerald sight
Dash of dog for ball
And skipping rope's bright blink
Lashing the light!

High in cloud
The sunset fruits are basketed
And fountains curl their plumes
On statue stone.
In secret thicket mould
Lovers defend their hold,
Old couples hearing whisperings
Touch in a handclasp, quivering.

For you sang out aloud
Arching the silent wood
To stretch itself, tiptoe,
Above the crowd. . .

> *You hold the word*
> *Unspoken.*

You breath. You be.
Bare, stripped light
Time's fragment flagged
Against the dark.

You dance. Explode
Unchallenged through the door
As bullets burst
Long deaths ago, your heart.

And song outsoars
The bomber's range
Serene with wind-
Manoeuvred cloud.

> *Light flight and word*
> *The unassailed, the token!*

Comrade

Once only did I sleep with you;
A sleep and love again more sweet than I
Have ever known; without an aftertaste.
It was the first time; and a flower could not
Have been more softly opened, folded out.
Your hands were firm upon me: without fear
I lay arrested in a still delight—
Till suddenly the fountain in me woke.

My dear, it's years between; we've grown up fast
Each differently, each striving by itself.
I see you now a grey man without dreams,
Without a living, or an overcoat:
But sealed in struggle now, we are more close
Than if our bodies still were sealed in love.

At English Bay: December, 1937

By the winter-stripped willows in the Park I walked
Gold-washed fountains in the sudden sun;
Brisk the air, white-capped the mountains,
Close at my feet the rim of the land's end—
Everything held in a silent axis, carved in sunlight
Except for the ocean pounding below me, relentless reminder:
Thoughts in my mind clear as heaven's azure
Till the heave, the roar of encroaching armies
Broke on my heart's shore.

Water that has washed the coasts of China,
Shanghai's city, yellow Yangtse;
Water that has cleansed the bloodied hands
And healed the wounds
Signed the death-warrant on too tell-tale lips
Sent to oblivion the iron ships;
Water forever restless, forever in struggle

As a man feels in himself his fevered spirit
Rising and falling, urging and being spent
Into new deeps and further continents—
Until he begins to move with others
Seizing the willows as banners—
Gold-washed fountains in the sudden sun!

(From the National Film Board of Canada production *Los Canadiennes*)

from Seven Poems

IV

On a night like this, the Ides of March perhaps,
Spring will arrest your muscles and a raid
Of hands will light on you, and cry out: "Choose."
Incisive fingers on your shoulder-blade,
Open sockets for stampeding news.

"Listen child." And you know the answer held
You face the pitiless eyes and open wide
Your own, like shock observers; as they say
The words no fluttering flag of fear could hide:
"The operation failed. He died today."

And if the words were different: "War's declared."
There is no difference, the thought is one.
This the expected shock, the Judas-kiss
A flower cup uncurling into sun
Childhood's leaves warned by the dark of this.

We grew, and munitions matched us, laboratories
Weighed the ingredients; magnifying glass
Revealed death's desert in a finger-nail
Of dust. Whatever door we sought to pass
Was marked with chalk. All sesames would fail.

This is not news, but a resolution passed
After hard labour, bitterness of sides.
Tenseness relaxed, you knew it all your days:
There would be one man missing, one who hides
His cunning hand from thunder with the "nays."

Impartially the chairman-undertaker
Smiling casts his vote, announces death
Speculates on population where
Our wombs are lacerated, lovers' breath
Is torn asunder in the cool March air.

We are the children long prepared for dust
Ready in bone, the wrist a pulsing pain:
On a precarious railway-rib we lie
Our limbs long ready for the armoured train—
Ears to the ground and bare eyes to the sky.

VI

The child looks out from doors too high and wide for him
On words spun large as suns, huge meanings sprayed on tree
And roadway, spreading fields, not to be caught and clapped
Together in a rosy nave, the sun no coin
For fingers to indent.
                        The child runs out to stare
At masterful young men who bat at tennis ball
At giants in kilt skirts whose march is purposeful
At mothers in cool gowns who move about like moons
Upon the eternal lawns, low laughter shimmering
About their curving mouths.
                        The child leans on the future,
Slender tree ungainly rooted there by private worlds
Who knew a private ecstasy unshared by him
But let the memory slip and reared a hedge
Of bristling phrases, last year's bills, and week-ends snatched
In secret hate; his room laid waste when radios
Are tuned, when rumour's blatant voice hits nerve,
Dries tissue, brittles down
The new unmoulded bone.
                        The child in cities toddling up
A stifling reach of stair, gains window-seat:
How consternation puckers up his eyes—at space
Unplanted, seed unwanted, wars unwarranted
Consuming his small, thankless growing place!

Words before Battle

When, in a Moscow hospital
You cried: "Abyssinia!" Barbusse,
And died—we few remembered.

The hot molten liquid
Of words poured out in hope
And defeat—these have burned us.

Now in self scrutiny,
Remembering your friend in song,
Lorca, shot like a dog—

Remembering thin tunics in Spain
Words riddled from the mouths
Of men by man-made steel,

Canadians from the Abraham Lincoln and Washington Battalions, Spain, June 1937.   (Public Archives Canada C-74967)

Remembering the Czechs beaten
To their knees without
A fight, gagged by the wayside:

Now we know our strength
Has been as the strength of one,
Our will as water, our words

Not bitter shafts of light
Striking the people; echoes
Only, of words to be said.

Now, precipitate
In darkness, we have found
Your cry unmemorized.

Energy has been spilled
On the floor, not conserved
In a glass jar for winter,

Struggle has been blind,
Relying too much on the fist
Bared to the teeth of guns.

It is not enough to be proud
And sure, shouting defiance;
It is not enough to ignore

The enemy's cunning, his sheer
Weight of steel, his mountains
Of iron and chromium

His breastplates gleaming
His bombers diving
His metal raining, driving—

It is not enough to foreshorten
Time's movement, to say:
"Tomorrow will be the day."

It was not enough for you,
Barbusse, nor for those slain
About Thermopylae.

And in this ominous
Barbed peace, we know:
It is not enough for us.

The Lizard: October, 1939

No one has come from the fronts we knew—
Shanghai and Yenan—for a long session:
Silent now the Madrid broadcasts. So was Vienna once
Blotted out. We remember her voices fading.
No one has come. Letters unanswered. The stricken
Refugees smothered then, after
Years of ditch stumbling?
The battling, thin tunics gored to death
In the country of the bull, in the country of the dragon?

In the sheltered rocks of our homeland, the Pacific waters
Hills shrouded with evergreen and the valleys yellow
With corn and apples; within the walls of our houses
Splashed with a vivid wallpaper,
Radios blare the censored version of our living:
Wrestlers rage, baseball bouncers rant,
The words of a recipe tinkle on the ear—
Lord Halifax speaks sprightly from London
Where the people run about gladly
Attending to air-raid precautions.

In the sheltered rocks, stealthily, a lizard
Slips hesitant into sunlight; tunes himself
To the wind's message. We slip out in pairs, as lovers
Strip ourselves, longing
To see bodies bare and flesh uncloseted,
To hear real voices again, to uphold the song
Of one coming from Madrid, Shanghai or Yenan
Bearers of good news
From the fronts we knew.

Vancouver 1939

*"All our perspectives had changed since that Sunday
morning when Churchill's voice came over the radio
saying that he was going to support Stalin. They were
joining together to defeat Hitler!"*

*My personal life was changing. I lost my job with
the provincial government because in August, 1937,
Duncan and I had married. My supervisor, Laura
Holland, a very fine and just woman, was most
sympathetic and let me work on, month by month, until Duncan found a
job. Then, the rules were, a wife had to quit hers. It was through his left-
wing activities and contacts that Duncan did acquire a job in 1938 at
Forst's, a Vancouver firm whose management was liberal-minded and
progressive — but I became quite depressed over the loss of mine.*

*Toronto was far away and my contacts with New Frontier were
becoming acerbic. However, it was in 1938 that my friendship began with
Jean and Alan Crawley, a deep friendship that buoyed me up through the
dark days to come. Moreover, the political struggle of the people versus
Big Business in British Columbia was extremely interesting. Vancouver
had become the centre of the long, drawn-out, longshoreman's struggle
and then it became the centre of the single unemployed's struggle for
"work and wages."*

*The most dramatic event was the out-of-work sit-down in the Art
Gallery, the federal Post Office and, for a shorter time, in the Hotel
Georgia. The P.A.C. rallied its writers and artists to visit the men on vigil
there, interviewing and sketching them. Trade unionist and C.C.F. and*

Communist wives provided a soup kitchen and rallied public support. (Irene Baird's fine novel, Waste Heritage, *gives vivid descriptions of these activities.*

But, after a month of holding out for action, the sit-downers at the Art Gallery and Post Office were met, at 5 a.m. on June 19, 1938, by the RCMP. Unless they would agree to leave peaceably they would be attacked with tear gas! Steve Brodie, the Post Office leader, argued that the men had to be formally arrested — then they would leave peaceably. The police refused. The brutal tear-gas attack was launched.

In the melee that followed men gasped for air, windows were shattered and many men, including Brodie, were beaten. No ambulances were called so private citizens picked up the wounded and drove them to St. Paul's Hospital. Others were taken to an emergency first-aid station set up by the strike committee.

Bloody Sunday
by Steve Brodie
(Published by the Young Communist League, Vancouver.)

Workers in Vancouver are beaten by authorities as they leave the Post Office where they had staged a protest against unemployment.(Public Archives Canada C-20596)

270

About the author

Although virtually unknown to the post-war generation except for a handful of students of history, Steve Brodie's name exploded into headlines with the audacious sitdown occupation of the Vancouver Post Office, Art Gallery and Georgia Hotel which he led. Following the removal by police of the sitdowners with tear gas and clubs and the brutal attack on Brodie himself, E.A. Lucas, with the assistance of the Civil Liberties Union, succeeded in obtaining the granting of fiat for Brodie to sue the Crown for assault, the first time such right had been granted in post-Confederation history. Despite massive public interest in the case, however, it never came to trial. Brodie later enlisted in the Canadian Army and his name, like the unemployed struggles, disappeared from the newspapers. He now [1973] lives in Victoria.

Sean Griffin: When, after reading Harold Winch's self-glorifying account of the Post Office sitdown in the Vancouver *Province,* I decided to write the real account of that historic struggle for the Pacific *Tribune,* I had no idea that among the audience for that article would be — Steve Brodie, himself. The last time I had seen him was more than thirty years before, only months, in fact, after Bloody Sunday.

As it turned out, he wrote from Victoria where he now lives, to express his appreciation. Some weeks and several letters later, the manuscript in the following pages came in the mail, painstakingly written out in longhand.

In the Thirties I knew Steve well. During the years that he was a leader among the unemployed, one of the many Communists and Young Communists working to organize and give leadership to the thousands of jobless, I was secretary of the B.C. Young Communist League and our paths often crossed. I knew him as a natural leader among the men with a great fighting spirit, a man who would not accept passively the suffering that had been thrust upon his generation.

Though a number of writers and commentators, realizing the renewed public interest in the depression years, have sought to record Steve's recollections of the event, none has publicized them. And Steve himself, having had long experience with the calculated tendency of such writers to omit, distort and even fabricate, feared that they would take his story and recast it in their own image. He wrote in one of his letters: "Since it is basically a working class story, I felt it more important not only to get the story down, but also to have a comparison if any of the others produce a distorted tale."

And unlike the accounts of Harold Winch and others, Brodie's story will stand the test of history.

By Steve Brodie

Towards the middle of May 1938, I felt that the men were becoming desperate and more and more doubtful that the organization was anything but a begging institution and I realized that something really defiant should be done, and that once it was successfully accomplished we should disarm the forces sent to deal with us by immediate submission to the law, once and for all forcing all governments to accept responsibility for the unemployed, or openly demonstrate that they preferred to act brutally and unlawfully. Although I hoped, against all hope, that they would at least go through the motions of civilized legal behavior, I dreaded their only known cure for protest.

I had suspected for some years that someone at the leadership level of the unemployed organization and the Party fraction was a police informer. I did not find out who it was until 1942 when it no longer mattered. To prevent leaks, I asked for and received a vote of complete confidence, in a select action committee. This committee was to be composed only of the five division leaders. Ernie Cumber was coordinator for the group, and the men were assured that in any action taken they would be led, not sent, by their division leaders.

We met in an old rooming house on Cambie Street, and after several ideas were discussed none of which were new, I introduced the plan to march on the Post Office, the Art Gallery and the Hotel Georgia. Many difficulties were raised, but since I had stepped out the necessary distances and had an exact time table made out, the plan received approval, reluctant at first, but as the sheer audacity of the move became more apparent, enthusiasm grew. Knowing the advantage of complete surprise, we agreed to go into action immediately after the convening of the daily meetings in our five separate halls. All the division leaders were aware that any error in timing, or any incident along the way where men got out of hand, could leave them open to severe penalties but they acted with resourcefulness and courage, daring much for no personal reward.

Norman Harris led Division III into the Art Gallery and immediately took steps to protect from damage the valuable art works there. Under extremely crowded conditions, one hundred men maintained perfect discipline for thirty days in spite of constant harassment by police and invitations to do battle. Press stories of defections made rations scarce at times, but morale remained high. Somehow, in a way which I have never understood, leadership seemed to pass from Harris to Harold Winch, then an MLA, and later MP. He appeared at 5 a.m. June 19, not at the invitation of the men, but as assistant to the chief of police. He claims credit for the fact that no clubs were used on the men, but fails to explain the use of tear gas on men who had surrendered to lawful arrest. As an elected official, surely he had a right to ask the chief of police to either carry out the law or wait until directly ordered by the attorney-general to proceed in a lawless manner. This would have exposed the entire plot to provoke rioting but, as usual, politics produced some strange bed fellows.

I make no apology for the statement, that had I been at the Art Gallery, the first illegal attack on men who were prisoners of the Crown would have been met in kind. If the handiest weapons had been valuable art objects, that would have been most unfortunate but believing then, as I do now, that people have value, while things only have a price, I would have made that illegal attack most expensive. I believe the insurance value at the time was over a million.

Jack Lucas with Division II joined with my Division I, at the Post Office. He took over responsibility for orderliness and general routine while my arguments with authority, and explanation of our position to press, police and public, made for an almost-round-the-clock job. A full meeting was held each evening, with widest discussion of what should and what could be done.

At each meeting, both Lucas and I requested a vote of confidence, offering to support anyone elected in our place. At all times we were assured of their support. Sometimes members of the public were present, and all workers in the mail section saw and heard everything that took place, yet the newsmen claimed consistently that the men lived in fear of some nameless punishment if they disobeyed their leaders.

On the first night, the reaction of the public was such that the police felt powerless to solve the problem in the usual way — with clubs. At 9 p.m. the men were addressed by Colonel W.W. Foster, chief of police. He congratulated us on our behaviour and discipline, said it had been a fine demonstration and asked us all to "go home."

When he was faced with unanimous refusal, I spoke on behalf of the men. I assured the chief that if we had homes to go to, we would hardly feel it necessary to occupy public buildings. I added, however, that if he felt our presence there was in any way a breach of the peace, we would, each and all of us, submit to arrest and face trial by magistrate according to law. He left to consult by phone with the attorney-general in Victoria. An agreement was made: no action would be taken that night as the crowds milling about downtown were in no mood to countenance any of the usual police methods of dealing with unemployment. It was eventually agreed by all authorities that this would be a nine day wonder, and if we were left, "to die on the vine," as the attorney-general put it, the men would drift away and the leaders would be dealt with in the usual manner.

All levels of government were shocked as week followed week, and public support remained strong. When business clubs and others who had never shown much concern, now called for public works as the only possible solution, they felt that their election slogan, "Work and Wages," was beginning to haunt them.

Three times during the thirty days, we were confronted by police orders to vacate, and each time we submitted to arrest, insisting however, that being equally guilty, we expected equal punishment. Never in ten years had all levels of government been in agreement on the issue of unemployment, but now they agreed that the buildings should not be cleared by lawful arrest and trial. A riot was necessary to provide the pretext for a few leaders to be railroaded for inciting, rioting and destruction of property. This had always worked in the past and support from press and pulpit, was assured.

* * *

An attack was planned for 5 a.m. Sunday, June 19 — Father's Day. As I slept on the floor, wrapped in a blanket, lent me by one of the night pickets, I was shaken awake and asked to go outside, as our pickets were uneasy at the large numbers of police gathering there. They gathered in groups on the street corners and those who had not been called in from a Saturday night booze party were passing around mickeys at a great rate, evidently trying to catch up with those already drunk. Laughing and poking each other's ribs with their billies; they seemed to be anticipating their job with great relish. I remarked at the time, they seemed like juveniles about to set fire to the family cat.

The outside pickets withdrew into the building where we observed members of the RCMP gathering in the mail sorting area. The press arrived just as the postmaster stepped out into the lobby accompanied by Major Hill, inspector of RCMP Division. His first action was to banish the press, who retired across the street, and wrote their "eye witness" accounts from inside a cafe. Their later stories of me rallying the men to fight, and shouting "every man stand fast," were pure fiction. Any such "boy stood on the burning deck" pose on my part would have made tear gas unnecessary. The men would have collapsed from laughter. Again, we held a meeting, where I received a vote of confidence as spokesman.

A proclamation was read, ordering us to depart to our homes, as we were now declared to be an unlawful assembly. Failure to depart would mean forcible eviction. I immediately reported to Major Hill that we were even more anxious to avoid damage to property and to ourselves than he was, so being now declared unlawful, we placed ourselves under arrest. To make certain that there could be no misunderstanding, I asked the men if they now willingly submitted to arrest. They shook the building with a loud "Yes." I turn to Hill and said "Sir, we are now your prisoners." He replied "I have no orders about arrest," whereupon I gave him a short lecture on the law, reminding him that being only policeman, he had no legal right to punish. That, I assured him, was the function of our courts, and asked again that he do his lawful duty, and place us under arrest. I offered to march with the men to any place he would designate where we would await trial by magistrate. When he refused, I asked the same of City Police Inspector Grundy. His only answer was, "We are here to keep you moving when you hit the street. There will be no arrests."

The next ten minutes were spent singing our marching songs, with mild cat-calling, and suggestions as to the use to which the police might put their bombs. Staff sergeant Wilson, who to this day swears he saw no unnecessary force used, threw the first bomb. Up until that moment, we had lived for thirty

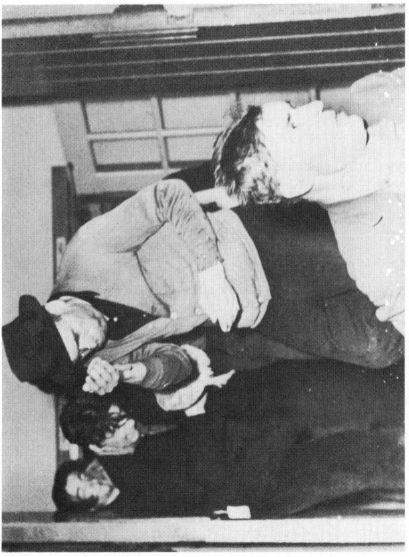

Men evicted from the Post Office in Vancouver, British Columbia, 1937. (Public Archives Canada C-79027)

days in that building without five cents worth of damage to property. Now as the lobby filled with gas, arrangements were made to purify the air by eliminating some three thousand dollars worth of plate glass, which helped to dissipate that choking cloud. From both ends of the lobby the RCMP attacked, equipped with gas masks and plying their whips in joyful abandon like the notorious Cossacks.

In the general melee, Jim Redvers slipped to the floor, and was immediately pounced on by two of Canada's Finest." He was kicked about the head so savagely, that one of his eyes was knocked out. His buddy, Little Mike, so named to distinguish him from Big Mike, as they both had unpronounceable names, took a severe pounding as he led Redvers out. He then made the mistake of asking a city constable to call an ambulance. The error cost him a slash which laid his jaw open two inches.

He carried that scar to his grave at age twenty-two. That grave is on the hill overlooking Dieppe.

Young Mike joined us at age seventeen, when the relief department in the Nelson district told him his share of the family relief was now cut off. In order to leave the entire $13.50 per month to his widowed mother and two kid sisters, he had to leave home. The cost to the government of Canada to maintain his grave is now more annually, than his family received altogether for three years. This doubtless will be explained away by inflation.

* * *

Sean Griffin: The brutality at the Post Office was a deliberate and cold-blooded act of police terror and as the news of it spread, it shocked the public much as the attack on the trekkers at Regina on Dominion Day three years before had done. Only this time, it was on Vancouver's own doorstep.

The atmosphere in the city was highly charged as people awoke to hear the accounts of the early morning events. Condemnation of police brutality was on everyone's lips. Radio stations reported every few minutes. On all sides, people voiced their indignation and horror at the outrage.

By Sunday afternoon, 15,000 people had gathered at Powell Street grounds in a giant protest rally to hear several speakers, among them aldermen from the city. The rally ended amid thunderous approval for a resolution demanding that the Pattullo government act immediately to provide work and wages — or resign.

As thousands began to leave the rally, word spread that several of the arrested men were being held at the police station a block away. A huge throng of people streamed down Cordova Street to the police station to demand that they be released. Later that evening 30,000 gathered at the CPR pier for a massive sendoff for 100 jobless who were on their way to Victoria to join others who had gone before. The crowd filled the streets from Granville and Hastings where the attack had taken place that morning, all the way down to the pier. Above the street, in the offices of the Federal Building, RCMP officers stood, filling the window spaces, hoping to intimidate the

276

crowd.

When the people saw them, they booed and jeered and several climbed nearby buildings to hurl rocks, driving them away from the vulnerable glass. It was not one of the more glorious chapters of the RCMP's history.

As the hundred men heading for Victoria marched through the crowd to a ferry, they received a tremendous ovation. Up on the deck, they began singing "O Canada" and the echo resounded among the surrounding buildings. As the boat pulled away, the huge throng joined them in singing "Hold The Fort." No one wanted to leave. It was one a.m. when the crowd finally broke up after a spokesman for the unemployed announced that the demonstration was over.

The long Sunday had ended but never would a government be able to remove the black mark that the authorities had left on history at 5 o'clock in the morning when they had resorted to open terror rather than accede to the people's demand for work and wages.

In Victoria, the unemployed lobby received a rousing welcome and people all over the island voiced their sympathies with the jobless men. But by the end of June, 1938, hundreds of police were swarming all over the capital city to remind the men of the power of the state.

The struggles of the unemployed in the thirties were not in vain. The Post Office sitdown, the on-to-Ottawa trek and hundreds of hunger marches and demonstrations combined with the battles of those fortunate enough to have a job to build their unions, left a deep imprint on Canada that would ever be felt in political change.

These struggles were instrumental in winning unemployment insurance and other social legislation such as pensions, health insurance and welfare. Above all, they made it clear that the people and particularly the working class, would not be cowed into accepting the conditions of the hungry thirties, a lesson that present-day monopoly and its government spokesmen should well remember in this period of inflation and renewed attacks by big business on the standards of living of working people.

It was a zooming time of high political excitement and controversy. For we weren't concerned merely with the local Canadian scene. Mass meetings and rallies were held for "peace and democracy" (thus the slogan had changed) and in defense of Republican Spain. The United Front policy initiated by the 1935 Commitern really seemed to be working. But nonetheless no help came from England to blockade Spain against delivery of German and Italian arms. Barcelona fell, Madrid fell. There was no word from China. The remnants of the Mackenzie-Papineau battalion were sent home. The Stalin-Hitler pact was a shattering psychological blow, not fully understood (as historians now believe). Russia's scheme was to awaken Chamberlain-led Britain to the dangers of the world threat of fascism. At the first world peace congress in Paris in 1937 Maxim Gorki had warned: "the enemies of humanism are preparing for a second world massacre." Well, it happened. Confusion reigned on the left. The Party went underground. When, in September, 1939 Britain finally declared war against Hitler I remember having a fierce argument with "Jim" Watts Lawson as to whether this war would really put an end to fascism, and should therefore be supported; or whether one should vote "Peace." I think that Duncan and I were of two minds — seeing both alternatives. We were by this time isolated from hearing any Party "line", as I imagine were most people who had been active on the left. Our solution was to withdraw, to settle down to family life on the North Shore. There, from an old house on a high hill we watched "the bush" change its depression face and become a maze of wartime houses, row on row, for the thousands of shipbuilders who moved in from all over the country . . . as I then recorded in the documentary poem, "West Coast."

Duncan and Dorothy Macnair with son, Peter.

278

from West Coast

FINALE

High on our hill we watched, and saw
morning become high noon, and the tide full.
Saw children chequered on the western beach
and ferry boats plough back and forth, knocking the nose
of tugboats, barges, freighters, convoys, cruisers:
the harbour a great world of moving men
geared to their own salvation, taking heart.
We watched gold sun wheel past the sombre park
slip beyond Lion's Gate, illuminate
cool purple skyline of the Island hills.
Then to the hulls and houses silence came
blinds down on tired eyes
dark drew its blanket over trees and streets
grey granaries and harbour lights; muffled the mountain-side.
Yet still, far, far below those lights pierced sky
and water; blue and violet, quick magenta flash
from welder's torch; and still the foreshore roared
strumming the sea, drumming its rhythm hard
beating out strong against the ocean's song:
the graveyard shift still hammering its way
towards an unknown world, straddling new day.

The home front against fascism had become a world struggle which we were into, willy-nilly. All our perspectives had changed since that Sunday morning when Churchill's voice came over the radio saying that he was giving his support to Stalin. They were joining together to defeat Hitler! This was a moment of intense emotion for us. Soon all the comrades who had been in jail were released. The unemployed men and women joined the army and the communists, though never permitted to go to the front, marched down the streets of Canada in battle dress. We were all in high hopes again that this time it truly would be a war that would change the world. Instead, we received Hiroshima.

Jean Watts Lawson marching off to war.

Index

Poems

Stories

Plays

Articles

Bibliography

ALLAN, TED and GORDON, SYDNEY. *The Scalpel, The Sword: the story of Dr. Norman Bethune*, New York: Cameron Associates, 1959.

BAIRD, IRENE. *Waste Heritage*, Toronto: Macmillan Co. of Canada, 1973.

BROADFOOT, BARRY. *Ten Lost Years, 1929-1939*, Toronto: Doubleday Canada, 1973.

BRODIE, STEVE. *Bloody Sunday*, (pamphlet), Vancouver: Y.C.L. Press, 1974.

DAVIS, N. BRIAN. *The Poetry of the Canadian People*, N.C. Press, 1976.

GRAY, JAMES. *The Winter Years*, Toronto: Macmillan Co. of Canada, 1966.

HOAR, VICTOR and REYNOLDS, MAC, *The Mackenzie-Papineau Battalion: Canadian Pact in Spainish Civil War*, Toronto: Copp Clark, 1969.

LEVERSEDGE, RON and HOAR, VICTOR, ed. *Recollections of the On to Ottawa Trek*, Toronto: McClelland and Stewart, 1973.

RYERSON, STANLEY and McNAUGHT, KENNETH. *The Dirty Thirties*, CBC, 1970.

Selected Articles by Dorothy Livesay

"This Canadian Poetry", *Canadian Forum* 24, April 1944, pp. 20-21.

"British Columbia's Imaginary Headache—The Japanese", accepted by *Star Weekly*, February 17, 1947.

"China's Co-operatives", *Canadian Forum* 27, November 1947, pp. 179-80.

"Writers Have Big Part in Making New World", *Saturday Night* 62, April 26, 1947, p. 17.

"Women in Public Life—Do We Want Them?", *Saturday Night* 64, July 19, 1949, p. 17.

"Summary" of Group C, "The Writer and the Public" section of Canadian Writers' Conference held at Queen's University July 1955; in George Whalley, ed. *Writing in Canada*, (Toronto: Macmillan, 1956), pp. 132-35.

"Race Relations in Northern Rhodesia", *Canadian Forum* 44, October, 1964, pp. 159-61.

"Making of *Jalna*, a reminiscence", *Canadian Literature* 23, Winter 1965.

"Polished Lens, Poetic Technique of Pratt and Klein", *Canadian Literature* 25, Summer 1965, pp. 33-42.

"Mazo de la Roche" in Mary Innes, ed., *The Clear Spirit*, published for the Canadian Federation of University Women by University of Toronto Press, 1966.

"Sculpture of Poetry; on Louis Dudek", *Canadian Literature* 30, Autumn 1966, pp. 26-35.

Notes on Creative Writing in *Vital English* published by N.B. Teachers Association, 1967.

"Clearing the Air", *The English Quarterly*, Vol. 1, No. 1, Spring 1968, Q3.

"The Documentary Poems: a Canadian genre?" in Eli Mandel, ed., *Contexts of Canadian Criticism*, (Chicago: University of Chicago Press, 1971); delivered at ACUTE, York University, 1969.

"Early Days", *Canadian Forum* 50, April-May 1970, pp. 34-36.

"Frenzies, lemans, concretemen!", *Canadian Forum* 49, January 1970, p. 230.

"A Prairie Sampler", *Mosaic* 3, Spring 1970, pp. 85-92.

"Hunters Twain", *Canadian Literature* 55, Winter 1973, pp. 75-98.

"Tennyson's Daughter or Wilderness Child? The Factual and Literary Background of Isabella Valancy Crawford", *Journal of Canadian Fiction*, Vol. 2, No. 3, 1973, p. 161.

Books by Dorothy Livesay

Green Pitcher 1928
Signpost 1932
Day and Night 1944
Poems for People 1947
Call My People Home And Other Poems 1950
New Poems 1955
Selected Poems 1957
The Colour of God's Face 1964
The Unquiet Bed 1967
The Documentaries 1968
Plainsongs 1969, 1971
Disasters of the Sun 1971
Collected Poems: The Two Seasons 1972
Nine Poems of Farewell 1973
A Winnipeg Childhood 1973
Ice Age 1975
The Woman I Am 1977